War in Europe

War in Europe

1450 to the Present

JEREMY BLACK

Bloomsbury Academic
An imprint of Bloomsbury Publishing Plc

BLOOMSBURY

LONDON · OXFORD · NEW YORK · NEW DELHI · SYDNEY

Bloomsbury Academic

An imprint of Bloomsbury Publishing Plc

50 Bedford Square	1385 Broadway
London	New York
WC1B 3DP	NY 10018
UK	USA

www.bloomsbury.com

BLOOMSBURY and the Diana logo are trademarks of Bloomsbury Publishing Plc

First published 2016

British Library Cataloguing-in-Publication Data
A catalogue record for this book is available from the British Library.

ISBN:	HB:	978-1-4742-3501-3
	PB:	978-1-4742-3502-0
	ePDF:	978-1-4742-3504-4
	ePub:	978-1-4742-3503-7

Library of Congress Cataloging-in-Publication Data
Names: Black, Jeremy, 1955-
Title: War in Europe : 1450 to the present / Jeremy Black.
Description: London : Bloomsbury Academic, an imprint of Bloomsbury
Publishing Plc, 2016. | Includes bibliographical references and index.
Identifiers: LCCN 2015029881| ISBN 9781474235013 (hardback) | ISBN 9781474235020
(paperback) | ISBN 9781474235044 (PDF) | ISBN 9781474235037 (ePub)
Subjects: LCSH: Europe--History, Military. | Military art and science--Europe--History. |
Armies--Europe--History. | Politics and war--Europe--History. | War and society--Europe-
-History. | Social change--Europe--History. | Europe--Military policy. | Europe--Foreign
relations. | BISAC: HISTORY / Europe / General. | HISTORY / Military / General. | HISTORY /
Modern / General.
Classification: LCC D25.5 .B485 2016 | DDC 355.02094--dc23 LC record available at http://
lccn.loc.gov/2015029881

Typeset by Fakenham Prepress Solutions, Fakenham, Norfolk NR21 8NN
Printed and bound in Great Britain

For Daniel and Megan Byles

CONTENTS

ABBREVIATIONS

ADD   Additional Manuscripts

BL   London, British Library

NA   London, National Archives

SP   State Papers

PREFACE

The priority in this book is the long-term of war and military developments. The book is not an attempt to offer a chronological account of campaigns and battles, the approach partly adopted in some of my other works, which, between them, cover the entire period. Instead, in this study, I focus on, first, long-term military developments, notably in the way war was waged and battle conducted; secondly, the relationship, more accurately relationships, between war and transformations in the European international system, particularly war as the cause and product of the latter; thirdly, the linkages between military requirements and state developments; and, fourthly, the consequences of these requirements, and of the experience of war, for the nature of society and culture, both élite and popular. These broad themes, nevertheless, have to be approached without any teleology or sense of inevitable development towards the situation that eventually occurred. Such an assumption, indeed method, is the great danger with military history, and, indeed, other branches of history, that focus on the long-term. To avoid this danger, there will be, after an opening chapter, a chronological organization in this book. This approach, however, is adopted without assuming that centuries represent coherent or causative units, or were separated by rigid divides, and that these units and distinctions were clear and valid. Indeed not: neither at the time, nor in terms of the past discussion of military history that is itself an important subject.

To allow for analysis of the four subjects mentioned above, the chapters will include substantial analytical passages. Alongside these will come discussion, where appropriate, of particular types of war, notably state-to-state, civil and naval. At the same time, themes and types overlap, and any rigid distinction is highly problematic. So also with the distinction between past and present. The topics highlighted resonate very strongly with current strategic concerns, including the porosity of war as a concept, the challenges of supposed technological advantage and the place of the state in all of this.

Europe is the focus of this book. It is about war and military development in Christian Europe, but does not cover the entire Western military tradition, and is not an approach to global military history from the Western perspective. Instead, the book deals with a portion of the West, a key portion, but a portion that excludes trans-oceanic European societies. Moreover, the Ottoman (Turkish) empire ruled much of Europe, more particularly most of South-Eastern Europe, throughout this period until it was heavily defeated in the First Balkan War of 1912–13. However, this empire is also excluded, because much of its military activity, notably from the sixteenth to the eighteenth centuries, and more particularly from the early 1510s to the 1740s, focused on its eastern frontier with Persia (Iran). In addition, the military relations between the empire and Christian Europe are best handled in studies dealing with relations between the West and the non-West as a whole. Europe is taken as including Russia, but the focus is on Russia's relations with other Western powers.

The range and quality of works on military history are such that any attempts to sum up a field are necessarily incomplete and tentative, not to say presumptuous. This is particularly so if there is any attempt to cover more than one subject, period or language, as, indeed, I seek to do. There are excellent historiographical works on narrow topics, for example Charles Esdaile's essay on the British army during the French Revolutionary and Napoleonic Wars.[1] Moreover, such pieces can make comments that are of more general relevance. Nevertheless, historians do not tend to range as widely as social scientists, or, at least, do not tend to do so unless they are part of the valuable speciality of world history. In many respects, this situation suggests that, alongside valuable detailed work, the way forward in historiography is to focus on conceptual issues, rather than summarizing an enormous range of work. That is the approach followed here. It helps explain why footnoting has been kept to a minimum, and is indicative of types of material rather than seeking to be comprehensive, impossible as that would be.

At every stage, it is necessary to remember that our subject is a harsh one. Jean Martin de La Colonie recalled of the successful British storming, under John, Duke of Marlborough, of the Schellenberg height in 1704:

> We were all fighting hand to hand, hurling them back as they clutched at the parapet; men were slaying, or tearing at the muzzles of guns and the bayonets which pierced their entrails; crushing under their feet their own wounded comrades, and even gouging out their opponents' eyes with their nails, when the grip was so close that neither could use their weapons.[2]

The battle, in which the British and their Dutch allies suffered about 1,500 dead and 4,000 wounded, led to a different form of suffering, as it was followed by the laying waste of much of Bavaria in an unsuccessful attempt to force Max Emmanuel, the Elector of Bavaria, to abandon his alliance with France. Both of these episodes tend to be ignored in general accounts, which focus, instead, on Marlborough's victory over a French–Bavarian army later in the year at nearby Blenheim.

History, as both the past and our accounts, in the present, of the past, is in a perpetual tension. Military history is particularly susceptible to the latter approach, and frequently in a somewhat naive fashion. In large part, this is because military history is a branch of history in which professional historians are notably weak. Instead, there are powerful cross-currents, especially from writers for an interested public, as well as from those trying to make the subject relevant to the modern military, and from social scientists using military history to support their theories. In each case, there is a tendency to ahistoricism. This is especially pronounced when there are efforts to find universal laws, and thus lessons, for example on strategy or leadership.[3] Such works are frequent, as indeed are collections of essays that are on common topics without sufficient efforts to search for discontinuities in the subject. Some scholars have made almost an industry in producing such long-range thematic works.

The limitation of assuming such common elements, without, at the same time, stressing the strong constraints and discontinuities arising from contexts, is relatively easy to discern. Less so is the related, but different, tendency to adopt a general analytical position that reflects the issues and ideas of a particular period. To some extent, such present-mindedness is an inevitable consequence of the way we think about history, but it also risks imposing a teleology on the past. This teleology takes two forms. First, there is an assumption that development towards a certain situation was inevitable, and, secondly, that this was the key theme. Moreover, there is a linked tendency to adopt analytical constructions that arise from this approach, and make apparent sense of it.[4]

The most dominant example in the Western tradition is the idea that, with time, there was a move, indeed development, if not progress, to the 'modern' military and 'modern' warfare, those, crucially, defined in terms of conventional warfare, regular militaries, bureaucratic organization, technological advance and industrial capability. In such accounts, the terms modern, industrial, total and conventional are commonly deployed, albeit with different priorities and varying causal links. The net effect, however, is the same. History is apparently cumulative and uni-directional, the past is anachronistic and problems are confronted and overcome by arriving at new solutions, outcomes, moreover that are understood as new and as solutions. Whether change is held to have occurred by means of revolutionary processes or in a more evolutionary fashion, and however revolutionary and evolutionary are understood and presented, there is a sense of the necessity of change. There is a focus on the new, a modernist bias and an unwarranted credulity with regard to models of progress, notably of the rise of the state, the rise of the West, gunpowder technology and Western military organization.

The standard approach entails ascribing the priorities of one age to another, and in a highly misleading fashion. For example, the focus on supposedly decisive battles which particularly characterized commanders and commentators in the nineteenth century led, when considering earlier periods, to an emphasis on battle, and on commanders who sought it, for example Gustavus Adolphus of Sweden (r. 1611–32). The element of decisiveness was generally exaggerated. Supposedly decisive battles were frequently more likely to be yet another blow in a series of blows (military, political and administrative) to prestige, authority and tax/manpower bases. As a result of the focus on battle, the role of other means of conflict was underrated. This was true in particular of sieges and of the small-scale conflict sometimes described as 'small war', conflict that was far more frequent than battles and sieges.[5]

More generally, and linked to the stress on scale and battle, the standard focus in discussion, both subsequently and at the time, was on symmetrical conflict, rather than on the need for armies to confront other forces, whether conventional or not, that sought to avoid battle. By focusing on such conflict, and on battle, there was an emphasis on particular commanders, strategies, tactics and other factors, rather than an engagement with the range of operations and contexts. This was misleading. Linked to the focus on conventional operations, there was also an emphasis on state-to-state conflict rather than on civil wars, or only on the latter when they approximated to conventional operations, or with that dimension stressed. This emphasis affected the understanding of war.[6]

The standard approach in the literature is readily apparent, but it is far less clear how best to formulate a new approach. This is a significant point because historiography ought to involve pointing the way forward to new challenges, issues and subjects for research and publication work, rather than solely looking back. The former is certainly more realistic as a reflection of present concerns than the manner in which historiography is often considered by academics. In focusing on the way forward, it can, of course, be difficult to detect clear schools and developments. However, the existing divided tendencies of military history can each be sketched forward as well as back. These include, and the tendencies overlap, the technological approach, the 'War and Society' focus, the 'Cultural Turn', the global perspective and the dominant attention to campaigns and battles. Each, indeed, seeks so to present itself, and, frequently to typecast others, that it is difficult to find much evidence of a coherent subject that can be termed military history. For example, in a criticism of the 'War and Society' focus, Norman Stone has commented on the tendency to focus on topics such as 'rape by soldiers, and other patriarchal activities'.[7]

There is also, very interestingly, the literature that seeks to link war to questions of state development and differentiation. This approach goes back to the stadial theories advanced in the eighteenth century, as Western commentators then attempted to devise a theory of history in which religion played no real role, a theory that did not rely on a providential account of Christian history and purpose. The stadial theories entailed a developmental model that today appears flawed, as well as prejudiced and Eurocentric; although it is not too different from many of the perspectives subsequently advanced by social scientists. In the essential argument, economic specialization led, and leads, to levels of society and related organization that have governmental and political consequences, as well as affirming and/or encouraging particular social and economic circumstances and trajectories. The nature of the interactions varied by commentators, as did the place and role ascribed to war and force, but greater military capacity was seen as stemming from these developments. An anonymous British pamphleteer claimed in 1719:

> No superiority in the field could be a match for their superiority of treasure; for money being the basis of the war, in the modern way of carrying such things on in the world, it has long since been a received maxim in the case of war, that the longest purse, not the longest sword, would be sure to conquer at last.[8]

The industrial dimension was more to the fore in the late nineteenth and twentieth centuries. In the *Times* of 22 May 1915, John Buchan, acting as a special correspondent with the British forces on the Western Front (that is France and Belgium) in the First World War, described a 'pandemonium of sound' that never ceased. He also presented an account of the 'mechanism of modern armies ... a gigantic business concern ... with more mechanics than Sheffield', a major centre of British metallurgical manufacturing.

In the eighteenth century, the developmental approach was notably prominent in the writings of Edward Gibbon, William Robertson and Adam Smith. In effect, this approach offered historical change itself as strategy; although the extent to which policy was planned was unclear in much of the writing. One of the most significant instances of policy being seen as important came with Gibbon's discussion of Peter the Great (r. 1689–1725). His adoption of Western governmental and military methods was presented by Gibbon, as making Russia a successful bulwark against any future irruption of 'barbarians' from the Asian heartland. It is instructive to note that a similar geographical challenge from the 'heartland', although this time from Russia, was construed by Halford Mackinder, Britain's leading political geographer, when he argued in 1904 that the means of waging war were in essence a product of forms of transport, and that these transformed geopolitics and thereby set strategic paradigms. Mackinder focused on the opportunities created for Russia for rail links, notably in the opening of a trans-Siberian railway to the Pacific.[9]

These varied works made explicit the generally implicit assumptions about space and development that, in practice, were highly influential in guiding ideas about war and military history. In essence, if the forces that war served and represented could be thus conceptualized, then war could be better understood. Due to the discrediting of geopolitics in the 1940s, as well as later criticism from the perspective of 'critical geopolitics', modern scholarship tends to be chary of addressing this dimension. That, ironically, leaves earlier assumptions still influential. In searching, as an aspect of historiography, for topics that would repay study, that of war and space, in the sense of spatial considerations, is one that bulks large. This is particularly the case because there are very different ways in which space can be conceptualized. For example, equal area cartograms, the usual pattern in considering space and, thereby, mapping, can be replaced by equal population cartograms, and these provide a very different cartography, as well as suggesting contrasting patterns of control, and resulting goals. The spatial dimension is an aspect of tasking, the tasking of military activity and of scholarship. As tasking, indeed, is a fundamental aspect of military history, so it is necessary to understand its parameters, role and dynamics. This process, to a degree, makes military history an aspect of total history. Rather than losing the value and distinctiveness of military history, that approach, indeed, is more appropriate than treating the subject as a totally different dimension. The latter may reflect the specialist characteristics of military activity, but does not address their purposes and contexts. In particular, the nature of the public–private partnership is an important one that deserves much attention. It is considered at length in the next chapter. This, then, is the prime historiographical challenge: how to relate military history to broader historical currents without ignoring the significance of its distinctive characteristics and particular patterns of change.

While working on this book, I have benefited from the opportunity to teach MA and BA History courses at Exeter, as well as MA courses in the Strategy and Security Institute there. I have also profited from opportunities to speak at the Naval War College in Newport, the Centre for Historical Analysis and Conflict Research at Sandhurst, the Foreign Policy Research Institute in Philadelphia, the New York Historical Society, the New York Military Affairs Symposium, Mary Washington University, Roger Williams University, the Citadel, the Guildhall in London, Rhode Island College, the Tavistock Festival, the Chalke Valley Literary Festival, the Waterloo bicentennial and the College of William and Mary, and to give the Dudley Keep Memorial Lecture at Winchester. While working on this book, I benefited from visiting Belgium, Bulgaria, the Czech Republic, Denmark, Estonia, Finland, France, Germany, Greece, Hungary, Ireland, Italy, Latvia, Lithuania, Malta, the Netherlands, Norway, Portugal, Romania, Russia, Serbia, Slovakia, Slovenia, Spain, Sweden, Switzerland and Ukraine.

Conversations with Kelly DeVries, Mike Duffy, Wayne Lee, David Parrott, Chris Storrs and Alessandro Stanziani have proved most instructive. I would like to thank Guy Chet, Xu Erbin, Dennis Showalter and Martin Thomas for commenting on all or part of an earlier draft. The time, commitment and friendship this represents are much appreciated. They are not responsible for any errors. I have also benefited greatly from the advice of three anonymous readers. It is a great pleasure to dedicate this book to Daniel and Megan Byles, who have proved for many years the very best of neighbours and whose neighbourliness is much appreciated by Sarah and myself.

CHAPTER ONE

Introduction

War was important. It transformed societies, moulded states, destroyed communities and struck deep into the experience of families. War was also complex as a phenomenon and varied as a means of activity and experience. In trying to provide an overview, some historians prefer unitary arguments, tying seemingly disparate military events, settings, cultures and developments into a coherent theme or superstructure. Although such an approach provides coherence and clarity, thematic descriptions and accounts, notably the established ones, such as the 'Military Revolution', the 'gunpowder empires' or the advent of the 'fiscal–military state', raise many questions. Moreover, there were events and processes that can undermine storylines of technological determinism, Western global dominance and bureaucratic centralization. History, indeed, is a messy process, and an understanding of the diversity of conflicts around the globe offers important correctives to the well-established, but overly simple, narrative of modernization, with its stress on the decline of cavalry and the rise, in contrast, of infantry, artillery and fortifications. Moreover, success and failure were the result of local conditions and demands, rather than reflections of the supposedly inherent benefits of certain technologies or formations. These points underline both the more general difficulties of establishing the relative capability of protagonists, and the need for fresh work on the subject.

Long-time developments, however, are not only present in retrospect. They can also be apparent to contemporaries. At the same time, the significance of change, while easy to suggest and a key part of the content and rhetoric of politics, can, in practice, be difficult to grasp. Aside from this difficulty, it can be highly problematic, amidst the 'noise' of many events in the present, to assess the situation in a way that matches the perspective of posterity.

War encapsulates this situation. In some respects, it is a grimly clear business, with its litany of battles and sieges, and its stark display of power in terms of numbers of troops and warships, and their readily apparent activities. We know war when we see it, and we can readily differentiate this conflict from the rhetorical ploys that are all-too-common today, such as war on poverty or cancer or crime. Yet, there are significant complexities, not least in terms of the overlaps between civil war and civil conflict, as well as the difficulties of distinguishing the latter from particular means of politics, social action or criminality. As another instance of the same problems of categorization, the modern 'War on Terror' has been very differently classified, not least with much discussion as to whether it truly is a war.

Turning to the more conventional understanding of war, and its changing character, it is both hard to grasp the particular significance of individual conflicts, let alone campaigns, battles or sieges, and also to separate out and assess capability, potential and developments, from the stark display of power and the need to provide and explain the lengthy narrative of conflict. The focus on narrative, indeed, can lead to an underplaying of analysis.

It may be comforting to believe that time brings wisdom, but, in practice, the situation is not thus eased. Instead, hindsight is very much a matter of the play of the present, with the pressing concerns of the latter framing the questions asked of the past and, as a related matter, the understanding and discussion of it. Military history, its content, sense of significance and power structures, can exemplify this process. For example, the concern with counter-insurgency (COIN) in the 2000s, as a result of American-led coalition interventions in Afghanistan and Iraq, led to a sustained reconsideration of the earlier military situation with an interest in earlier episodes of such operations, for example the Napoleonic conflict with insurgents in Spain in 1808–13, and the later difficulties the British had repeatedly encountered in successive interventions in Afghanistan in the nineteenth century.

This shifting concern with particular types of war is a clear-cut instance of a more general analytical process reflected in changing concerns, categories and prioritization. There is also a broader question about development, that of significance and the related prioritization in the discussion of events and their causes. The teleology that has been long dominant was that of the relationship between war and state development. Reflecting the character of history as an academic discipline in the nineteenth century, this linkage was long-established. This was particularly so in German historiography, notably the work of Otto Hintze (1861–1940), Professor of Political, Constitutional, Administrative and Economic History at the University of Berlin. The linkage was re-expressed in 1990 by the influential American sociologist Charles Tilly (1929–2008), with his argument that war made the state and the state made war. Allegedly, moreover, states accumulated coercion in order to protect and control capital. At the same time, the bureaucratic and political processes involved helped lead to the enhancement of public goods, such as better communications.[1]

It is an instructive guide to the character of modern military history that many have heard of Charles Tilly, but not of Jean, Count of Tilly (1559–1632), one of the principal generals of the Thirty Years' War, victor over German princes and Danes at Wimpfen (1622), Höchst (1622), Stadtlohn (1623), Lütter (1626) and Wolgast (1628), only to be defeated at Breitenfeld (1631) and the Lech (1632) by the Swedes under Gustavus Adolphus. He was fatally wounded at the latter, not a risk that faces modern military historians.

Charles Tilly's concise statement appeared to answer the question it raised, as well as providing military history with a relevance for those who doubted the value of the subject. State-building was presented as dependent on states taking over control of formal military activity and seeking to limit unofficial activity, and states as employing military power in order to enhance their power and prestige and, crucially, those of the social groups that they reflected.

The relationship was organized in accordance with time and space axes, with the development seen as occurring across time. This provided a developmental and teleological dimension, one that was held to be particularly characteristic of Christian Europe. This situation was believed to arise from the large number of states Christian Europe contained, the related failure of projects of imperial hegemony or at least of great-power dominance, and the resulting high rate of military activity as independent states frequently fought each other. This situation, it is widely held, led to a distinctive rate in Christian Europe, both of military activity and improvement, and of administrative sophistication and political consciousness, in order to support this improvement.

The 'military revolution' argument, for modernizing military change and governmental consequences from the fifteenth to the eighteenth century, was a major part of this thesis.[2] The entire analysis provided a way to consider Western exceptionalism, and to provide a long-term explanation for Western imperialism and, subsequently, the military power of the United States. With the 'military revolution', history was apparently explained in a theory and adage that appear to work across time while apparently telling you all you needed to know about military affairs and its processes of development. As with many interpretations, there is, indeed, a degree of substance to the linkage of war and states, and it forms an aspect of the subject and argument of this book. Indeed, part of this book is devoted to considering Tilly's valuable theory.

At the same time, there is also room for reconsideration. In part, this reconsideration reflects the nature of hindsight, or rather the shifting perspective of the present. The emphasis on state development as inherently progressive and positive was one that was apparently appropriate for the nineteenth century, not least as higher education, the source and focus of much comment, was then inflected with themes of state benefit. Aside from the degree to which academics in the period were highly patriotic, universities across much of Continental Europe, and notably in Germany, were closely linked to the state and its purposes. Leopold von Ranke (1795–1886), Professor of History at Berlin from 1825 to 1871 and the key figure in the development of German historiography, very much pursued this relationship. As an instance of the focus on the state, and its regular forces, there was a reflex (which still dominates modern historiography) to paint mercenaries with a broad and denigrating brush. The image of mercenaries, indeed, acts as a modernist tool that serves to transmit coded messages regarding modern national armies, modern states and military professionalism within the context of nation states.

Moreover, the emphasis on the state received additional impetus in the twentieth century, again in part because of close links between the state and higher education. In addition, the key role of the state in social welfare, as well as a widespread belief from the 1940s in Keynesian economics, ensured that government was regarded as a social good even if there was a reaction, particularly in Germany, after the Second World War against any relationship with what was defined, and indeed stigmatized, as militarism. In Western Europe, the reaction was linked to a radical critique of power from the Left, notably from the 1960s, one, furthermore, that had longer-term influence when young radicals became older policymakers or wielders of academic power.

Confidence in the capability of the state, as opposed largely to confidence in its intentions (although the latter were also doubted), became even less pronounced from the 1970s as, from a different political direction, neo-liberal views became more prominent. This trend was very much the case in the 1980s. The consequence of neo-liberalism was not only a doubt that a trajectory leading to a stronger state was inherently good, but also, more specifically, work suggesting that the public provision of military services was not inherently more efficient. The focus here was not on fighting, but rather on other aspects of military activity, notably logistics, although the role of private military contractors led to calls to note the value and potential of mercenaries.[3] Britain and America are not among the signatories of the UN Mercenary Convention of 1989, which prohibits their use. It will be instructive to see whether, in the future, the current use of mercenaries, will alter the inherited nineteenth-century reflex.

This issue has been given an historical dimension that focuses on the 'early modern period', the late fifteenth to eighteenth centuries. In this period many dynasties and individual monarchs owed their position to victory in battle and war, including the Yorkists (1461, 1471) and Tudors (1485) in England, William III (1688–91) and the Hanoverians (1715–16, 1745–6) in Britain, the Bourbons in France (1589–94), Spain (1701–15) and Naples (1734) and the Romanovs in Russia (1611). Alongside the emphasis on the formative role of monarchs who acted as war leaders, comes a stress on broader political and social networks. In part, these were a matter of the clients, allies and supporters, willing or otherwise, of the new monarchs.

At the same time, there was also an emphasis on the extent to which effective governance required co-operation not only for political, but also for governmental reasons. Thus, military recruitment and, in particular, logistics were frequently only effective if they involved public–private partnerships. Recruitment entailed issues of command, and thus the broader question of fighting capability. It was suggested that privately contracted forces could be more effective, as well as innovative.[4] Moreover, as another example of partnership, much government was local, with the local landowners who wielded authority and power in effect exemplifying the partnership, which worked across the social hierarchy. Thus, aristocrats were provincial *gouverneurs* in France and Lords Lieutenant in England. This system worked to raise and support military forces and to defend localities.[5]

A different element of co-operation was provided by the basis on which the military served. In a pattern that reflected the nature of society, control and discipline were often very harsh, but there was also a conditional quality to social relations. The notion of appropriate behaviour required good kingship and good lordship, and the military counterpart was an expectation that soldiers should be treated appropriately, notably with the provision of promised pay and supplies. Frequent mutinies led to compromise, as rulers and generals had to propriate their troops. This process had an affect, not only on the operations of military organizations, but also on the conduct of campaigns. There was discussion in the sixteenth century of alternatives, in the shape of militias or conscript armies of civilians, but the emphasis remained on paid professionals. Many of these mercenaries were from foreign lands, although the understanding of 'foreignness' was far less fixed and significant in this period than was to be the case by the late nineteenth century.[6]

Indeed, the situation with military service was to change as governmental control increased and public culture changed. The emphasis between these two elements is unclear and varied, and this variation affected the extent and nature of the conditionality of military service, and what that meant in terms of a public–private partnership. Moreover, the contours of particular political environments played a role. Thus, between 1890 and 1918, developments in the Austrian, British and Russian empires can be profitably contrasted. Despite pressure for Irish separatism, large numbers of Irishmen (both Catholics and Protestants) volunteered to serve for the British Crown in the First World War. That was a form of conditionality of service different to that of the conscripts in the Austrian and Russian armies. However, the collapse of the latter two in 1918 and 1917, respectively, indicates that conditionality was also a factor there.

So also with the eagerness of German soldiers to fight on in late 1944 and early 1945. That the army did not collapse, despite major defeats at the hands of rapidly advancing Soviet and Anglo–American forces, was in part due to the conspicuous terror deployed by the Nazi regime, as well as the more specific total failure of the military coup against Hitler in July 1944. However, there were, in practice, other elements also at play, although the tendency to blame Nazi terror subsequently proved more convenient. A determination to defend the 'Fatherland' increased as Allied forces approached the German border, while, among Germans, there was also a widespread degree of ideological support, often fervent, for the Nazi regime.

Conditionality has also been present since 1945. Precisely because modern armies are more embedded in the societies they are meant to protect and the states they represent, these armies are greatly affected by social trends. Democratization, in particular, acts as a solvent to unquestioned obedience, and also encourages a willingness to challenge tasks and methods. This was true not only of the democratic states of Northern and Western Europe, but also of the totalitarian states of Eastern and Southern Europe after 1945. Indeed, concern about the views of the army affected conservative military figures, in Greece, Portugal and Spain, considering coups to seize control or, conversely, the retention of power after 1970 in the face of democratic demands. This concern also affected Communist leaders in Eastern Europe assessing the use of force to resist pressures for change.

To a degree, albeit in a very different context, the idea of modern states as limited by social conventions, political assumptions and legal norms, not least in the use of force, repeats the pattern under which so-called 'absolutist' rulers in the seventeenth and eighteenth centuries co-operated, including in their control of the military, with local supporters and agents, both within their territories and outside them. The latter was a process encouraged by the degree to which sovereignty in many areas, notably much of what would later become Germany and Italy, was fragmented and shared, and central power correspondingly limited in theory as well as practice.[7]

Both the nature of states in the period and the character of politics, domestic and international, forced this reliance on coalitions of interest. However, rather than treating these states and coalitions as inherently flawed, and notably by later, especially modern, and particularly current, standards, it is important to note their capacity to maintain military forces and support war. The broad nature of the coalitions, and the need to sustain and defend them, ensured that this was indeed war as politics, and politics as war, and, in some respects, more so than was to be seen later. This puts a valuable perspective on the idea of progressive development towards subsequent effectiveness.

The thesis of a public–private partnership that can be readily seen in the sixteenth to eighteenth centuries, however, has not been adequately worked through for the nineteenth and twentieth centuries, and, in part, this book is a call to do so. In the particular case of democratic capitalist societies, military capability requires not only a public–private partnership in terms of agreement over policy, but also active co-operation in order to ensure the necessary capability. Moreover, although the political, social and economic contexts can be very different, the same is also true for totalitarian states. The search for co-operation, indeed, is a key element of strategy, which, broadly conceived, is a question not so much of military moves as of the pursuance and use of capabilities. Economic prosperity, social stability and political effectiveness are all aspects of this equation. This equation links the ability to ensure stability and engender wealth successfully to that of employing them to provide a military that secures prosperity and furthers national goals, at least as defined by the government. Stability is understood as a key aspect of prosperity.

The historical pedigree of this approach is readily apparent. What has been referred to as mercantilism when applied to the seventeenth century, an approach that the French proved especially adept at following, was more generally the case, as governments strove for an economic development that would directly contribute to military strength, as well as indirectly providing settings for military activity. Mercantilism looked towards present Chinese and, indeed, Russian attitudes on the appropriate relationship between state and economy.[8]

In Britain, this process was exemplified by the Royal Navy, not only because it protected trade and was the most expensive branch of the military, but, also, because it for long represented the most advanced industrial activity carried out in Britain and, indeed, a source of industrial development.[9] Moreover, the major naval dockyards at Chatham, Portsmouth and Plymouth were the largest building complexes in Britain. In many respects, the navy in the seventeenth and, even more, eighteenth centuries reflected a co-operation between public and private. The dockyards themselves were state concerns, but much shipbuilding and repair was contracted out to private shipbuilders, and notably so in wartime when there was a need to raise naval capacity rapidly, for example during the War of American Independence (1775–83), which, after France entered the war in 1778, became, in part, a large, complex and threatening naval conflict. Earlier, in 1749, as a result of long war service against France and Spain, including damaging operations in the Caribbean, the British battle-fleet in good condition had been greatly reduced, and the dockyards could not cope with requirements for repair and replacement. This problem was overcome in the early 1750s, not least through using the private sector to build new ships.

Public provision should not be regarded as necessarily more (or less) efficient. The 1749 visitation of the royal dockyards in Britain revealed corruption and inefficiency. There was resistance in the Navy Board to proposals for radical reform, but there was considerable success in making the existing machinery work more smoothly. As a result, the naval mobilization of 1755 proceeded relatively smoothly. The public–private partnership heavily involved in the contracting out of army supply had also improved. The supply system that provided stores for naval construction, as well as foodstuffs to the Victualling Board (established in 1684) for naval operations, was even more a case of co-operation, in which the private sector played a key role. So also with the use by the Transport Board of merchantmen to move troops and, even more, supplies overseas. The effectiveness of these systems and their improvement helped enable Britain to deploy its forces effectively. Contractors understood the market better than bureaucrats and were less constrained by politics. This system could be further seen with Britain's overseas bases where, again, the Royal Navy rested for its effectiveness on both private local providers and contractors operating at long range.[10] So also with the significance of British privateers, private ships, authorized by the government (and thus not pirates), that provided the vital tool for commerce-raiding. The manning of the navy was a particular version of public–private partnership. Using forcible seizure through press gangs, the wartime navy was able to conscript experienced sailors from the British large merchant fleet, and then protected the nation's trade.[11] The crucial area of gunpowder production and distribution was another sphere of public–private co-operation. Greatly fluctuating demands created problems both for gunpowder makers, who were private, and for the Ordnance. In Prussia, where small-arms workshops were established by the government in 1722, their management was entrusted to the Berlin firm of Splitgerber and Daum, which was also used to expand the production of Prussian iron.

The process of partnership was also, but very differently, the case for the largest source of manpower at the service of the British system, the East India Company. Based at Leadenhall Street in the City of London, and in large part operating at the behest of its shareholders, and to their profit, the Company deployed military forces. This situation was not unique in Britain, being also the case, for example, with the Hudson Bay Company and the Royal African Company, each of which also had to protect fortified trading bases, such as those in West Africa from which slaves were traded. However, the scale of the East India Company was unprecedented in the British world. The Company ran a navy, of both warships and merchantmen, and used it to protect interests, for example against privateers in the Gulf and off the west coast of India, as well as to trade. The Company's naval system reached to major bases at Portsmouth and Bombay (Mumbai), to staging posts, notably the island of St Helena in the South Atlantic, and to trading stations past India, especially on Sumatra and in Canton (Guangzhou).

However, it was on land, overwhelmingly in India, that the Company was most potent. In 1782, it had an army of 115,000 troops, a force greater than that of the British army at this point. The discovery that Indians could be trained to fight effectively in the Western manner was critical. Moreover, this combat-ready army, which rose to 154,000 strong in 1805, was engaged in a number of wars from the 1750s to the 1810s, notably with the Marathas, Mysore and in Bengal. The latter was to provide a solid source of revenue and manpower, and to enable the Company to act as an effective territorial power.[12] India also served as the base for British operations elsewhere, including the capture of Manila in 1762, Djakarta in 1811 and Kandy (in Sri Lanka) in 1815. This remained a key pattern in the

British empire until Indian independence in 1947. Without these troops, Britain, thereafter, proved a far weaker power.

Looked at differently, the army depended on the profitability of the British position in India. The Indian troops in British service were all volunteers, and, even in the Second World War, there was no conscription in India, unlike in Britain. Although individual soldiers were not paid much, the total burden of pay was considerable, while much money had to be spent on equipment and supplies. Moreover, in order to dominate India, the Company needed to control the military labour market and be able to out-pay all potential rivals, a situation that mirrored that in parts of Europe during the early modern period. The Company eventually succeeded in doing so at the expense of the Marathas, the key opponent in west India, in a series of wars that left the British with the controlling position by the end of the 1810s. Thus, on a pattern also seen in Europe, the prosperity able to produce and utilize the necessary revenues was a key element in strength, alongside the more narrowly 'military' factors of training, equipment and leadership.

As with the Royal Navy, military capability served for the East India Company to protect the economic interests essential, not only to this capability, but also to national prosperity. Support for trade was a fundamental concern, and this meant the ready use of force against brigands, privateers and pirates, and to intimidate potentially hostile foreign powers. Thus, the Bombay Marine played a central role against Maratha privateers, notably the Angria family, although, finally, the job had to be entrusted to the Royal Navy. Similarly, North American colonial authorities and others had to turn to the Royal Navy to deal with pirates such as 'Blackbeard'. In both political and administrative terms, the British system proved able to create the world's most powerful empire, as well as to see off the French challenge, notably to see off Napoleon, who was finally defeated in 1815.[13]

Despite constitutional and practical differences, there were similar patterns of co-operation in other states, notably France. In particular, merchants were crucial to the operations of their armies and fleets. So also with other East India companies, most prominently that of the Netherlands.[14]

The closeness of the relationships in this period saw the British military, government and the business community work together. Frequently, this was a matter of direct tasks, such as merchants entrusting the movement of bullion to naval commanders, while, in Britain, troops were used for this purpose. More generally, the very structure of the British fiscal system rested on military strength. In the eighteenth century, the principal source of gold in what was overwhelmingly a metallic currency system was the Portuguese colony of Brazil. Britain's ability to dominate trade with Portugal and Brazil was crucial to gaining the gold that helped the government to recruit and support foreign military assistance and to borrow money at a low rate of interest, and that enabled merchants to finance trade with areas in which there was a negative balance of trade, notably Russia, Turkey and China. Naval dominance was the background to this global engine of trade. However, Britain's primacy in the Atlantic system rested, not only on the Royal Navy, but also on the deployment of the army to the Continent. The key destination was to assist Portugal against attack by Spain and/or France, notably in the 1660s, 1700s, 1762–3, 1808–13, and, with the focus now on civil war in Portugal, the 1820s.

An understanding of mutual benefit was a central element in systems of military support. This was particularly so in paying for the British military as annual supplies had to be granted in Parliament. Indeed, the cost-benefit of the military was often brutally contested in Parliament in the eighteenth century, with foreign policy and the value of the respective services being particularly contentious, not least in debates on the Addresses to the Crown, the key occasions at the start of the session. The navy did best in these debates, in part because political anxieties about what the government might do with the military focused on the army in Britain, but, more particularly, because it was easier to show that the navy secured economic interests.

The eighteenth century in Britain thus served to demonstrate the need for explicit discussion of the value of the military for broader national goals, and the impact of being able to conduct such discussion. Naval supporters were prominent in the mercantile community. Conversely, the army generally lacked protagonists at this scale, while it was only when the army's beat of securing national security was focused by readily grasped threats from France, as in the late 1750s, 1790s and 1800s, that public backing rose. This though led to the key expression of partnership in the shape of the militia and the volunteer movement. The number of militia rose to over 100,000 in the mid-1790s, and volunteer numbers were comparable.

At present, in contrast, the British governmental system has not worked well to articulate the relationship between military force and prosperity or security, and the same is true for most other European states. Again, the concrete character of trade makes this relationship easier for the navy to articulate, and piracy, notably in the Indian Ocean, has provided a readily comprehensible example. In practice, until security can be understood as a public good in a 'rules-based' system[15] requiring military capability, indeed very much so, it will be harder today to make the case than it was in the eighteenth century. The example of Britain, therefore, indicates the complexities of the public–private partnership and how they serve to offer a context within which to consider more familiar narratives and analyses.

Accounts of capability, however, let alone clinical accounts of battle need to be read alongside an understanding of the actual horrors of the fighting, including the use of case-shot against close-packed rows of soldiers. The Battle of Minden in 1759 was an impressive British victory, but one British participant wrote to his father:

I thought formerly I could easily form an idea of a battle from the accounts I heard from others, but I find everything short of the horrid sense, and it seems almost incredible that any can escape the incessant fire and terrible hissings of bullets of all sizes, the field of battle after is melancholy, four or five miles of plain covered with human bodies dead and dying, miserably butchered dead horses, broken wheels and carriages, and arms of all kind ... in the morning on the ground in our tents were pools of blood and pieces of brain.[16]

The shaping of European history is a matter of space and theme, as well as time and theme. Finding patterns in the geographies of events and developments involve conceptual and methodological problems, just as do those relating to the chronologies of events and developments. Moreover, these patterns are a matter not only of scholarly analysis, but also of political controversy and polemical comment. The extent to which these are (and were) differentiated are far from clear and, in practice, there is frequent overlap. It is instructive to turn to a statement made in the British House of Commons in 1778. Charles Jenkinson, a key government official who became Secretary at War that year, declared that:

the great military powers in the interior parts of Europe [Austria, Russia, Prussia], who have amassed together their great treasures, and have modelled their subjects into great armies, will in the next and succeeding periods of time, become the predominant powers. France and Great Britain, which have been the first and second-rate powers of the European world, will perhaps for the future be but of the third and fourth rate.[17]

This argument, which reflected, in part, the successful co-operation of Austria, Prussia and Russia in the first partition of Poland in 1772, a major transfer of territory, was not, however, the focus of Edward Gibbon, who, like Jenkinson, was an officeholder and an MP. Looking, in his *Decline and Fall of the Roman Empire* (1776–88), at the West as a whole, Gibbon thought it unlikely that 'barbarian' invaders would succeed anew, as they had done at the expense of the Roman Empire, in part because they would have to overcome a Russia that in his view had been Westernized under Peter the Great, and, more generally, due to improvements in Western defences, thanks to cannon and fortification techniques.

The issues raised by the two men reflected both a strong sense of volatility, a volatility underplayed in much social science work with its ahistorical characteristics,[18] and the tendency to relate this volatility directly to questions of military capability. Moreover, there was the question of how best to understand the dynamic of military developments and, in particular, whether the key issue was developments within Europe (and, if so, why) or, rather, the pressure on the West of external powers. The latter raised the issue, mentioned in the Preface, of how external powers were, and are, to be understood and, in particular, whether the very linkage helped make such powers part of a European military system. If the West is understood in terms of a Romano–Christian nexus, then the Ottomans (Turks), despite taking over Constantinople (Istanbul), in 1453, and the Eastern Roman Empire, were clearly an external challenge, which helps explain the discussion of their role in Chapter 2, notably in conflict with Spain. The challenge was not simply that of the quantity of force brought to bear against the West, but also of different military methods that were effective and remained so until the nineteenth century, albeit with a lesser impact after the early 1680s. There was no significant disparity between Turkish and Western abilities to mobilize and finance major campaigns until the late seventeenth century. The Turks were effective in feeding and supplying their troops, and their logistical ability was very important to their operational capability.

The role of this challenge on developments within the West invites consideration. In particular, there is, repeatedly, the question of the relative significance of a Western core as opposed to a periphery, with the former understood in terms of developments produced by conflict with other Western powers, whereas non-Westerners played a role in the latter. This theory is superficially attractive, and is linked to a tendency to primitivize developments in Eastern Europe, not least by suggesting that the Turks were somehow bound to fail and/or were more primitive in their fighting techniques, and that this affected their opponents, with, indeed, detrimental long-term consequences for force structure and fighting quality. That approach, which is sometimes particularly directed against the long-standing use of cavalry in Eastern Europe, and notably in Poland and Hungary, is misleading in its account of Eastern Europe. This approach also underplays the extent to which, far from being limited to Eastern Europe, or Mediterranean powers in addition, powers in conflict with non-Western opponents included Portugal and Spain in the sixteenth century, and, as a result of trans-oceanic operations, England, France and the Dutch, thereafter.

Moreover, conflicts on the periphery, however defined, might well have had a greater impact on the core than a model that privileges developments within the latter might claim. Methods and organizations devised to deal with these conflicts had an impact elsewhere in the West. Austria and Poland acted as crucial intermediaries, notably in maintaining a role for light cavalry. In the eighteenth century, the Russians developed and used successfully against the Turks the infantry columns subsequently employed by the French.

There are also problems with assuming that non-Western powers were less sophisticated in an administrative fashion. It is indeed the case that the limitations of the technologies and organizational forms for the exercise of power at a distance was, and remained, a factor affecting the ability of decentralized imperial regimes that were too large and heterogeneous to develop into more effective states with a degree of bureaucratic efficiency.[19] Yet, the level of effectiveness seen in China was very impressive. In addition, as discussed in the next chapter, Europe also included a hostile expanding imperial system in the shape of the Turkish empire. Its strength was based upon the resources of a far-flung empire, on an ideology that saw war against the non-believer as a duty, and on a society structured for its effective prosecution. Turkish forces were deployed in accordance with a grand strategy based on a considered analysis of intelligence and policy options and drawing on a formidable and well-articulated logistical system. Moreover, alongside non-Western powers, Western states also pursued empire, in Europe as well as overseas.[20]

Success against the Turks helped give Austria and Russia greater relative power. Jenkinson's 1778 prediction might have appeared prescient in 1815 when, indeed, his son, Robert, 2nd Earl of Liverpool, was Prime Minister. On the third anniversary of Napoleon's costly victory over the Russians at Borodino, a victory that opened the way to Moscow, Tzar Alexander I, in the presence of the rulers of Austria and Prussia, reviewed 150,000 Russian troops at Chalons in France. Nevertheless, the enhanced governmental effectiveness and greater state authority (compared to Western European states) of what became the leading states of Eastern and Central Europe did not so clearly have the consequences Jenkinson predicted, which underlines the repeated difficulties of anticipating circumstances. Most obviously, Russia, Austria and Prussia failed to overthrow the empire of Napoleonic France in 1805–7, and only did so in 1812–15 due to Napoleon's military and political maladroitness, both in invading Russia and in failing to benefit from the rivalries between the three powers, and due to the key role of Britain. Aside from the pressure exerted from blockade by the British navy, and the more direct contribution of the British army under the command of the Duke of Wellington, the economic and fiscal system, already referred to, generated the funds that enabled Britain to subsidize its allies while also providing crucial commercial links.

If, in 1945, Soviet forces (the largest part of which came from Russia) conquered Berlin, Prague and Vienna in the defeat of Germany, a defeat that also entailed the overthrow of Hitler's alliance system, with the conquest of Bucharest, Sofia and Budapest, they did so, not because of the weakness of Western Europe, but due, in part, to the assistance of pressure on Germany from Western powers, crucially the USA and Britain.[21] In this case, the divisions of Jenkinson's 'interior parts' were notable: Hitler's German empire, which included Austria and the Czech Republic, fought the Soviet Union.

The Cold War represented a continuation of the geopolitical advance of what Halford Mackinder termed the 'Heartland', with the Soviet Union greatly helped by the economic and manpower strength of Eastern Europe, and notably by the industrial base of East Germany, which was occupied from 1945. Nevertheless, in practice, the global dimension played out very differently from the late fifteenth century to developments in Europe, for, however powerful these states of the 'interior parts', notably Russia, but also Austria and Prussia (and later Germany), were on the Continent, the trans-oceanic world was competed for by Atlantic states, with Britain (later the USA) ultimately dominant. This contrast, and the variations arising from differing perspectives on it, is of more general note. Indeed, the nature of the present, military, geopolitical and ideological, remains up for contention, and this is even more so for speculation about the future. Each, in practice, contributes to debate about the past. Thus, teleological accounts of change should be seen as an aspect of this contention, rather than as an immutable proof subject to analysis.

Periodization is also subject to contention, notably the consequences flowing from the adoption of differing divides and periods, and, linking to this, from the emphasis placed on these. For example, a stress on a division in 1792, the outbreak of the French Revolutionary Wars, can involve an emphasis on ideological factors and on related organizational changes, notably a greater degree of mobilization of the resources of society, but also on the tactical and operational changes adopted by the French Revolutionary forces. Although each of these aspects as developed by the Revolutionaries is generally presented as more effective than their *ancien régime* predecessors, this approach represents a seriously misleading assessment of the latter. It also offers a preference for war-waging through battle and attack that does not capture the range of cultures of war at issue, not least the potency of the defensive option.[22] Moreover, in 1815, Napoleon, the heir of French Revolutionary methods, collapsed in total defeat and failure before *ancien régime* forces, which suggests that a periodization focused on 1792 is inappropriate. Indeed, 'why focus on failure?' is a question that repeatedly emerges when considering Louis XIV, Napoleon and Hitler for, in each case, initial success was followed by eventual defeat. In that context, their opponents deserve more attention. A focus on 1792 is also one that makes sense for Western Europe, but not for Eastern.

Alongside important contrasts in perspective, and chronological discontinuities within the period covered by this book, there are also major notes of continuity. These are provided by the dominance of military service by men and by the degree to which the ability of Western societies and states to finance military activity increased in the late fifteenth and sixteenth centuries, and remained considerable thereafter. This ability, in the late fifteenth and sixteenth centuries, was due to political consolidation, administrative development and economic growth, as populations recovered from the traumatic mid-fourteenth-century epidemic of bubonic plague known as the Black Death, an epidemic that, with the addition of repeated attacks, ensured that the population remained low through the fifteenth century. The revival of population numbers was not directly linked to the rise in the place of infantry in European armies and warfare, as that reflected a number of factors (both narrowly military and others), but the two were related.

An emphasis on a discontinuity in the fifteenth century that was followed by the change discussed above should not serve to suggest that there were not important developments that spanned the fifteenth century. Indeed, alongside the dynamism of continuing themes as the causes of conflict, such as Crusading,[23] there were important medieval anticipations of many features of what was to be seen as characteristic or even revolutionary about sixteenth-century warfare. At the same time, the successful use of siege artillery and the raising of permanent standing forces gathered pace from the mid-fifteenth century.

A range of factors contributed to the development of artillery, with governmental strength, however precarious, being one of them. Technological changes were significant in order to find a rapidly burning mixture with a high propellant force, and thus to transform what had initially been essentially an incendiary into a stronger explosive device. The use of potassium sulphate, rather than lime saltpetre, possibly from about 1400, helped limit the propensity of gunpowder to absorb moisture and deteriorate. Moreover, around 1420, 'corned' powder was developed in Western Europe, the gunpowder being produced in granules that kept its components together and led to it being a more effective propellant, providing the necessary energy, but without dangerously high peak pressures. Iron cannonballs were supplemented by canister or grape shot. The employment of improved metal casting techniques, which owed a great deal to a different, but related activity, the casting of church bells, and the use of copper-based alloys, bronze and brass, as well as cast iron, made cannon lighter and more reliable. They were able to cope with the increased explosive power generated by 'corned' gunpowder, while improved metal casting also permitted trunnions cast as an integral part of the barrel, which improved mobility and rates of fire.[24]

Charles VII of France (r. 1422–61) employed artillery with results, notably in rapidly conquering Normandy from Henry VI of England in 1449–50, although, as with the fall of Constantinople to the Ottoman ruler Mehmed II in 1453, far more than the use of cannon was involved in this success. Charles' successor, Louis XI of France (r. 1461–83), proved particularly successful in developing an effective military system. Moreover, the increased ability, thanks in large part to cannon, to operate rapidly and to purpose in fortified regions, such that it was possible to overrun an entire region in one campaign increased strategic options and the political threat posed by war.[25]

The process of political consolidation and administrative development, one associated with the 'New Monarchies', notably in France, England and Spain, was to be greatly challenged from the 1520s, as the impact of the Protestant Reformation increased domestic divisions. However, the demographic growth of the sixteenth century, while stemmed in the seventeenth, in part, in response to global cooling and its impact on crop growing seasons, yields and resistance to disease, resumed from the mid-eighteenth in a continuing trend that contrasted with the earlier period of Western history. This was a crucial element in Western military history, and one of lasting significance. Again, the degree of emphasis, whether on inherent continuity, or on the discontinuity of seventeenth-century crisis, is open to debate. Long-term trends can conceal key short-term factors. Yet, the rise in population was a fundamental motor of change, albeit one that operated differently to the situation in other parts of the world. Alongside differing circumstances in modern Europe, notably due to the role of immigrants, this rise continues to be such a motor at present and will be so into the future.

CHAPTER TWO

The Fracturing of the European System, 1450–1600

If all periods are subject to change, this was especially the case in the late fifteenth and, even more, sixteenth centuries. The impact of the Ottoman (Turkish) advance in Europe, especially from the 1450s, interacted, combined and clashed with that of the Protestant Reformation from the 1510s, as well as that of the rapid and major expansion of the Western world, particularly from the 1490s. These developments were on an unprecedented scale for Christendom. Invasions of Europe comparable to that of the Turks had been briefly seen with the Mongols in the thirteenth century and, before that, the Magyars of the tenth. However, it was necessary to go back to the Moors of the eighth century in Spain and Portugal to see a long-term change, political and religious, of the scale wrought by the Turks in the Balkans. The significance of the Turkish challenge, an involuntary challenge unlike those facing Western expansion, ensures that in this chapter the wider global context of European history attracts particular attention. As further instances of developments on an unprecedented scale, there was no earlier comparison with the Reformation nor with trans-oceanic expansion. Conflict played an important, although differing, role in each of these.

Moreover, the developments of 1450–1600 interacted. For example, the expansion of the Western world led to a major increase in the availability of bullion as a result of the Spanish conquest of the Aztec and Inca empires and the subsequent exploitation of gold and silver deposits, notably silver in Mexico and at the 'silver mountain' of Potosi in Bolivia. This bullion ensured that Spain had more money and credit with which to pursue its ambitions in Europe, and made the protection of the shipping route from the New World, notably that from Vera Cruz in Mexico, a strategic necessity.

The situation, which resulted from the changes discussed in the opening paragraph, created military needs and, therefore, opportunities. These can be presented as beginning a new period in Western military history, one, indeed, that serves for the opening chronological section of this book, a section that also seeks a focus on conceptual, methodological and historiographical issues. Indeed, an emphasis on military needs and opportunities, in short on tasking, is more appropriate than the argument that new military technology, in the shape of the large-scale use of firearms and cannon, both on land and at sea, as well as fortifications designed to resist artillery, brought in a new age of war and served to create new needs, opportunities and anxieties, both military and political. In short, rather than as is suggested in the last sentence, technology, instead, should be discussed in the context of political and ideological needs and opportunities. The perception of these helped establish tasks, and these tasks framed the response to technological possibilities.

Outlining contrasts in routes into the subject underlines the extent to which there are significant procedural and analytical choices involved in covering military history, and for other periods as well as this one, not that the options are all of equal merit. These choices must be addressed explicitly in order to clarify the subject intellectually and to offer a mature exposition. Choices relate to what to cover and, more significantly, as generally unstated, what not to cover. They relate to where, and how, to place the priority. There are also fundamental choices in exposition and choices in analysis. As examples of a far from exhaustive list, should the emphasis be on land capability or on its naval counterpart; on offensive ability or on defensive strength? Usually the answer, in each case, is both; but, accepting that obvious conclusion, how does that settle the more problematic case of where to place the emphasis and how to handle it?

What approach should be taken to the equations of cost, and what to the different, but related, issues of economic, social and political, context and impact? To possess a fine military capability but, in doing so, to incur major political costs in order to sustain it, and thus to endanger internal stability as Spain did in 1640, is frequently a poor trade-off. Nevertheless, looked at differently, there is always risk of political and social instability, and this military capability may lessen its consequences. Thus, alongside problems, indeed serious problems, the added military strength of the state can bring many benefits. Moreover, the debate about imperial overreach, or what is presented as overreach, in the case of leading powers, such as Spain in the sixteenth century and Britain in the early twentieth (and certainly if handled in a sophisticated fashion, rather than by means of argument by assertion), underlines the highly problematic character of military power. In doing so, the difficulties of forming a judgement and, even, framing a pertinent analytical context, are amply displayed. Partly for that reason, the focus in this chapter is on Spain, the leading Western power, and certainly in the late sixteenth century.

There is, in addition, as with other topics, the change and changes, indeed inherent uncertainty and dynamic, provided by military developments, and the question of how best to assess developments when considering military power. Is innovation a key constituent of the latter and, if so, how is it to be evaluated? Was the likely pattern of development clear-cut, and, if not, why not? Could another course have been followed and, if so, with what consequences? Why were other courses not followed? How are the costs and risks of military change to be assessed? How far is the emphasis to be on the early stages of innovation, and how far on their later diffusion? What view is to be taken of the public–private partnerships discussed in the last chapter, and how did their potential and the contemporary perception of them alter during the period?

A conceptual introduction based on questions, and on questions that cannot really be readily answered, ensures, in the case of this book, that the subsequent discussion is offered as a basis for propositions that are necessarily incomplete and always open to debate. It is possible to argue, simultaneously, that European military power by 1600 was impressive compared to the situation in 1450, but that so also was the power of other parts of the world;[1] while, whatever the overall assessment, not all sectors of European military power should be seen in this light or as impressive. Moreover, the military was only able to deliver specific outcomes. Yet, the latter has also been true of military power across history, and this limitation is not best approached in terms of overreach and systemic failure. This consideration of 1450–1600, in turn, offers perspectives on the following period, not least establishing the question of whether, and to what extent, the same, or a similar, analytical construction should be used.

The questions already offered are made more significant, both individually and as a group, because of the practice of discussing the period, and notably in Europe, in terms of a military revolution, indeed the military revolution that got the concept of such revolutions going.[2] This practice comes with the implication that the ability to frame, respond to and keep responding to the potential of such a revolution was central to power, and, moreover, that military proficiency and development should be discussed in terms of this supposed revolution, as should the political history of the period. Thus, the analysis is apparently readily provided: terminology, in part, serves to this end.

In practice, the somewhat dated and seriously problematic thesis of the early modern military revolution requires critical discussion and scrutiny. This discussion should take place at a number of levels: European and global, land and sea, offensive and defensive and chronological, being an incomplete list. In terms of comparative context, all these factors invite close attention, but there is also the question of the frame of reference: Western (in the sense of Christian Europe), European (in a geographical sense) or global; and, whichever frame is adopted, how are they to be defined and how is space in terms of analytical attention to be distributed? There is also the key issue of the use of language, as applying the term revolution serves to provide a metaphor rather than to offer an analysis. Metaphors are potent, but that is what they are, and the metaphor of revolution is both highly resonant and overused, both in this and in other periods.[3]

The geographical issue is made more pertinent by the long-standing tendency to treat European developments in terms of the broader trajectory of what was referred to as the 'gunpowder empires'.[4] While understandable, that approach offers only an inadequate introduction to the global context. In particular, employing, as so often, an 'epistemology of opposition in which the two sides are delimited in terms of essential differences from one another' is mistaken.[5] Thus, it was possible for Spain, the leading Western military power in the sixteenth century, to make spectacular gains over some non-Western opponents, notably the Aztecs and Incas in the New World, and not at the expense of others, prominently the Ottoman Turks in the Mediterranean. So also with Portugal, which made spectacular gains in the waters and coastlines of the Indian Ocean, but proved unable to sustain its positions in Morocco and, differently, Mozambique.

The early modern period can be taken as essentially 1450–1750, although it is capable of other bookending dates including 1789. In an influential argument, the historian William Robertson, in his *History of the Reign of the Emperor Charles V with a view of the Progress of Society from the subversion of the Roman Empire to the beginning of the sixteenth century* (1769), was to date the onset of the modern European system to the outbreak of the Italian Wars in 1494 and the establishment, he claimed, of a balance of power.[6] In so far as there was such a balance, it was challenged most clearly in Europe by Spain and the Turkish empire.

The key contrast throughout the period between Spain, the leading Western power, and other contemporary major world powers is that of a unique global range and related ambition on the part of Spain, the state that is the focus of most discussion of military change in the sixteenth century. As it was well aware, the Spanish empire had a unique range among major global powers. This was notably so after the acquisition of the Portuguese throne by Philip II of Spain (r. 1556–98) in 1580 after a rapidly successful campaign by land and sea. At the same time, the choice of words is indicative. The use of acquisition does not suggest the role of force which in fact was very important to what was a successful conquest after King Sebastian had been killed (and his army totally defeated) at the Battle of Alcazarquivir in Morocco in 1578 fighting the Moors. Spain's global range brought significant economic advantage, as well as the ability to act as a regional force in a number of separate areas across the world, and to an hitherto unique extent. In a very different context, this prefigured the situations of nineteenth-century Britain and the modern USA. Modern China currently lacks this capability and ambition, and the same was true of early modern China, as well as of the Mughal empire in India.

In addition to acting as a regional force in a number of separate areas, there was also, for Spain, as for Britain in the eighteenth century, the possibility of thinking of more global coordination. The practicality of the latter, however, was gravely limited, before the steamships, coaling stations and telegraph networks of the late nineteenth century, given the technology of the earlier period (notably for the speedy and reliable transmission of messages and the movement of troops), and also the resources available. So also with bold ideas, for example of a Turkish advance in 1569 on Astrakhan which the Russians had conquered a decade earlier,[7] and of Spanish action against China. The latter ideas were a product of fantasies by Spanish officers already hanging about in the Far East. They were rejected out of hand by Philip II and the government in Madrid. The Spanish presence in the Philippines, established from 1565, was in practice weak and, by the standards of the modern state, limited, and the same was true of the Portuguese presence in the Far East.

Indeed, there was no reason to think that, in normal circumstances, Spain would have managed to overthrow the Incas of the Andean chain of South America in the 1530s, let alone the far more powerful Chinese. In the former case, the aftermath of a devastating civil war was the key context, and this was also the situation for the Manchu overthrow of Ming China in the 1640s. As with the Spanish overthrow of the Aztecs in modern Mexico in 1519–21, local divisions weakened the responses to the outsiders and produced assistance for them. The Incas and the Aztecs were the two major powers in the Americas, although their ability to influence developments there more widely was limited, notably due to their lack of naval power. American peoples had boats, both on the Atlantic and the Pacific, but no naval power to compare with that of Spain. The success of the Manchu, which was matched by that of the Mughals in conquering the Lodi Sultanate of Delhi in 1526, and by those of the Turks, serves as a reminder that the Christian Europeans were not necessarily the most impressive conquerors on land.

Whatever the limitations of Spain in the Far East, the period did show that it was possible to act militarily at a distance, and to do so successfully. This became a characteristic of the European Atlantic powers, and one that requires consideration as a crucial aspect of the distinctiveness of this power. Issues of military effectiveness are linked to it. Moreover, among the major world powers, only the Western European ones, and notably Portugal and Spain, had the capacity to act in more than one hemisphere in the sixteenth century. In addition, whereas the Turkish empire sought distant power projection, into, and in, the (Persian) Gulf and the Indian Ocean,[8] it did not match the consistent effort being made by Spain to deploy power at a greater range. In addition, the Turks failed in the Gulf and the Indian Ocean, and did not persist in their efforts there.

The net effect was a contrast, in terms of distance, between a transoceanic Spanish and an essentially trans-Mediterranean Turkish empire. This was a contrast linked to that between an empire that drew heavily on precious metals and one based more exclusively on land and trade. The latter contrast was also the case with the seventeenth and early-eighteenth-century reliance of the Dutch and British empires on maritime power and trade, rather than simply on territory. Thus, in India and West

Africa, trading bases were sought, and not extensive lands. This, in turn, helped influence the ethos of overseas military activity. On the other hand, territory was a goal in both North America and, for the Dutch, in Brazil.

A focus on capabilities, including technological advance, leaves to one side the extent to which the latter were, and should be, considered in terms of goals and, thereby, military tasking. Although it is possible to point to important similarities between the imperial powers of the period, they were not always similar or, indeed, readily comparable. For example, the means and purposes of dynastic aggrandizement and ambition in the case of the Habsburgs were different to those of the Ottomans (Turks), Safavids, Mughals and Ming, not that these were identical. Indeed, to write of 'Asian' is to suggest an essential identity that did not exist, a point that can be even more clearly made in the case of 'non-Western'.

The character and extent of differences are not fixed and can be debated. For example, it is possible to describe dynasticism in contrasting fashions. The nature and dynamic of Philip II's policies in his later years is a subject for which there are more plentiful sources than for the other cases discussed. Nevertheless, despite the availability of these sources and the considerable scholarship deployed, these policies have been presented both in terms of messianic imperialism but, more convincingly, with reference to the idea of traditional dynasticism.[9] The issues of manifest destiny and universalism also emerge for both the Habsburgs and the Ottomans (Turks) for earlier in the sixteenth century. There are instructive parallels between the two.[10]

The ambitions of the Emperor Charles V (r. 1519–56;[11] Charles I of Spain, r. 1516–56), father of Philip II, focused heavily, but not exclusively, on honour and glory. His reputation played a major role in the choices he made, not least in resolving the conflicting priorities of his various dominions, which included Spain, Sicily, Naples, Sardinia, the Milanese (Lombardy), the Low Countries (Belgium and the Netherlands), Franche-Comté and Austria. In this stress on reputation, Charles followed the emphasis on prestige and rank seen with his predecessors and contemporaries.[12] With its focus on honour and dynastic responsibility, and its concern with rank and *gloire*, the political culture was scarcely cautious or pacific. The nature of this culture did not dictate outcomes, but it did ensure a bellicosity that lent itself to the aggressiveness of young rulers. A focus on renown was also seen with warriors. Whether old or new, forms of warfare served to display valour and other traditional knightly skills. Moreover, such skills were still pertinent for the leadership required from officers. The stress on individual prowess was not incompatible with organized systems of warfare. For example, fighting at sea in part served to display the merit of the prominent warriors who commanded the warships and led the boarding parties. The same was true with fortifications in that those who led storming parties into breaches, or who resisted attack in these breaches, acquired great renown.

As with other dynasties, the international situation involved choice while also affecting choices. For example, if Ferdinand of Aragon (r. 1479–1516), one of Charles' grandfathers, had not, in the 1500s, pursued the interests of his forbears in southern Italy, then it would possibly have remained in the French orbit, and this outcome remained a prospect both in the 1520s and the 1640s. Such a development would have compromised the Spanish position with the Papacy, and thus the position of the Habsburgs within Spain, in Italy, and in ideological terms as defenders of Christendom. Ferdinand could, however, have devoted more attention, instead, to expansion in North Africa and the political and ideological tasks, challenges and opportunities this represented.

The rivalry between Aragon and France in Italy looked back to competing ambitions in the thirteenth century. This was an instance of the degree to which dynastic, political and geopolitical rivalries did not begin in the early modern period but, in many respects, were a continuation of those in the later Middle Ages. So also with the competition between the Burgundians and the kings of France and those between England and Scotland. Indeed, the interaction of these older identities and tensions with newer ones helped to give a dynamic quality, as well as complex character, to the politics of the period.

If the issue of goals directs attention to political culture at the decision-making level, there is also the question of its wider resonance. Most notably, the societies of the period had hierarchical and deferential political cultures, and were far more opposed to disruptive change and the ethos of modernization than later societies were to be. As a result, new technology was resisted, shaped or channelled into socially acceptable patterns. This conservatism scarcely prevented change, but it affected both its content and pace. This was the case both within the West and in the non-West.

In part, conservatism can be discussed in terms of different national military traditions, such that France had less infantry firepower than Spain in the early sixteenth century, while the Poles and the Mughals put a far greater emphasis on cavalry than the German rulers and the Ming respectively. A focus on traditions can make the system as a whole, as well as individual countries, appear anachronistic. However, it is necessary, in this as in other cases throughout the period covered by the book, to avoid an easy turn to suggesting anachronism. First, as with other instances, such a conclusion underplays the great significance of political and social contexts. Secondly, arguments of anachronism greatly risk adopting a teleological, as well as misleading, approach to military development. Not least, these arguments underplay the extent to which weapons were part of tactical systems that helped incorporate innovations into existing patterns of use and already-established practices of training and command, and were seen accordingly. At the same time, the Europe of the Renaissance was capable of thinking through new solutions even as it looked back to Antiquity in its search for validation, as with the attention devoted to Flavius Vegetius'

De Re Militari, a Roman text of the fourth century. This was a major source for fifteenth-century manuals.[13]

Printing made earlier manuscript works more accessible and was an important aspect of the potential for change that was so apparent from the fifteenth century. The use of movable metal type by European printers from mid-century ensured that the already frequent circulation of military manuals was stepped up. This was important not only for a self-conscious revival in the Renaissance of Greek and Roman knowledge, but also of making more recent manuscript works more accessible. Thus Leon Battista Alberti's *De Re Aedificatoria*, with its call for sloped and lower fortress walls, was written in the 1440s but first printed in 1485. The prestige of the Classical world was such that a 'return to the past' served to validate new emphases. In particular, from 1487, the Roman writers Vegetius, Aelianus Tactitus, Frontinus and Modestus were published by Eucherius Silber in Rome. In turn, Julius Caesar's *Comentarii* were published in an Aldine edition in 1513, and this served as the basis for another Latin edition published in Paris in 1543. Published in Lyon in 1594, Guillaume Du Choul's study of Roman fortification and military discipline appeared in new editions in 1555, 1556 and 1567. Ideas and vocabulary associated with Classical Rome were applied in order to validate developments. For example, Battista della Valle's *Vallo Libro Continente Appertinentie à Capitani, Ritenere e Fortificare una Città con Bastioni*, a very popular work on fortifications that went through eleven editions from 1524 to 1558, drew heavily on Classical sources.

The Classical world, however, could provide only limited guidance to many of the challenges and opportunities of the period. The trans-oceanic was not the sum total of Europe's maritime power, which was also significant more locally. However, serious constraints were posed by the need to maintain naval capability. These constraints involved the requirement to build and maintain ships in the face of serious environmental pressures on ships' organic components. Philip II, like his fellow monarchs, did not adequately appreciate the constraints.[14] Nevertheless, there was also the ability on the part of Spain and France to sustain significant fleets both in Atlantic and in Mediterranean waters, an ability that was important to their rivalry. The range of maritime environments was great, and that of the tasks therefore required was considerable. Thus, under Philip, Spain deployed fleets in the Azores and the Mediterranean, both western and eastern, the Tagus, the English Channel and the North Sea, as well as in more distant waters.[15] This deployment was of a different order to other Western powers in the late sixteenth century. The distinctive aspect of the Spanish mobilization of resources was both its depth, encompassing widespread social, political and financial networks, and its extraordinary wide reach, both on land and at sea. As a result, Spain was a major military power in many geographical contexts, but also had very heavy costs and numerous opponents, indeed a unique number as far as contemporary Europe was concerned.

The deployment of force offers a measure of relative power and one of considerable significance. War was the more active stage of such a measure. In this case, the most significant rivalry for this measure was that in the Mediterranean; as Spain was most strongly opposed there by a non-Western power, the Turkish empire. In this case, it is possible to look for direct comparability for Spanish military power, and to consider specific outcomes. This is a process that is not practical for distant empires such as China and the Mughal empire. Moreover, the Mediterranean should be seen as a key and integral sphere of Western power, rather than as a detached sphere or one separable in terms of the specific equations of naval and amphibious power.

Just as in the Balkans, the struggle with the Turks focused existential issues of identity so that the struggle became the end product of what had been the long Spanish theme of conflict with Islam. This was a theme that was integral to Spanish history, identity and ideology, lay as well as religious, at this point, and a theme that very much bridged the medieval and the early modern, two periods generally seen as opposed. The *Reconquista* of Spain and Portugal, the overthrow of Moorish rule, was followed both by campaigning into North Africa (with which it overlapped) and by a discriminatory policy towards those of Moorish origins living in Iberia. Final Spanish success in 1492 against Granada, the last Moorish territory in Iberia, for what was seen in Spain as the new 'Chosen People', was followed by the stepping up of conquest in North Africa, as the Mediterranean was not regarded as a barrier. Captured positions such as Malaga, which fell in 1487, became important bases for this conquest. Moreover, the strategic[16] and ideological assumptions of the *Reconquista* remained valid.

At the outset of the sixteenth century, the Turks were not yet established in the western Mediterranean, as they were to be on the coasts of what is now Algeria and Tunisia. Instead, the Spanish military machine had been well-honed by the long war for Granada, while Spain's opponents were weak and divided. On the coast of North Africa, the town of Melilla was gained in 1497, followed by Mers-al-Kabir in 1505, Oran in 1509 and Bougie, Tripoli and the Peñón d'Argel position dominating Algiers in 1510. Spain still holds the first, as well as Ceuta.

However, as so often, comparability between two powers has to be set in a context of contrasting exigencies, for it is rare that powers compete without any other alternative commitments. Thus, the situation for Spain in the Mediterranean deteriorated in the 1520s as Charles I of Spain focused much (though far from all) of his attention on his role as the Emperor Charles V, the heir to the inheritance of the anti-French Dukes of Burgundy and, less centrally, that of the Habsburgs. He devoted more resources to war with Francis I of France (r. 1515–47), notably in northern Italy, than to competing with the Islamic powers, and this was particularly clear on land. This was the decade of Charles' crushing defeat of Francis at Pavia (1525), as well as of more decisive success against French forces in Italy in

1529, decisive in that it led, with the Treaty of Cambrai of that year, to a longer peace than that which had followed Pavia. In fighting Francis over Italy, Charles was fulfilling the goal of Ferdinand of Aragon as well as of his other grandfather, the Emperor Maximilian I (r. 1493–1519).

Gunpowder weaponry was significant in the fighting, albeit less so than might have been anticipated. Slow loading made artillery of limited use in battle, however valuable it was in battle. Nevertheless, the Spanish deployment of musketeers made a major difference in successive battles, first in the Italian Wars and later in the early stages of the Dutch Revolt. This was notably so because this emphasis on firepower was not matched by others. The Spaniards employed their infantry flexibly and effectively, concentrating firepower and practising volley fire.[17] At the Battle of Cerignola in 1503, a greatly outnumbered Spanish army provided a striking demonstration of the value of new weapons. Their commander, Gonzalo de Córdoba, a veteran of the conquest of Granada, held his men in defence behind a trench and earth parapet. This stopped three attacks by the French cavalry, exposing them, and the Swiss pikemen in support, to heavy Spanish fire from arquebuses: handguns in which the powder was ignited by a length of slow-burning match. Córdoba's revival of the art of field fortification thereby transformed tactical possibilities, although, as a reminder of the difficulty of judging success, this was possible largely because the French attacked rapidly and without due care, failing to bring up their artillery against the Spanish fieldworks, which would have been vulnerable to cannon. The effectiveness of firearms was linked to their mobility and rate of fire. As a consequence, cannon were most effective against a static defence, whether in the field or fortifications. Cannon offered little against light cavalry.

Demonstrating the importance of the tempo of a battle and of seizing the initiative, the Spaniards at Cerignola then mounted a successful counter-attack, with infantry providing fire and movement, and then cavalry, and thus completed the victory. Cerignola began a series of battles that involved the use of a variety of weapons, weapons systems and tactics, in the search for advantage. The different combinations of infantry, cavalry and artillery owed much to the precedents created by the organization and sophisti-cation of combined arms systems in the late fifteenth century, especially by the Burgundians. Close-proximity action remained the crucial nature of conflict in both battle and 'small war'. Firearms did not greatly lessen that as they were not sufficiently effective to clear the battlefield. Although firearms could do considerable damage, hand-to-hand combat and cold steel remained important in both infantry and, even more, cavalry fighting.

The Turkish advance was tangential to Habsburg power in the 1500s, but less so by the 1520s. The character of a dynastic model of power, however, was that, although it is possible to focus on prioritization, Charles was also deploying collective power, both against France and the Turks. Thus, Spain, which at this point was a dynastic union that is difficult to define politically, was devoting resources and military power in the 1520s

and 1530s not only against France, but also to war with the Turks, both in
the Mediterranean and in holding the Hungarian frontier. Individual careers
demonstrated this, and suggest the links that could result. Thus, Alfonso
d'Avalos, Marquis of Vasto (1502–46), an Italian-born Spaniard, not only
served in Italy against the French, including at the battles of Pavia (1525)
and Ceresole (1544), but also campaigned against the Turks in Hungary in
1532 and served on the successful expedition against Tunis in 1535.

In turn, the Turkish empire became far more important as a Mediterranean
force, which enabled a marked increase in its power-projection, as well as
greatly affecting the geopolitics of Southern Europe. Indeed, a key aspect of
the military history of Europe in this period was that Christendom was very
much subject to the agenda of a non-Christian power. The rapid and totally
successful Turkish conquest of Egypt in 1517 was particularly significant
and served to underline the extent to which Europe was part of a wider
power system, in political, religious and economic terms. This conquest,
which was affirmed when rebellions were crushed, greatly strengthened the
Turks as a naval power, and also ensured that they were able to ground
their Mediterranean position on strong economic underpinnings, especially
the agriculture and commerce of Egypt. This grounding proved significant
for Turkish power projection, both further west in North Africa and into
the Indian Ocean. There was no previous experience of Islamic power on
this scale. As a consequence of the replacement of the local Islamic regimes
in North Africa by direct Turkish influence, the Spaniards were pushed
onto the back foot and came to fight a defensive, reactive struggle to retain
footholds and influence.

The Spanish presence in North Africa was far weaker than that of
the Turks, and required large infusions of support. Such a dependence
highlighted the importance of alternative commitments, for they affected
not only the ability to provide these infusions, but also the willingness
to do so. The same was to be true of the American-Soviet rivalry in the
Mediterranean in the late 1960s and early 1970s. Similarly, Spanish
support had to be provided to southern Italy and to Malta. Conversely, the
absence of such support led to the loss to the Turks of Italian-held islands
in the Aegean, including Naxos in 1566, and, finally, that of Venetian-ruled
Cyprus in 1570–1.

As an instance of the partnerships of power and empire, the use of local
agents proved a key element, one that, from the 1520s, gave the Turks a
crucial advantage. Corsairs, notably Hayreddin, 'Barbarossa', proved very
significant. He not only recaptured the Peñón in 1529, but also gained
control of Algiers and its hinterland. His submission to the Turks extended
their power, and Suleyman the Magnificent's commitment to North Africa
and the Mediterranean was shown in 1533 when Hayreddin was appointed
Kapudan Pasha, the admiral of the Mediterranean fleet, as well as the
Governor-General of the new province of the Archipelago: the Aegean
islands and coasts.

Hayreddin's success was at the expense not only of Spain, but also of other Muslim rulers, and this issue further greatly complicates the issue of comparability. Thus, in 1534, illustrating the then unique mobility of naval power, he drove the Spaniards from the Greek coastal fortress of Coron and attacked the coasts of Spanish-ruled southern Italy, but also occupied Tunis, overthrowing the semi-independent Hafsid dynasty. This was an aspect of the marked consolidation of power in the western Islamic world (which was where the Turkish empire was located), a consolidation that made the Turks such a serious challenge to Spain. Within Europe, despite the consolidation represented by the Habsburgs, no Christian power matched the range the Turks could deploy. The situation would have been more challenging still had Morocco been absorbed into the Turkish world, but this did not occur. Partly as a result, Morocco was able to focus on a distinctive trans-Saharan policy, sending an expedition to Timbuktu in 1590–1 and, thereafter, developing a presence in the valley of the River Niger.

In this, as in other cases, it is unclear how best to define 'Spain' and, related to this, how the composite Spanish monarchy can best be defined. For example, does the ability to gain military commitments from Naples and Sicily, and still more to draw upon resources from client-allies, notably Genoa, Tuscany and the Order of Malta, constitute 'Spanish' power? This point is also valid for later periods and other states.

Hayreddin's capture and of Tunis from Mulay Hasan, its pro-Spanish ruler, in 1534 was no mere raid. Tunis was occupied, and this established a new site for struggle, and thus for the assessment of relative power, while also underlining the extent to which the southern shore of the Mediterranean was not in a separate military and political sphere. Indeed, Europe as a concept was highly problematic on this side. The Mediterranean is a more helpful reality, albeit one that leaves the conceptualization of Europe difficult. Moreover, Mediterranean influences and interactions ranged widely, including across the Sahara and into Mesopotamia in modern Iraq.[18]

The extent to which individual battles and campaigns can be used to measure relative power is highly problematic. Nevertheless, these clashes are significant, and were seen as such by contemporaries, notably in establishing an impression of power. Hayreddin's capture of Tunis in 1534 led to a response from Charles I of Spain (Charles V) in 1535. Launched with 82 war galleys and over 30,000 troops, this expedition was in large part paid for with Inca gold from South America, which repaid loans from Genoese bankers. This was an instance of the crucial public–private partnership in finance. Moreover, the ability to move money represented an important aspect of the military system. Charles was accompanied by large numbers of Spanish and Italian nobles in an expedition that attracted considerable attention in Christendom, prefiguring the efforts to relieve Famagusta in Cyprus in 1571 and Vienna in 1683.

Mounted in ferociously hot conditions, this expedition displayed amphibious capability, as well as success in fighting on land. Although defended by a large Turkish garrison, the fortress of La Goletta at the entrance to the Bay of Tunis was successfully besieged. A week later, nearby Tunis was captured. Following a pattern also seen in the Americas, for example with the co-opting of Aztec and Inca aristocrats, Charles installed a pro-Spanish Muslim ruler in Tunis, while Spanish troops remained at La Goletta until 1569.

The continued difficulty in assessing significance, and, specifically, of arguing from the particular to the general in military capability, is shown, however, by the next expedition, that led against Algiers by Charles in 1541. This was the key Muslim naval position in the western Mediterranean. This expedition was a considerable logistical achievement: 65 galleys, 450 support vessels and 24,000 troops sailed from the island of Majorca in mid-October. However, while landing the troops, the fleet was badly damaged by an autumnal storm, an abrupt indication of the operational limitations of force projection and notably of the rarity of large protected anchorages. With about 150 ships lost, the troops were soon re-embarked.

This failure led to a strengthening of Turkish activity as confidence mounted. In 1542–4, Hayreddin with 110 galleys co-operated with the French, raiding Catalonia (1542), capturing Nice (1543) and harrying the Italian coast (1544). This co-operation serves as a reminder of the extent to which leaving out the non-Western dimension can lead to a failure to understand the context of the military and political dynamics between Western powers. In addition, the city of Tripoli, held, thanks to the support of Charles, by the Knights of St John (a point which underlines the problem of defining Spanish power), fell to the Turks in 1551. The Knights had moved west after losing their headquarters of Rhodes to the Turks in 1522. All of these were blows against Spain and its allies. Each year until 1556, and again in 1558, the Turks sent out large fleets, although, for logistical reasons, they returned every winter to Constantinople. In 1560, a substantial Spanish force dispatched to recapture Tripoli was defeated with heavy losses at Djerba.

In 1571, in turn, the Turks were heavily defeated by a Spanish-Venetian fleet at Lepanto off the west coast of Greece, losing maybe 30,000 dead as well as 243 ships. However, the resilience of the Turks was fully displayed in 1574, when a large Turkish fleet carrying 4,000 troops rapidly captured La Goletta and Tunis, despite the great sums Spain had spent on each position. Among the key factors in the Spanish failure there was the distance between the forts, which prevented them assisting each other, the extent to which the Turks received a great deal of support from the local Arab population, and the absence of Spanish naval intervention. Thus, tactical, strategic and operational factors all played a role.

So also with the Turkish failure at Malta in 1565. This failure owed much to command divisions, logistical issues, the resilience of the defence by the Knights of St John and their local supporters and the ability, eventually, to relieve the besieged capital, Valetta, with a major force of Spanish troops from nearby Sicily. That the Turks employed a large wooden siege tower against the fortress of Birgu, only for it to be destroyed by cannon firing chain shot, was of far less significance, just as Turkish artillery did not play a crucial role in the capture of Constantinople in 1453.[19]

More generally, up to 1574, the number and scale of amphibious operations mounted in the Mediterranean by the major combatants was impressive. The size of armies that were transported, the distances they were moved and the speed of transit were all striking, and highlighted a degree of competence and capability that was largely due to the experience of the commanders and sailors involved, and to the major resources and impressive infrastructure behind them, and both on the Christian and on the Turkish side.[20] Yet, at the global level, this competence can also be seen in the world, notably with the bitter campaigning by Japan, Korea and China as control over Korea was contested in the 1590s. This campaigning reflected a considerable capability and major effort.[21] At the same time, a key element was that it was not sustained. The unprecedented scale of these campaigns produced serious strains and the problem of how to sustain warfare on this scale.

A contrast is instructive. Between the 1640s and 1670s, the Mediterranean again saw major battles and campaigns involving regional naval powers, notably the Turks, Venice, Spain, France, the Dutch and the English. With the exception of two expeditions that led to the fall of Taiwan, this was not the case in East Asia during the century after those in Korean waters in the 1590s. The capability shown when the Chinese invaded Taiwan was not seen in more distant Chinese operations, and was not matched by Japan or Korea in the seventeenth century.

As a result, there was nothing on the East Asian or global scale to match Spanish success in the New World, not only the initial conquest stage, but also the subsequent widespread expansion in Central and South America. This expansion is impressive. It was stopped in part by a lack of resources and also by the serious resistance encountered, notably in Chile and northern Mexico, but also because the Spaniards appreciated that further effort, in the face of ferocious guerrilla warfare, was not worth it, to try to occupy underpopulated, resource-thin regions, and notably once the silver-rich areas of Northern Mexico had been secured. There was no comparable process in Europe, for underpopulated areas, such as Lapland and Ukraine, were affected by the rival claims of imperial powers: Sweden, Russia, Poland and the Turks.

The scale of Spanish military activity, and the major problems and heavy burdens to which this activity gave rise, help explain a continued and, in part, increasing reliance on military outsourcing, and a dependence on private resources and capital, in order to sustain military activity. Spain was better able than her enemies to sustain the new challenge of large-scale and protracted warfare because, thanks to its imperial position, range and connections, Spain had the advantages of New World silver, credit facilities, and the capacity to mobilize resources as a composite monarchy, to elicit co-operation and support, and to use 'soft influence', as well as pressure, even intimidation, in order to draw in the resources of other states. These advantages and strengths outweighed the inefficiencies and limitations of early modern Spain. It is instructive to compare and contrast this situation with that of Britain in the eighteenth century. The British ability to elicit co-operation included for example the use of subsidies in order to attract Continental allies, although the independent views of the latter came foremost.

Repeatedly, in the sixteenth and other centuries, it is the non-linear character of military activity that emerges, a character that arose in response to the succession of different challenges, as well as to the possibility of winning allies and obtaining support.[22] In short, a task-based approach to military history is crucial, as is an understanding of tasks in the variety of political contexts that pertained. Beginning in the mid–1570s, Spain turned from conflict with the Turks in order to take the leading role in the Wars of Religion within Western Europe. This provided a new version of the commitment to the Low Countries and the concern about France. These conflicts stemmed from the Protestant Reformation, which had begun in 1517, leading to conflict from the German Peasants' War of 1524–5. From the 1560s, conflicts to which the Reformation contributed became more common outside Germany and this encouraged Spanish interest in Europe north of the Alps. The Dutch Revolt from 1566 against Philip's rule added a strong personal dimension. So also did the appreciation that religion, in being linked to aristocratic discontent and urban opposition, was a key element in power politics there and elsewhere.

Similarly, as instances of changing tasks, in the late sixteenth century, China, its relations with the Mongols settled, became newly-active in (eventual) support of Korea as an opponent, in the 1590s, of a newly-united Japan and its adventurism. In addition, the Turks fought the Safavids of Persia (Iran) anew from 1578 to 1590. Contemporary views are significant in explaining the assumptions within which power was perceived and understood, and thus effective.

As a result, far from their being a trade-off between Spain and the Turkish empire, the latter reached its greatest extent territorially at the same time that Spain's reconquest of much of the Low Countries, initially successful intervention in the French Wars of Religion, ability to thwart the repeated English attacks on Portugal and the Spanish New World, and continuing dominance of Italy, all suggested that it too was approaching an apex of unprecedented power. Thus, it is mistaken to place Spain on a terminal trajectory by the 1590s, and such an assessment would have meant little to most contemporaries, to their perceptions, and their fears. The same was to be the case for Britain in the 1890s.

Assessing the respective capability of the Spanish and Turkish military systems in these years is difficult, not least because they did not fight on land at any scale. Instead, it is a question of comparing their operations against other powers. For example, the Turks' victories over the Safavids in 1578 and 1583–5, and their subsequent advances against them in 1587–8, nicely match those of the Spanish Army of Flanders under Alessandro Farnese, Duke of Parma, notably the capture of Antwerp in 1585. However, the latter are far more prominent in military history, which raises interesting questions of the cause and value of relative assessments and the significance that is placed upon them. In both cases, there was also the same problem of consolidating these advantages. Despite initially heroic levels of military success, Spain had lost the Northern Netherlands by 1609 and the Turks Baghdad by 1624, although the Turks were to regain it, while Spain was not to do so with the Northern Netherlands. France was a more immediate diversion of Spanish strength than the Austrians were for the Turks.

Turning to military factors, the attempt to use developments in fortification technique and military tactics as a measure of capability, for example in charting a supposed European military revolution, are unconvincing as well as teleological. The combined arms tactics that are important to the discussion of this revolution were, as ever, far easier to attempt than to execute successfully under the strain of battle. The contrasting fighting characteristics of the individual arms – muskets, pike, cavalry, cannon – operated very differently in particular circumstances, and this factor posed added problems for coordination. So also did the limited extent to which many generals and officers understood these characteristics and problems.

More generally, as with other instances, military adaptation is the appropriate term, rather than revolution. Nevertheless, the effective use of weaponry required a discipline that rewarded the use of professional troops, such as those of Charles the Bold, Duke of Burgundy from 1467 to 1477, and his eventual Swiss vanquishers. The latter focused on pikemen whose rapidly-advancing columns proved deadly to infantry and cavalry opponents alike as at Novara (1513), although pikemen were vulnerable to firepower as at Bicocca (1522) when defensive Spanish firepower caused heavy losses among the attacking Swiss.

The teleological and triumphalist language of governmental development and military revolution can be very misleading. Far from war being necessarily won by planned action, let alone long-term military development, it was frequently the side that was less handicapped by deficiencies that was successful. As a result, coping with problems was the major skill of command. This was true both on campaign and on the battlefield, and on land and at sea. On campaign, providing supplies was both difficult and vital, while, on the battlefield, the retention and use of reserves amid the uncertainty of battle was often crucial.

Military adaptation and the related eclecticism, synthesis and fluidity,[23] took place in a variety of contexts. Thus, it is necessary to consider developments in terms of particular circumstances and the more general practice of fitness for purpose. Armies were mixed infantry/cavalry forces, and contained infantry and cavalry troops that used firearms as well as those that did not, and also those that used earlier missile weapons, such as bows and arrows. The varied response to firearms should be understood not in terms of military progress, administrative sophistication or cultural superiority, but, rather, as a reaction to the different tasks and possibilities, within a context in which it was far from clear which weaponry, force structure, tactics or operational method was better. Firearms fitted into established patterns of warmaking, rather than transforming them, in large part because they represented new iterations of the firepower already offered by archery.

In contrast, artillery offered an enhancement of capability, and notably against fortifications. This encouraged investment in the latter, investment which was knowledge-driven. For example, Cesare Borgia (c. 1476–1507), the illegitimate son of Pope Alexander VI and the successful Captain-General of the papal army in 1499–1502, asked Leonardo da Vinci, a gifted physical geographer adept at surveying among his many skills, to examine the papal fortresses. He provided accurate maps, for example of the city of Imola in 1502, that were useful tools with which to plan defences.

Cavalry was more prominent in Eastern than in Western Europe, but it developed in a different fashion. Whereas in France and the Low Countries, pistollers played a major role, as firearms were adapted for mounted use, cavalry shock tactics continued to be central further east. This contrast led to differences in weaponry and protective clothing. However, in 1456, at Staraia Rusa, Vasily II of Muscovy was able to defeat an army from the powerful city-state of Novgorod that was strong in lancers, by making good use of mounted archers, in part provided by Tatar auxiliaries. Yet, in Russia, in the sixteenth century, the cavalry increasingly used the sword not the bow.

Cavalry arms were not the sole regional contrasts. In Ireland and Highland Scotland, infantry shock tactics were far more important than elsewhere in Europe. Weapons, moreover, did not necessarily dictate tactics. The pike could be used either for attack or in defence. Moreover, there were important continuities. It is noteworthy that in 2015 the impressive History and Archaeological Museum at Constanţa in Romania describes the weapons of the fourteenth to seventeenth centuries as medieval.

Although the Turks had no equivalent to the *trace italienne* (the new system of fortification developed from the fifteenth century), nor to the extensive and costly fortifications constructed along the coasts of Naples and Sicily against Barbary raids (and still easily visible, for example at Trapani in Sicily), or built in the Austrian-ruled section of Hungary, they did not require any such development as they had not been under equivalent attacks. When the Turks needed fortresses, they constructed them, as in Syria, Palestine, Eritrea and Yemen;[24] but the different nature of Ottoman attitudes towards territory, and of fighting practice, had an effect on their response to frontier positions. In particular, the Turkish emphasis on field forces and mobility, as well as their interest in expansion, ensured that they were less concerned with protecting fixed positions.

In contrast, Western losses of fortresses to the Turks early in the sixteenth century, for example of Modon (1500), Belgrade (1521) and Rhodes (1522), as well as a lack of confidence in mobile defence, encouraged the introduction of the new angle-bastioned military architecture despite the cost it entailed. Thus, what might appear advanced, and what certainly required governmental effort to create and sustain, arose from military weakness, rather than strength. This has often been the case more generally. In this case, the effort can be seen as an important aspect of the response to weakness.

In short, capability has to be related to tasking and problems, and means to goals. Indeed, no clear superiority for Western forces on land over the Turks was to be demonstrated until the repeated defeat of the Turks by the Austrians and their allies in 1683–1717, notably at Vienna (1683), Zalánkemén (1691), Zenta (1697), Peterwardein (1716) and Belgrade (1717).[25] It is far from obvious that a comparable Western superiority existed in India until the 1750s and, more clearly, late 1790s and 1800s,[26] and in China until the late 1830s and, more clearly, 1860. Prior to that, rather than assuming any Western superiority, whether or not based on (or amounting to) a military revolution (however the latter is defined), it is more appropriate to note the more complex, contingent and varied nature of relative military capability.[27] In particular, the range of Asian trajectories indicates the danger of treating the Turks as if they defined the non-West, or served as an appropriate example. This point is linked to the risk of explaining eventual Western domination in terms of a Western exceptionalism that is asserted rather than demonstrated. Furthermore, as with the range of Asian trajectories, it is important to note that the same is the case for the West.

It is also highly necessary to give due weight to the non-military factors that help account in the case of individual powers for differences between success in particular regions. This point can be seen if the Dutch Revolt is considered. The serious difficulties Spain encountered in the 1590s in trying to maintain the tempo of success against the Dutch seen the previous decade cannot be best explained by Dutch tactical changes, notably the introduction of volley fire, an introduction important to discussion about military modernization, if not revolution. Instead, the nature of the political struggle in the Low Countries, in the shape of the contrast between output (military success) and outcome (political result) was crucial, as was the strongly competing commitments of the Spanish government and military. The commitment in, and against, France, which became far more significant after the assassination of Henry III in 1589 threw open the French royal succession leading to the prospect of a Protestant king (Henry of Navarre who became Henry IV). This proved a major bar to the continued pursuit of successful operations against the Dutch by the Spanish Army of Flanders.

Issues of strategic choice in prioritization and policy repeatedly arose. Nevertheless, it would be wrong to see this as a necessarily insuperable factor, for Spain continued to experience failure in the Low Countries after war with France and England ended in 1598 and 1604 respectively. This failure, in part, reflected the accumulated strain of many years of conflict, notably serious financial strain.[28]

At the same time, it is appropriate to note Dutch strengths. Alongside tactical changes, especially an emphasis on firearms drill and tactics, came an increase in the size of the Dutch army, from 20,000 men in 1588 to 32,000 in 1595. Moreover, the availability of resources was significant not least in order to ensure pay, and thus maintain cohesion and prevent mutinies. Resources were linked to an impressive supply system, tactical delivery and operational effectiveness. Thus, 10,000 cannonballs were fired by the Dutch in their successful two-month siege of Groningen in 1594.

So also with England. At the close of his reign, Philip II suffered not only from the absence of a coordinated strategy linking Spain's various commitments, but also from the lack of consistency in policy towards England – whether to overthrow the Tudor dynasty, a policy that entailed allying with English Catholics, or to force the English out of the war. This lack was related to a contrast, already referred to, between emphases on religious crusading and on pragmatic considerations. A lack of strategic clarity, even wisdom, was linked to a reactive policy of responding to English threats to the Spanish empire, a policy which gave the initiative to the English. Their strengths, particularly at sea, were part of the equation. Moreover, the English were able to subdue rebellions in Ireland despite Spanish support for the latter.[29]

Developments in the West locate, generalize and limit the Spanish military experience. These developments certainly made gunpowder weaponry normative, which is to say that drill, tactics and assumptions were all increasingly focused in a particular way, while remaining far from identical. Indeed, it is mistaken to see this period, which involved experimentation in infantry tactics and formations, in terms of a single model of effectiveness and a uniform direction of change. The Thirty Years' War (1618–48) was to reveal the extent to which there was no such model or direction. Instead, greater standardization occurred at the close of the seventeenth century with the development then of an all-firearms infantry using linear formations. Nevertheless, in Western Europe, already by 1600, there was, in armies and navies, a greater uniformity in weaponry and tactics than had been the case a century, and, even more, 150 years, earlier. In the case of Russia, firearms became more significant. By 1480, the Muscovites deployed arquebusiers and, by 1494, Italian cannon-founders had established a casting yard in Moscow. However, it was not until 1514 that Muscovite artillery was sufficiently powerful to help determine the fate of a siege, that of the major Polish-held fortress of Smolensk. That year, the use of artillery and arquebusiers helped the Poles defeat a larger Muscovite army at Orsha, and this led Vassily III to focus attention on developing an arquebusier force. The tactics employed were less formalistic than those developed in Western Europe, but the warfare was well suited to the Eastern European circumstances of great distances and small populations.

Rather than assuming that there was a paradigm form that should have been adopted, it is helpful to focus on the alternative concept of fitness for purpose as a defining context, goal and means for military activity. This issue relates more specifically to the value of the concept of an early modern military revolution. This value can be questioned, and that is the case whether the early modern military revolution is understood as a Western or a global phenomenon. The debate on the revolution has possibly run its course in terms of advancing new perspectives.[30] Nevertheless, the conceptual and methodological poverty of much military history, or rather the limited number of analytical terms, are such that there is likely to be continuing resilience in the concept. Concepts are convenient as well as apparently appropriate. The idea of an early modern military revolution ably serves the purposes of discussing developments within the West, notably those involving Spain, Sweden and the United Provinces, of establishing criteria by which developments elsewhere in the West can be classified and assessed, and of considering the situation on the global level.

These criteria and issues are linked in discussion of military history, at least in the case of Spain, but the extent to which this link is appropriate is not clear. Indeed, there is a fair amount of argument by assertion in much of the discussion of the military revolution. This issue of approach is not tangential to the debate, but, in practice, integral to it, as argument by assertion captures a key element of the methodology at stake. It is very difficult to compare and contrast different military environments, and, notably, across the range of their activities, or, rather, difficult to do so if to a point that enables the construction of a viable general thesis. In addition, this process is commonly accompanied by that of elision, notably the failure to consider instances that do not match a general theory, or, in contrast, but to the same effect, minimizing those that do so.

The two processes can be seen with Geoffrey Parker's classic 1988 study about the military revolution, a study that focused on Spain although, to a degree, covering the world. They were already present with Michael Roberts' original 1955 lecture, published in 1956, as that lecture worked by neglecting most of Europe, indeed Christian Europe, and leaping instead between specific limited examples, particularly Sweden, and an ambitious general theory of military development. More widely, work on early modern military history at the global scale often lacks an adequate theoretical and methodological approach. At the same time, there is a strong incentive to fit developments anywhere and everywhere into such an approach. This incentive can lead to schematic accounts, such as those of Roberts and Parker,[31] or, more recently, and focused more on Eurasia as a whole, Kenneth Chase and Alessandro Stanziani.[32] Each of these accounts has great merit, but, however, is far from comprehensive. Instead, they are selective as to outcomes, and suggestive as to the analysis of process.

There is also a key methodological problem in terms of the weight to be placed upon simultaneity when establishing developments. In particular, it is unclear whether simultaneity has any particular significance. On one level, this is absurd given the importance of global climatic developments that occurred simultaneously producing striking common denominators, a theme in Parker's more recent work.[33] Moreover, similar points can be made about demographic expansion. On the other hand, comes the long-standing stadial approach, with the suggestion that a similar context had contrasting consequences for societies that were developing at a different rate. The problems with an uncertainty of conceptual context emerge when considering whether, in turning to details, there is more to assess than simply one episode after another. That is certainly an implication of an empirical approach, but such an approach, and the related stance, make it difficult to assess the significance of particular events. As a result, they can sit in somewhat of a void.

Turning to the process of change, there is the question of how best to distinguish between changes in weaponry and their wider context, specifically the training, systematization and large-scale deployment of such weaponry on land and at sea. In establishing the importance and relevance of developments, the rate of change is also a major issue. This is particularly the case if the rate is to be reified and then somehow compared across cultures as well as periods. On top of that, there is the question of background and, notably, whether the late medieval centuries are to be considered as a period of stability or, a key alternative, stable change (*i.e.* change that could be handled without major discontinuities); or, instead, whether a far more intense period of transformation can be seen in the fourteenth and fifteenth centuries. If the last, then the consequences of this transformation for the following centuries become an issue, and not only in terms of the questionable theory of a military revolution or simply that of a new departure.

To take solely the West (i.e. the Christian European states), although the issue is also pertinent elsewhere, if we see the major innovations as prior to 1500, and as followed essentially by incremental change and diffusion, then it is still necessary to evaluate the respective significance of the changes in the two periods, and to do so also if comparing with non-Western cultures. In this context, it is worth noting that many of the changes associated with the sixteenth century, such as larger armies and navies, permanent forces under the control of the state, a military infrastructure, greater military expenditure, new tactics and the *trace italienne*, all had important medieval precedents.[34] This was true both for Spain, as it became the Western world empire in the sixteenth century, and for the remainder of the West. In particular, paid armies and trained infantry, as opposed to forces raised by feudal means and with the key element being cavalry, had a considerable lineage, and notably with the significant development of both in the fourteenth century. There is a tendency, however, to treat archers as progenitors for the subsequent introduction of hand-held gunpowder weaponry and, more generally, to present the development of infantry, especially when armed with bows or handguns, as the route to military proficiency. This teleological approach has led to a slighting of the variety of medieval warfare, not least the value of cavalry, and to a misleading account of the changes in this warfare, which included those through the use of pole axes, pikes, field fortifications, wagon forts, and the continued development of heavy and light cavalry.

There is the related possibility of subsuming changes, however significant, within what can be seen as longer-term continuities or patterns across the world, such as the similarities between the successful Mongol invasion of China in the thirteenth century, and that by the Manchu in the mid-seventeenth century. Each depended in part on divisions within China. This interplay of change and continuity is a frequent problem, one that returns us to the question of emphasis. This problem also raises the question of the imagery of change, notably whether it should be seen as cyclical (and if so how) or not.

To centre the account of military development on the West poses serious intellectual, conceptual and methodological questions. Yet, to adopt that approach, sixteenth-century developments in the West certainly appear to have opened up contrasts, both within the West, and between the West and the non-West, that may have been significant. That a focus on firearms was less apparent elsewhere in the world, with the significant exception of Japan (where it is unclear how normative gunpowder weaponry really was), is not necessarily a sign of weakness or slow development, even if that may appear a pertinent judgement from the perspective of the late nineteenth century. This approach, however, is questionable as criteria and apparent significance change greatly and is less than helpful if judging sixteenth-century forces on their own merit. Indeed, tactical flexibility in some contexts meant a mix of weaponry very different from that of leading Western armies. This point is underlined if considering Japanese firearms and other infantry weaponry in the period.[35]

In the sixteenth century, the learning curve in the use of firearms entailed an understanding of their limitations as well as their potential. Interlinked problems with range, accuracy and killing power affected their tactical potential and use, while there were serious separate issues arising from supplying powder and shot, and keeping the former, in particular, in a usable condition. Rate of fire, logistics and cost were all crucial issues, as were versatility of use and tactical awareness, and the presence of an influential social group and military interest committed to firearms. A considerable body of experience and knowledge existed for the exploitation of all manner of bladed weapons, but a similar knowledge and skill base had to be built for firearms. Tactics countered the limitations of handguns, notably the use of densely packed soldiers fighting at close range so as to build up the volume of shot likely to hit a target, thus offsetting the effects of low individual accuracy. Moreover, the use of firearms became more important as they were integrated into combined arms tactics. As a result, firepower came to have greater significance than the manpower offered by other infantry. However, that approach can represent a misleading primitivization of other infantry weapons and forms. That would be inappropriate, not least given the significance and professionalism of pikemen in the fifteenth, sixteenth and seventeenth centuries. Indeed, the reliance into the nineteenth century, as at Waterloo (1815), on infantry squares to see off cavalry attacks was a testimony not only to firepower but also to the tactical value in the defence of cold steel, in this case bayonets not pikes. This proved especially valuable against cavalry as horses were deterred from charging home.

Turning to organization, it can be argued that Western forces acquired a tactical and organizational superiority, most famously with the Spanish *tercio*, a unit formation, a superiority that enabled them to use gunpowder weaponry tactics more effectively than their opponents. Dutch infantry formations became more closely packed and more effective in their use of firearms from the 1590s. While valuable, and clearly applicable in some cases, this argument suffers, however, from a degree of Eurocentricity in its application. The thesis, a popular one in recent years, focuses on the ability to keep cohesion and control in battle, and to make effective use of units. This disciplined unitization of armies is generally discussed, in terms of the West and of related intellectual developments, and there were certainly important relevant developments in Western armies and navies. However, this approach scarcely covers such major changes elsewhere as those introduced by Abbas I of Persia (r. 1587–1629),[36] or in seventeenth-century China with the Manchu-banner system.

To take one example of an area of contextual development that attracts attention, printing plays a key role in the account of change in the West. It was indeed important in strengthening the consciousness of a specific military tradition, and thus a distinctiveness that owed much to the linked literature. Printed manuals on gunnery, tactics, drill, siegecraft and fortification spread techniques far more rapidly than word of mouth or manuscript. This was a spread that linked Spain to the more active worlds of print in Italy and the Low Countries, and Eastern Europe and Scandinavia to the more active world of print in Germany. Moreover, manuals enabled a degree of standardization that was important for cohesion and standardization and, therefore, the utilization of military resources. Maps permitted another form of the sharing of information. More generally, printing and literacy fostered discussion of military organization and methods, and encouraged a sense of system as well as a certain degree of reality.

Printing certainly transformed the writing about war in the West, but this was also seen elsewhere. In late Ming China, there was a military manual publishing boom that encompassed the compilation of technical manuals, training works, encyclopedias and campaign histories. Japan was also affected. Indeed, the oldest extant fully fledged drill manual for firearms was a Japanese one that appeared in 1595. In contrast, there was no comparable development in the Turkish and Safavid empires. Similarly, the latter two saw scant use of printed maps. The impact of print culture on the conduct of war at the time, however, is less clear than a smooth account of heightened effectiveness might suggest. This is even more apparent if the question of success is considered. Ming China succumbed to Manchu invasion in the mid-seventeenth century, while, although the Koreans during the Japanese invasion expressed their fear of Japanese volley-fire, the Japanese failed in Korea in the 1590s. These Asian examples challenge the claim that print culture had a significant impact on military success at the time, and also underline the most general difficulties in assessing military capability.

There is a broader problem with the primitivization of the conceptual methods and organizational effectiveness of forces that were neither Western nor Oriental. Rather than presenting these forces as hordes, as was, and is, frequently done, it is instructive, instead, to note their flexibility in battle conditions and the persistence of cavalry-based armies. The repeated success of Afghan forces in the eighteenth century, in Persia and in India, is notable, and this success continued into the 1790s. This point is more generally pertinent when observing the degree to which there were a number of dynamic powers in the world whose success is not necessarily explicable in terms of a Western-style military revolution or, indeed, of developments that paralleled those in the West. Thus, comparison with Spain does not have the apparently fixed basis of clear-cut criteria of strength, effectiveness and development. In the case of cavalry, it remained particularly important in Eastern Europe, but became less so in Western Europe as a whole, although cavalry remained significant in the French Wars of Religion, making full use of the new wheel-lock pistol.[37] Issues of cost, environment and effectiveness all played a role in these contrasts, but so also did social assumptions and the extent and nature of state control and governance.

In an interesting supplement to his work on the supposed early modern military revolution, one that moves attention somewhat from Spain, but also places it in a wider context, Parker argued in 2007 that capital-intensive military innovations were a characteristic of Western society, and, therefore, by extension, an explanation of distinctive capability. He employed this concept as a way to link the Greeks of the fifth century BCE, the Renaissance West and more recent Western warfare, including the development of the atom bomb. Adopting a cultural approach, Parker related this emphasis on research and technology to a willingness to spend and an ability to pursue the intellectual understanding of natural processes and possibilities. In contrast, he argued that there was a shortage of the necessary flexibility in cultures that lacked diversity and openness.[38] This approach represented a valuable broadening of the technological approach, although, again, it risked primitivizing non-Western societies. Moreover, while Parker's approach offered much of value for the eventual 'rise of the West' by 1850, it was less easy to apply to particular events in the sixteenth and, even, seventeenth centuries. What may appear links were frequently less clear in reality.

As a reminder, indeed, of the number of possible contexts, a key similarity across the world, one, moreover, arguably, that should take analytical priority over differences between cultures, was that of the willingness of leaders and combatants across much of the world not only to kill large numbers, but also to accept heavy casualties. Moreover, glory was presented as involving both. This willingness, which was amply seen in the case of Spain, and owed much there to the potent practical and psychological legacy of the *Reconquista*, was part of an important continuity with preceding and subsequent centuries. In contrast, this attitude has been far less common in the case of regular forces over the last half-century. A functional explanation of this contrast draws attention to the cost of training modern troops, but social, cultural and ideological factors are more significant. Concepts of duty and fatalism, in the contexts of a much harsher working and demographic environment, and in markedly inegalitarian systems, were significant across the world in the early modern period. This situation acted as a key enabler of bellicosity and of the normative character of war. As a result of the continuation of this crucial cultural dynamic from the Middle Ages, however defined, into the twentieth century, and across the world, it is less helpful to think in terms of paradigm shifts in warfare, at least, in this respect, prior to the last half-century. The effect of culture on the conduct of war challenges the understanding of technology and of the impact of logistics on war by those who write in terms of a military revolution. These emphases are not incompatible, but there is a crucial contrast in focus.

Turning to a very different argument for a major discontinuity, the most influential single writer on geopolitics, Halford Mackinder, a British geographer, in a famous lecture delivered in London in 1904, presented the early modern period as a key transition in global history, one leading to what he termed 'the Columbian epoch', a transition that did not only affect the New World, but also Asia. There, according to him, the transformative role was 'first played by the horsemen of Yermak the Cossack and the shipmen of Vasco da Gama'.[39] To Mackinder, writing in the broadest of possible terms, this was a crucial reconfiguration of power:

> The all-important result of the discovery of the Cape route to the Indies was … in some measure to neutralise the strategical advantage of the central position of the steppe-nomads by pressing upon them in the rear … endowed Christendom with the widest possible mobility of power, short of a winged mobility … The broad political effect was to reverse the relations

of Europe and Asia, for whereas in the Middle Ages Europe was caged between an impassable desert to south, an unknown ocean to west, and icy or forested wastes to north and north-east, and in the east and south-east was constantly threatened by the superior mobility of the horsemen and camelmen, she now emerged upon the world, multiplying more than thirty-fold the sea surface and coastal lands to which she had access, and wrapping her influence round the Euro-Asiatic land-power which had hitherto threatened her very existence. New Europes were created.[40]

This account has interest in terms of the discussion of the long-term signifi-cance of the period, but it does not provide much of an indication to the immediate military situation then; although there is the important caveat that the new trans-oceanic links rapidly became highly significant in terms of providing the capacity to gain and move bullion, and thus to finance military operations, and were seen in that light. The financial history of early modern warfare has been partly written, notably in terms of the movement of New World bullion, but there is still much work to be done and this requirement extends to the comparative financial dimension. In particular, the assessment of Spain, the Turkish empire, the Mughal empire and China in terms of the availability of funds and credit is a key approach. Western Europe was able to utilize a wide-ranging resource base, one that was enhanced by trans-oceanic expansion. There was heavy forest cover and abundant mineral resources in Western Europe, both of which were essential for naval construction and metallurgy. There was also access to larger quantities of cheaper metal than was available elsewhere, and some of this metal, in the form of nails, was used to hold Western European ships together. Western Europe, with its water mills, windmills, heavy forge work and mechanical clocks, had one of the most advanced industrial systems of the time. Along with a relative openness to new ideas, this economic strength helped Western Europeans in their adaptation and improvement of technology, not least that developed elsewhere.

The availability of funds and credit was linked to the success of government in co-operating with private entrepreneurship and, more generally, in thus financing war, a theme greatly advanced by David Parrott in his valuable discussion of early modern Europe, notably seventeenth-century France.[41] This was a long-term trend. Thus, in the fourteenth and fifteenth centuries, Byzantine armies 'were supported by small baggage trains and it was expected that most of the soldiers would cover their expenses through their own means'.[42] The spoils of war were significant in providing the means for war, not least in motivating troops and providing the basis for privateering.[43] These elements remained the case. Thus, in 1815, French troops at the Battle of Waterloo were encouraged with the prospect of benefiting from the fall of Brussels if they were victorious.

This issue highlights the extent to which, as ever, warfare was impacted in political and social contexts. The ability in the sixteenth century to win and use political support, specifically the backing of major landowners and also of the merchant oligarchs who dominated towns, was generally more crucial than bureaucratic systems; although, looked at differently, political support and bureaucracy had, and have, variable meanings depending on the context.[44] Co-operation was particularly apparent in the case of action against peasant and urban rebellions, as the private forces aristocrats could raise proved very necessary in these cases, not least in confronting opponents often operating across a considerable area. Thus, in 1514, the Crown and the nobility co-operated to suppress a large-scale peasant uprising in Hungary. The rebel army lost impetus when it focused on the siege of the castle at Temesvár and was then easily defeated by a force led by the *Vajda* (Prince) of Transylvania (now north-west Romania).

Alongside administrative development and political co-operation at the state level came an insistent and ferocious pressure on available resources that would have led most monarchs and ministers to smile at my remark that there were more resources to tap. The problems with raising sufficient funding to sustain high levels of operational warfare were faced by all the major combatants during this period. They were particularly the case with civil wars. Thus, in late-sixteenth-century France, lack of finance resulted in the steady decline in the effectiveness of the royal army, notably its artillery, during the Wars of Religion that lasted from the early 1560s to the late 1590s, and in a reduction in the size of forces deployed by the combatants.[45]

Moreover, desertion was relatively easy in civil wars and was a regular occurrence as both leaders and men returned to their estates and their homes. When combined with epidemics, the impact on army numbers could be devastating. For troops on campaign in foreign lands, this option was not so convenient, and this factor helped account for the prevalence of mutinies when pay was not forthcoming and credit with the local communities was withdrawn. At the same time, troops could desert from one army and join another, including its rival. The military labour market was intensely competitive and could be highly volatile. In the Dutch rebellion against Philip II, military entrepreneurs raised armies of their own accord in the 1560s and 1570s, but this worried the economically dominant urban oligarchs because they feared that mercenaries would leave them to their fate when their pay was in arrears or, even worse, betray their town to the Spaniards. To try to ward off this danger, the oligarchs declared that supreme command over the troops lay with the provincial States (Parliaments) and the States General, and the right to appoint officers was assigned to the former. The army thus served as the military expression of the rebellion.

There is a clear slant in the literature, one reflecting the focus of subsequent centuries. This entails an emphasis on state-building as understood in modern terms, and on the military means that are related to this. Each emphasis deploys subliminal assumptions about progress and, thereby and therefore, capability. These assumptions can be seen in the literature on the Western 'military revolution', which deserves unpicking accordingly, and also in the literature on global military history, and whether or not it is presented in terms of such a revolution. There were, and are, clear social assumptions, assumptions generally discussed as desirable, notably in the ability of firearms to level social distinctions and to destroy the castle walls of powerful landholders. Thus, Louis XI of France successfully employed cannon against rebellious barons in the War of the Public Weal in 1465–9. Military capability and the consequences of internal conflict were linked, in the classic account of military-political developments, to a newfound political cohesion and governmental means and purpose that, together, served as the basis for the early modern, and then modern, state, and notably so in Europe. This process allegedly began with the 'New Monarchies' of c. 1460–1520, although other points and periods of departure have been discerned and there were specific trajectories in particular states. In Transylvania, a developing proto-state under the suzerainty of Hungary in the sixteenth century, the Princely Chancellery was in charge of fiscal matters, and the mobilization, supplies and pay of the army, as well as the maintenance of border fortifications.

Furthermore, in a feedback mechanism, it was argued that the pressures of external conflict, in particular its cost, helped lead to the new situation, the new-model state; and, in turn, sustained it. In short, a form of Social Darwinism (competition resulting in the survival of the fittest), combined with the reading back of the resource-based account of military proficiency and success seen in many accounts of the two world wars and the Cold War, led to a focus on the relationship between state-building and war. There clearly was such a relationship, indeed one that was causal in both directions. However, aside from the relationship not excluding other causal links, this approach faces difficulties when being used to consider the issue of relative military capability between states. Linked to this, there are specific problems in applying a gunpowder-based approach to comparative power and state-building.[46] Thus, in southern Spain, Granada's fall in 1492 owed much to largely German-manned Spanish artillery and offensive artillery tactics, but took a decade of campaigning and was also a product of serious divisions among the defenders. The absence of support for Granada from North Africa was also significant. Moreover, Spanish military capability was not simply a matter of firepower.[47]

Again, in contrast with the grit of events and specifics, the standard approach to state-building[48] also suffers from its schematic character, rather as the thesis of the 'Decline of Spain' does for the seventeenth century. Indeed, there is room to consider why historians, notably in the Anglosphere, working on Spanish history appear to favour such schematic accounts. As a parallel, models of military development that assume some mechanistic search for efficiency, and for a related maximization of force, do violence to the highly complex process by which interests in new methods interacted with powerful elements of continuity, as the notion of effectiveness was framed and applied in terms of dominant cultural and social patterns, a pattern that continues to the present. However innovative, military technologies repeatedly ended up accommodating entrenched conceptions of power and social relations.[49] In the early modern period, a stress on the value of morale and on the importance of honour came naturally to the aristocratic order that dominated war-making. Traditional assumptions about appropriate conduct were very important in force structure and tactics, and this was particularly so for individuals conscious of lineage and reputation, and not psychologically committed to change. Referring to dominant cultural and social patterns, and using terms such as accommodating, should not imply that there were no significant reasons for continuity in military arrangements.

The consequences of the misleading and teleological treatment of the state, both as a whole and more specifically in the early modern period, are a particular problem in that they seriously affect the consideration of military developments. There is a misleading tendency to treat 'the state' as an essentially bureaucratic entity, and one automatically seeking greater power. This account underplays multiple divisions and their close relationship with social dynamics,[50] as well as the varied understandings of the idea of power. Moreover, the accompanying role of court and aristocratic factionalism and of military entrepreneurship[51] is such that accounts of statecraft in terms of supposedly modern concepts, both of decision-making and concerning the rationale of power and goals, are misleading. This is a corollary to the similarly misleading emphasis on rationalism and efficiency in the literature on the military revolution, indeed its inherent 'Fordism', with its focus on allegedly optimal production of military resources and methods.

These points about states relate moreover to empires in that consensus also played a role. Thus, the Austro–Ottoman Thirteen Years' War (1593–1606) repeatedly indicated the significance of a form of coalition warfare, in the shape of the importance, yet unpredictability, of subordinate parts of imperial systems, notably Wallachia, Transylvania and Moldavia. Thus, Transylvania changed sides to back the Ottomans in 1599, only to be defeated by the Wallachians.

Reform often centred on the search for a new consensus with the socially powerful, rather than on bureaucratic centralization, not that the latter process was without its ideological tensions, legal difficulties, serious administrative limitations and grave political problems. The pursuit of a new consensus was centralizing – in that it focused the attention of regional élites on the centre – but not centralized. Indeed, military strength was not largely a matter of bureaucratic sophistication and development, although that was an element. Instead, the co-operation of key social groups with rulers was necessary. This role helps explain the degree to which the inherent strength and adaptability of economies, societies and states may have been more important than the particular characteristics of their military systems. Linked to this, rather than seeing the type of army as establishing capability in some overarching thesis of proficiency through change and of change in proficiency, it is pertinent to focus on the concept of fitness for purpose in particular circumstances, notably political as well as military circumstances, or, rather, with the two understood as closely linked. The crucial ability to combine force with appropriate political factors characterized the use of some militaries regarded as at the cutting edge but also others that were very different. For example, most of the Spanish army that suppressed the 1591 Aragonese revolt was scarcely professional, instead being recruited by the Castilian nobility from their estates, but it was successful.

Nevertheless, on the European scale, competitive military systems also put a premium on the size of armed forces and the sophistication of their weaponry, which enhanced the position of rulers able to elicit and deploy the necessary resources. Paid soldiers were the vital element in Western Europe, but obligatory levies played a major role. Such levies, however, did not necessarily provide effective forces for the field forces of rulers. As so often there were regional variations. The service basis for landownership that provided Russia with cavalry was given a new iteration by the granting of *pomestie* land by Ivan IV, while, in 1497, John I of Poland confiscated the estates of landowners who had refused to take part in the campaign against Wallachia that year. This practice was not matched in Western Europe. However, obligatory levies were generally more important in local defence than in expeditionary warfare, and obligation could be as much owed to the local community as to the distant ruler. The value of citizens' militia could also be shown in operations against the ruler, as with the successful defence of the Dutch town of Leiden against Spanish siege in 1574. The military activity of local forces overlapped with the maintenance of law and order. The dynamics and tensions of kinship played a role in both.

The compromises between rulers, élites and local communities that were important to order within states could also become the base of a degree of centralization into major organizations. This was not on the scale of the nineteenth and twentieth centuries, but, nevertheless, military administration was developed. Western European warriordom, its ethos and practices, depended heavily on clerks. Spanish bureaucracy was particularly impressive. However, the Turks proved successful in achieving a concentration of resources, and in deploying them with less need to consult local élites. This success was crucially important to the logistical sophistication that underpinned Turkish operations.

Governments also sought to set norms for the military. The enforcement and acceptance of discipline was a significant aspect of state control of war and was to be central to the transformation of martial élite culture as knights became officers. This process helped to ensure the continuation of ancestral political and social privilege, but their technically different battlefield roles required a more predictable and disciplined response, and this response helped improve the effectiveness of Western forces. Training became more significant, as it was only thanks to training and discipline that different types of troops could combine effectively in battle tactics. Advances in technology themselves were often of limited use without such combination, as was shown by the need for vulnerable handgunners to combine with pikemen.

If war was a forcing house of change, it was also designed to prevent it, both in terms of changes in territorial power and in the prevailing political, social and ideological practices and norms. Armies suppressed rebellions, and maintained, or strengthened, social and spatial patterns of control. This was particularly so at the expense of peasant risings, as in Hungary in 1514, Germany in 1525, Transylvania in 1596 and Lower Austria in 1597, but also of urban discontent. The control of towns was a military and governmental process within states and as rulers sought to extend their authority. This was seen most clearly when town walls were breached and when town militia were subordinated to royal garrisons. Thus, rebellion by the city of Ghent in Belgium was overcome in 1492 and 1540, with the latter followed by the construction of a citadel. The city of Groningen acted as a centre of regional opposition, resisting Habsburg attempts to bring it under control in 1505–6 and 1514. In turn, in 1536, the city successfully resisted an attempt by Duke Karel of Gelderland to take control.

The linked extension of fortifications under the control of the ruler was seen in Eastern as well as Western Europe, but it took a number of forms, not only that of the *trace italienne* seen in particular in Spain and Italy. In Moscow, the inner walled Kremlin, a term dating from the fourteenth century, was joined by the connecting *Kitai Gorod* (fortified city), the walls of which were built in 1534–8. To the east, north and west, the *Tsargorod* (city of the Tsar) was protected by white stone walls with earth added. Five miles long and with 28 towers, these were built in 1583–93. An outermost earthworks and twelve major gates were constructed in 1591.

In practice, whether building fortifications or deciding on war, the ambitions of rulers were the key element in the military history of the period, and not least with Philip II. Although he commanded in the Low Countries against the French in the 1550s, and in 1580 reviewed the Spanish army before it invaded Portugal, he was not a warrior like Gustavus Adolphus of Sweden (r. 1611–32), and thus did not implement policy and engineer military developments as the latter did. Nevertheless, Philip was crucial to Spain's military history. His ambitions, and those of other rulers, such as Henry VIII of England, Francis I of France and James IV of Scotland, were significant to any assessment of capability, as they established the goals that were formulated. Each of these monarchs was proud to serve in person and James was killed, alongside much of Scotland's nobility, in the English victory at Flodden (1513). In peacetime, the emphasis on hunting as well as on tournaments and other forms of mock combat dramatized valour and prowess.

War proved the most established way to gain the renown that was then repeatedly displayed. The ceremonial entries of French monarchs celebrated royal valour and success, while Titian painted a splendid equestrian portrait of Charles V to celebrate his victory at Mühlberg in 1547 over John Frederick, Elector of Saxony, the leading German Protestant prince. Less prominent rulers also sought to gain fame and enhance their position through war. Francesco II Gonzaga, Marquess of Mantua, presented his performance at the Battle of Fornovo in 1495, where he had fought bravely and captured many prisoners, albeit failing to block the French march north, as a victory; and Andrea Mantegna's painting the *Madonna della Vittoria* (1496) was produced accordingly. Francesco also displayed what he saw as an apt comparison, Mantegna's earlier series the *Triumphs of Caesar*, an exemplary reference. Rulers, both Western and non-Western, frequently played an active role in the development of weaponry and tactics.[52]

The major role of glory and honour was such that military activities that provided both were necessarily effective in a fashion that, however, can be difficult to compare, both across space and time, as so much depends, in judging individual states, on the political and cultural context. So also for the value and values brought to the social élite by military service, a value and values that was readily apparent in Castile, the political core of Habsburg Spain,[53] as well as in other states. The hierarchy and collective discipline of officership could work, and could be made most effective, if it rested on a definition of noble honour and aristocratic function in terms of military service. Nobles were treated as especially suited to this service thanks to their nobility. This process was encouraged by the presentation of war in glorious and chivalric terms. Chivalry certainly remained strong as both concept and idiom. The definition of aristocratic honour with reference to military service was encouraged by the emphasis on honour, service and glory by, as well as for, rulers. This very much remained the pattern in the following century.

The bleak character of military service,[54] also remained the pattern, as did the brutality of war, and the often harsh and murderous treatment of civilians, as in war between Scotland and England, for example the English campaigning in Scotland in the 1540s. The people were deliberately harried as a display of power and an attempt to assert control. The pressure on the Huguenot-held town of Sancerre when besieged by Royalists in 1572–3 during the French Wars of Religion led to the ejection of the poor, to cannibalism, and, eventually, to surrender on terms. The eating of human flesh was also seen in the German city of Augsburg in 1635 during the Thirty Years' War.[55] Prisoners could be killed in cold blood, as at the Dutch city of Haarlem in 1573: about 2,000 Dutch troops had their throats cut after their surrender to the Spanish Army of Flanders. Similarly, the slaughter of civilians, for example, cutting the throats of the population of the town of Zutphen, led many other troops to surrender.

There was also a deliberate assault on religious sites as part of a process of destroying the values of opponents, a process to be seen anew with French Revolutionary, Napoleonic and Communist forces and in

Yugoslavia in the 1990s. Thus, in Viviers in France, the cathedral was plundered by Protestant soldiers in 1562 and the roof of the nave was pulled down five years later. Clerics were slaughtered by both sides in the Low Countries and France, and worshippers were intimidated, if not killed. Image-breaking was important to the process of gaining control, as in the Dutch city of Utrecht in 1578. Religious activity, education, publications, censorship, marriage, the household and poor relief were battlefields, so the conflict was as much about soft power as hard power.

However, cannibalism was rare, and was held up as both exceptional and a warning of what could happen. On many occasions, civilians were not slaughtered. The enslavement of captives was common along the border between Christendom and Islam, but was not frequent within Christendom. Indeed, the impact of wars may have been overstated. Certainly, battle-field casualties were relatively small, while most cities were not sacked.[56] In addition, as a very different aspect of public–private partnership, violence was endemic to society, rather than being simply a product of war. Accepting these caveats, war, nevertheless, was generally brutal in its impact, and, in part, because of its being waged by societies that did not enjoy a comfortable margin in resources. Moreover, in war there was a clear willingness to treat civilians as prey.

CHAPTER THREE

The Creation of Lasting Standing Forces, 1600–1700

Within Christian Europe, despite much talk of empire and the threat of empire, there was no hegemonic power in the seventeenth century to match that of Manchu China or Mughal India, each of which were areas of far greater population. The branches of the Habsburg dynasty that ruled Austria and Spain appeared close to a hegemonic position in the late 1620s, after successive successes over German Protestant opponents and the Dutch, and again in 1634 after their joint victory over the Swedes at Nördlingen in southern Germany. This victory appeared more dramatic because earlier Swedish victories at Breitenfeld (1631) and Lützen (1632), and the advance of Swedish forces as far south as Bavaria in 1632, had created an impression of the Swedes as ushering in a new military order. Subsequently, the Austrians were able to negotiate a favourable German settlement with the Peace of Prague (1635). That year, France and Spain went to war, but this did not usher in the failure of Spain. Instead, in 1636, Spanish troops advanced deep into France. In turn, as a later instance, Louis XIV of France (r. 1643–1715), with the largest army in Europe, seemed also to wield hegemonic power in the late 1670s and early 1680s, and was held by critics to aim at it until his forces faced repeated defeats in the 1700s. Louis' own propaganda made boastful claims of his influence and power.

In each case, however, the position of these rulers was precarious and they were swiftly challenged as an aspect of the multipolar nature of the European system. The Habsburg position was attacked by Gustavus Adolphus, King of Sweden (r. 1611–32) from 1630, and by France in 1628 to 1631 and from 1635. Victorious over the outnumbered Swedes at Nördlingen, the Habsburgs, in turn, were under great pressure by the late 1630s and, even more, the early 1640s. The Spanish defeat by the French at Rocroi in 1643 did not mean that Spain was doomed to failure, but, alongside serious, long-term revolts in Catalonia and Portugal in 1640 against rule by Philip IV of Spain, it marked an abrupt change from the situation in 1634–6.

In turn, Louis XIV was challenged by the growing power of Austria, once it had defeated the Turks outside Vienna in 1683, and by Britain, after it was taken over by Dutch forces under William III of Orange following his successful invasion of England in 1688. The defeat of the Turks was followed by the Austrian conquest of Hungary, a hard-won success that was finally confirmed by victory in 1697, although attempts to take forward this success into the Balkans could not be sustained. Meanwhile, supported by domestic opponents of James II, William III's invasion and seizure of the throne was another instance of the potentially decisive nature of warfare in Europe. So also was his subsequent total defeat of James' supporters in Scotland and Ireland in 1689–91, a defeat that led to the creation of Britain as a state defined by conquest and co-operation, in a way in which medieval rulers and Tudors had been unable to secure.

The growing power of Leopold I of Austria (r. 1657–1705) and of William III encouraged other rulers to turn to them and away from France. This was to affect the policy of Savoy-Piedmont, of a number of German rulers and of Portugal. The successes of Leopold and William were not to be reversed. This outcome demonstrated not only political factors, but also the greater effectiveness of campaigning compared to earlier in the seventeenth century. Such an aggregate assessment invites qualification, but can nevertheless be seen. It was comparable to the rise of military effectiveness in the fifteenth century, a rise not generally matched in the sixteenth century.

Other instances of military decisiveness included the conquest of the British Isles by Parliamentary forces in 1642–52 during the civil wars of that period, and the capacity of the Swedes to crush the Danes in 1643–5 and 1657–8 in rapid and overwhelming campaigns. Conversely, the time taken by the Parliamentary forces scarcely suggested decisiveness, while the Swedes did not have comparable success against Poland and Russia in the 1650s. Indeed, the scale of Poland and Russia helped limit the opportunities for decisive campaigning, although it did not prevent bold plans for changes in dynasty, ruler and territorial control. Thus, in the mid-1650s, Sweden, Brandenburg and Transylvania planned to seize and partition Poland, only to fail in 1657 in part because most of the Polish nobility backed the King. In the face of intractable resistance, the Swedes withdrew while the Transylvanians were defeated. This failure fatally weakened Transylvania.

In general, battles were usually won, as in the previous century, not by the use of a particular weapons' system, but by experienced and motivated troops whose dispositions had been planned and organized, as with the major victory of Gustavus Adolphus of Sweden, over outnumbered and outgunned Catholic German forces at Breitenfeld in 1631, a hard-fought battle. In battle, experienced and well-deployed infantry were usually safe against frontal attack, although the tactics employed left room for both musketeers and pikemen to show their skill. For example, pike formations were more open than normally assumed, suggesting that the effectiveness of pikemen depended on individual skills in hand-to-hand combat as well as the sheer weight of mass. Pike conflict was an elaborate and dynamic method of conflict.[1] The threat of a tactical impasse in infantry warfare led to the particular need for skills in generalship and for flexible and effective cavalry, both of which were offered by Gustavus Adolphus and in England by Oliver Cromwell.

Innovative ideas about deployment and tactics were not necessarily superior, as was shown in the Thirty Years' War (1618–48). Units and tactics associated with what would subsequently be seen as military modernization and the 'Military Revolution' did not necessarily win, underlining the extent to which the thesis faces serious problems if scrutinized closely. If armies were evenly matched, battles, whatever the precise tactical deployment, were either inconclusive encounters or were determined, amidst the chaos, change and contingency of combat, by other factors, such as terrain, the availability and employment of reserves, and the results of cavalry clashes on the flanks, which were frequently decided by which side attacked first: cavalry were far more effective in attack than in defence. These clashes could lead to the victorious cavalry assaulting the enemy infantry in flank and rear where both pikemen and musketeers were very vulnerable. This was the case in the French victory at Rocroi in 1643 and in the Parliamentary triumph over the Royalists under Charles I at Naseby in 1645, the latter the decisive battle of the English Civil War.[2] As a result of this possibility, the ability of commanders, such as Cromwell, to retain control over cavalry so that they acted in a disciplined fashion was crucial. In Eastern Europe, cavalry continued to play a greater role. This was especially so in Poland. There, another aspect of difference was that many cavalry still wore mail armour.

At the same time, the contrasting results of battles, and notably of Rocroi and Naseby, reflected the need to set campaigns in the context of broader currents including commitments on a number of fronts, strategic pressures and the ability to go on mobilizing resources. In confronting Spain, France was weaker in these respects, than the Parliamentary side in English, but neither result was preordained. That Parliament introduced impressive fiscal devises, particularly the Assessment and excises, no more made victory certain than the efforts of Spain and France in the 1630s and 1640s to increase their fiscal yield and control.[3] These efforts need to be put alongside the effective use of contributions systems to ensure that wartime forces could be sustained by living on the areas they occupied and intimidated. Organized by military contractors, these systems sustained a major increase in troop numbers in the 1620s, an increase that changed the character of what became the Thirty Years' War, increasing the scale of conflict and permitting its continuance.[4] There was no equivalent to the peace through exhaustion seen on a number of occasions in the sixteenth century, although then also wars could last for many years.

Numbers alone were only of value if they fought well and were handled ably. The latter point encouraged the hiring of mercenaries and the related recruiting of experienced commanders. The hiring and conduct of mercenaries, however, were controversial, a situation that had long been the case. The loyalty, or lack thereof, of mercenaries frequently led to concern, although the changing of sides has to take note of the porosity and mutability of the sides. For example, Danish-born Heinrich Holk served Christian IV of Denmark and held the major fortress of Stralsund against the leading Austrian general Albrecht Wallenstein, only for Holk to change over to the Austrian army when Christian left the war in 1629 and to fight under Wallenstein who, as the foremost military entrepreneur, offered a better guarantee of continued and paid employment.

Mercenary leaders and units could be unreliable both politically and on the battlefield. The Swedes agreed in 1609 to provide Tsar Vasilii Shuiskii of Russia with mercenaries in return for an alliance against Poland and an agreement to surrender claims to the Swedish-ruled province of Livonia. However, the following year, the mercenaries, their pay in arrears, switched sides at the Battle of Klushino, and this threw open the road to Moscow for the victorious Poles who had benefited from the shock charges of their cavalry. As another disadvantage, mercenaries were often hired at a considerable distance from the zone of hostilities. This caused delay in starting operations, and also created the problems of having to fight their way through and of being reluctant to move so far that it made a return home difficult.

It is necessary, however, to appreciate the highly problematic character of the nationalist and teleological assumptions that made mercenaries appear poor soldiers, assumptions that were particularly voiced from the 1790s, in part as an aspect of the politics of the French Revolution. Dwelling on the deficiencies of mercenary service leads to a failure to explain why reliance was placed on mercenaries. Alongside betrayal, they could provide loyal service, as with the many Scots in Dutch, Swedish and Russian service. The nature of many modern mercenaries, as social, political and economic marginals outwith the structures of a clearly organized civil society, has led to a failure to appreciate their predecessors. As with 'regular' soldiers, many, in practice, were raised by gentlemen from traditional connections: clients, retainers and tenants.

Moreover, mercenaries were accustomed to war and had the group cohesion and experience that was crucial to success in combat. It required training and familiarity to employ a pike or a musket effectively, while artillerymen and cannon founders were frequently mercenaries, and steps were taken to ensure procurement of such troops, notably the habit of hiring experienced men from units that were being disbanded. These men expected better pay than new recruits, but were less likely to desert, not least as they encountered difficulties in readjusting to civil society. New recruits, indeed, were largely trained by a process of being exposed to more experienced men.

It is misleading to present mercenaries and operations involving them as if they did not change in their character, and thus can be readily assessed and, as a result, contrast with allegedly more modern, state-directed, national patterns. Such a presentation is misleading because the use of mercenaries indicated a major capacity for change. This was seen, for example, during the Thirty Years' War. By the 1640s, the armies involved were smaller and more mobile than those of the late 1620s and early 1630s (although there was also considerable variety among the latter), as well as being more battle-hardened and resilient. Smaller size meant that logistics could be better managed, which thereby increased the ease of direction and the flexibility of usage. French and Swedish forces were able to advance far into the Empire. In 1647, the Swedes campaigned as far south as Bregenz at the eastern end of Lake Constance.

As with most developments in military history, it is unwise to cite simply one set of causes, in this case for smaller armies. A combination of heavy earlier losses and, especially from the 1620s, the population downturn of the century (or, at best, demographic stagnation) made it hard to recruit sufficient soldiers. This was a European-wide problem and one, moreover, that could not be countered by recruiting soldiers from outside Europe. Cultural norms played a role. Christian societies shipped slaves to plantation economies in the Americas, but were unwilling to raise slave forces comparable to those seen in the Islamic world.

Militias, as well as other forces recruited at the outbreak of hostilities were regarded as less combat-ready than mercenaries, in terms of both experience and training. When tested on campaign, militia repeatedly lacked the skill of professionals. However, a reliance on less expensive militia ensured larger forces, which helped explain the Swedish reliance on militia from the 1540s. Even so, the Swedes also used mercenaries.

Western rulers in the sixteenth century sought to move towards professional standing armies that combined the experience of mercenaries with the reliability of subjects. However, in wartime, as during the Thirty Years' War, these armies tended to be supplemented by both militia and foreign mercenaries. The administrative capability, in terms of information, local officials and police enforcement, that systems of conscription could call on with considerable success from the late seventeenth and, even more, eighteenth century, was less in evidence earlier on. As a result, rulers both created standing forces and raised additional forces by drawing on mercenaries, as well as by using the important and long-standing sub-feudal pattern of encouraging aristocratic officers to recruit from their own connections and tenants. The situation was less fixed and regular than was to be the case by the late nineteenth century. Instead, armed forces varied greatly, not only between peace and war, but also within individual years of peace or war. A complex interaction of opportunity and motivation, involving factors such as the reliability of pay, the season and the proximity of the harvest, encouraged recruitment or desertion, and, as a result, the size of units could vary greatly.

Albeit in very different contexts, the problem of potential tactical impasse was to recur frequently in warfare in Europe, in large part due to the symmetrical character of this conflict, for example during the First World War. In other words, the use of similar weaponry, and by similar formations operating with similar tactics, made it difficult to obtain a capability advantage as a consequence of weaponry, formations and tactics. If such an advantage was created, as with the use of the oblique attack by Frederick II of Prussia, Frederick the Great, in the 1740s and 1750s, then opponents moved to counter it or sought to do so, as in that case. In the nineteenth and twentieth centuries, the deployment of new and improved weapons was rapidly countered. Similarities extended to command practices and culture, recruitment, logistical infrastructure and governmental context.

At the same time, it proved possible to deliver military verdicts. In 1672, the French declared war on the Dutch Republic on 4 April. Thanks, in part, to the support of the local ruler, the Elector of Cologne, the French forces crossed the Rhine and invaded the United Provinces from the vulnerable east (as opposed to the fortified south), only being stopped when the dykes were breached on 20 June. The politically and economically crucial province of Holland had been saved, but the French had made a far greater impact in one campaign than the Spaniards had done in over a quarter-century of war (1621–48), including advancing to capture the major city of Utrecht. However, this campaign also indicated the difficulties of translating output, in the form of success in battle, into outcome, in the form of an end to the struggle in which one side accepted the will of the other. The Dutch offered terms, but an over-confident Louis, hopeful that the war would widen to include Spain, which he wanted to despoil, issued excessive demands, including major territorial gains and the acceptance of Catholic worship. This was unwise.

Moreover, there was a crucial domestic political dimension. An Orangeist coup in Holland in July 1672 brought the anti-French William III of Orange to power as *stadtholder*. He was to prove Louis' staunchest opponent and was unwilling to accept a settlement under which he became hereditary ruler of the United Provinces in return for yielding to French demands.

In turn, in 1673–4, the conflict changed shape, in part because of Louis' over-confidence and his maladroit handling of others, but also because the coalition that Louis had created was unstable. In 1674, his major ally, Charles II of England, deserted him. The broadening out of the war saw both conventional warfare between regular forces, notably in the Rhineland and the Spanish Netherlands (Belgium), and also a large French expedition to Sicily to assist the rebels there against Spanish rule. The terms of the treaties of 1678–9, collectively known as the Peace of Nijmegen, reflected French success, particularly in the Spanish Netherlands (Belgium), but not on the scale of that in 1672. The difficulty in fixing victory was to be a major problem in many conflicts, and notably when they involved a number of powers.

The same situation of similarity in fighting method pertained with navies. Sailing warships and galleys, the two types of vessel employed, generally fought vessels of the same type, and were armed and handled in a similar fashion. Success owed much to skill in handling vessels, to persistence under fire and to chance episodes, such as setting light to gunpowder on opposing ships. The resulting explosion was the easiest way to destroy a warship for, being built of wood, they were difficult to sink. Naval warfare in the seventeenth century saw significant developments. These included tactical, operational, strategic and organizational changes, as well as in the respective standing of the individual powers. In 1600, Spain was the leading naval power in Christian Europe, despite having encountered serious challenges from Turkey, England and the Dutch over the previous three decades. In contrast, in 1700, England was the leading power. It had passed France in the 1690s, while France, in turn, had passed the Dutch in the 1680s.

These changes did not reflect the development of unique types of warship, armament or means of fighting, but, instead, the building of more ships than rival powers. In turn, these ships had to be maintained and anchored in dockyards that represented major investments in capability, and the necessary organization accordingly. The dockyards included Chatham, Portsmouth and Plymouth for England, Brest and Toulon for France, Karlscrona for Sweden and Copenhagen for Denmark.

In naval tactics, there was an emphasis on broadside fire, which, in turn, led to line-ahead deployment and movement. As with combat on land, there was a contrast between the tactics and deployments outlined in manuals and those that arose in reality. Moreover, there was a contrast between the 'small war' that constituted most operations and large-scale battle. The latter was relatively uncommon (at sea as well as on land), whereas clashes between individual ships, blockading stations and attacks on commerce were all more common. Line-ahead tactics at sea suited the views of commanders translated from the army, which was a common aspect in the command system, but the need to maximize the number of guns that could be brought to bear through broadside fire was a key element. It was seen, in particular, in the three wars between England and the Dutch, those of 1652–4, 1665–6 and 1672–4, as well as in the battles of the Nine Years' War between French and Anglo–Dutch fleets, notably Beachey Head (1690) and Barfleur-La Hougue (1692).

Both battles and naval campaigns could have major consequences, not least as warships, cannon and trained crew could not be rapidly replaced. After the loss of many warships at Barfleur-La Hougue, which ended an invasion attempt on England on behalf of the exiled James II, Louis XIV could have rebuilt his fleet. However, under pressure, in the Nine Years' War, the War of the League of Augsburg (1688–97), from a major coalition, he preferred to concentrate on the army, while, at sea, the French focus shifted to privateering attacks on English and Dutch trade. This serves as a reminder of the role of choice in strategy, force structure and doctrine. Commerce protection became a major goal for England and the Dutch, but this did not preclude the strategic use of naval power. Overwintering in Cadiz, the English, from 1694, increased their power projection into the Mediterranean, a step that had major military, political and economic consequences. Until Malta gained independence in 1964, England (from the parliamentary union with Scotland in 1707, Britain) remained a major Mediterranean power: naval power-projection overcame the limitations of geographical position.

Alongside the more complex pulls of specific strategic cultures, particular national traditions, and the complexities of fitness for purpose, the recurrent issue of symmetry in war on land and sea reflected the multipolar character of Europe, and also its cosmopolitan culture. For example, *La Nouvelle fortification de Nicolas Goldman* (1645), a book published in French in Leiden by the major Dutch publisher Elzevir, was written by a Leiden mathematician born in Breslau, the major city in the province of Silesia, then ruled by the Austrian Habsburgs (now Wroclaw in Poland). Publication in widely read languages, such as French and Latin, and the related ability to read other Western languages, meant that manuals and other books, and the ideas they offered, could be readily disseminated. Printed manuals on gunnery, tactics, drill, fortification and siegecraft spread techniques more rapidly than word of mouth or manuscript. Publication also helped ensure that military service could be governed by written regulations. Contemporary writings on war reflected the sense that not only were there lessons to be learned, but that they needed learning. There was a process of mathematization through an engagement with ballistics, although the interest in mathematics was long-standing, reflecting as it did the increased use of quantification in Western society for the understanding of space and time, and the concern with regularity, harmony and precision seen from the Renaissance.

Service in the armies of other rulers had a comparable impact in spreading ideas and practices. Thus, in the early seventeenth century, there was a widespread service of Italians in the armies of the Emperor, as well as of France and Spain, and of Scots in Dutch and Swedish forces. The latter helped ensure that, in a long-standing process, Continental examples were transferred to the British Isles, which underlined processes and issues of adaptation.[5] Moreover, valuable experience was obtained that proved important during the mid-century civil wars. On the basis of his experience on the Continent, Donald Lupton suggested discarding the pike and focusing on muskets.[6] Subsequently, Patrick Gordon, a Scot, proved a key means of the dissemination of military practice to Russia in the late seventeenth century.

The use of countries in this fashion is misleading, as much of the service was personal in character, and was generally understood in this light. As such, the service was a reflection of long-established and strong ideas, ideals and practices, notably of patronage and clientage. The emphasis on individual links did not match the later stress on the state as an abstract entity. Such a notion existed, and had intellectual and legal form. However, the degree to which the state corresponded to an abstract notion or a mathematical system was limited. This point has major implications for ideas of modernity and accounts of modernization, both of which are inclined to underplay individual and other sub-state links and also to adopt a teleological approach.

Towards the close of the seventeenth century, the development of the bayonet altered warfare in the West, primarily in tactics but also with wider implications. The early plug bayonet, which was inserted in the musket barrel, and, therefore, prevented firing, was replaced by ring-and-socket bayonets: the bayonet was attached to the outside of the barrel. This allowed firing with the blade in place. This capability led to the phasing out of the pike, which was now redundant: pikes offered protection against cavalry, but not against infantry wielding firearms carrying bayonets. Bayonets were a better complement to firearms in fulfilling the pike's defensive role, and, moreover, had an offensive capability. This change was largely carried out in the 1690s and early 1700s. The ability to change weaponry, and on such a scale and so rapidly, reflected the capability of states to rearm their soldiery, a capability that was organizational and also a reflection of the state of metallurgy and the scale of industrial capacity. This is a change that deserves more attention than it generally receives, and, in particular, more attention to the processes involved.

Already, there had been a move away from the use of the pike, with the proportion of pikemen decreasing during the century as that of musketeers increased. Thus, in the Austrian army, the proportion decreased during the Thirty Years' War to a third by 1670, with the pike abandoned in the 1690s as the bayonet was deployed. The proportion in French infantry units fell from half at the start of the century to a third by 1650, a quarter by 1680, and a fifth by 1690, and formations accordingly became longer and thinner.[7] At the Battle of Neerwinden in 1693, the French successfully used their bayonets in attack. Brigadier-General James Douglass argued that the British and Dutch suffered from a lack of socket bayonets whereas the French army was able to be 'both pushed and fired at once and of a much better defence than our pikes were'. After the battle, Douglass pressed for permission to arm his troops with socket bayonets.[8]

As pikes were replaced by muskets equipped with socket bayonets, so matchlock muskets were replaced by flintlocks, which were more reliable and fired faster. Fire rates improved, notably with the adoption of platoon firing.[9] Western armies were not to experience a comparable change in weaponry until rifled guns became the norm in the nineteenth century.

It had been very complicated to coordinate pikemen and musketeers in order to ensure the necessary balance of defensive protection and firepower. The new system involved trial and error but led to the longer and thinner linear formations, and the shoulder-to-shoulder drill in order to maximize firepower, that were to characterize Western infantry in the eighteenth century. The new weapon did not greatly encourage attacks because bayonet drills were, for a long time, based on pike drills, with the weapon held high and an emphasis on receiving advances, although they were also used offensively on occasion.[10] Although challenged greatly by column advances, notably, but not only, from 1792, linear deployments and the supporting drill remained important for much of the nineteenth century. However, the deployments were made too dangerous by the enhanced firepower stemming from new weaponry that encouraged the development of the so-called empty battlefield in which troops adopted an open order and sought to avoid exposure to fire.

In time, the line of close-packed infantrymen was to appear anachronistic, as was the square formation adopted when infantry were threatened with attack in flank or rear. Indeed, that the square lasted longer in trans-oceanic imperial campaigns against non-Western opponents helped underline this apparent anachronism. This was but one of a series of real and apparent anachronisms, although the extent to which a practice was anachronistic was frequently a matter of perception and circumstance.

Alongside the frequent habit of referring back to the Classical world,[11] as when the use of the pike was justified[12], the idea of anachronism was a prime way in which change was experienced and conceptualized, which thereby created ideas of modernization. For example, in the seventeenth century, across much (but not all) of Europe, ruined castles provided contemporary travellers and painters with potent images of decay, apparently representing the end of feudalism. Castles offered specific sites of military transformation, and made it appear necessary and inevitable. Whereas castles had often been on hilltops, looking down on the countryside, and remote from towns, modern *trace italienne* fortifications were generally on the flat and frequently near towns. Dutch painters, such as Jacob Ruysdael, depicted ruined castles as a world that had past, ivy climbing over stone walls, as also with dissolved monasteries. In England, the sight of ruminating cattle amid the dilapidated walls of Melbourne Castle, in Derbyshire, would surely have horrified John of Gaunt – one of its early owners – had he witnessed such a spectacle back in the fourteenth century. But by 1597, the place was of more use as a pound (holding area) for trespassing cattle; it was demolished for stone in the 1610s.

Under the Tudor dynasty (r. 1485–1603), the English social élite increasingly looked to the Crown. They were encouraged by the removal of those who did not or who could be suspected of such an intention, as well as by the distribution, from the 1530s, of Church lands to those willing to support Henry VIII (r. 1509–47). In 1521, Edward, 3rd Duke of Buckingham was arrested and executed for a disloyalty supposedly indicated by his castle works at Thornbury, a site far removed from the frontier. As a result of changes under the Tudors, England was largely demilitarized. Military training and a coterie of armed followers became less important to landowners. The shift from castle keep to stately home was symptomatic of an apparently more peaceful society and a product of the heavy costs and military redundancy of castle-building. Town walls and castles fell into ruin, unless on the coasts or Scottish frontier, where Berwick's fortifications were strengthened under Elizabeth I (r. 1558–1603). John Speed described Northampton Castle in 1610: 'gaping chinks do daily threaten the downfall of her walls'.

When James VI of Scotland (r. 1567–1625) became James I of England (r. 1603–25), the Union of the Crowns apparently removed the need for fortifications near the Scottish frontier. When James visited once mighty Warkworth Castle in Northumberland in 1617, he found sheep and goats in most of the rooms. In Wales, many castles were abandoned, and fell into disrepair and ruin, while others were enhanced, not with fortifications, but with comfortable and splendid internal spaces, especially long galleries, as at Raglan, Powis and Carew Castles. In contrast, Beaumaris, one of the most impressive works of Edward I (r. 1272–1307), was described as 'utterly decayed' in 1609, while a 1627 survey of its once mighty fellow Conwy, revealed that it was in a lamentable state.

'We had planted four-mortar pieces in one place, and two mortar pieces at another, each mortar piece carrying a granado shell twelve inches in diameter'; so wrote Joshua Sprigg, an eyewitness to the Parliamentarian siege of Raglan Castle in South Wales. By the time of the mid-seventeenth century civil wars in the British Isles, cannon were more effective, while defensive positions were generally not state-of-the-art. Nevertheless, fortified positions could hold out against attack unless it was pressed hard, and much effort was invested in fortifications. Castles in the early stages of the English Civil War of 1642–6 were major sites of local control. They provided good bases for garrisons, and many were brought back into habitation and use accordingly. For example, Banbury Castle was refortified and established as a garrison to protect the nearby Royalist capital at Oxford from attack from the north. The Parliamentary garrison in Warwick Castle dominated that county, while Hartlebury and Dudley Castles were major Royalist sites in neighbouring Worcestershire. The walls of Rockingham Castle were improved, while Warkworth Castle was garrisoned.

Most particularly, thanks to a formidable effort in 1642–3, allegedly including both 20,000 citizens working without pay as well as special taxes to cover other costs, London was turned into a super-castle. It had a rapidly constructed eleven-mile-long defence system, comprising an earthen bank and ditch, and a series of twenty-eight forts and two outworks. This was very different to the London of its earlier fortifications, notably earlier walls and the Tower of London, for the wider perimeter encompassed a more far-flung city. Moreover, a medieval royal castle was no longer part of the defensive equation. As a reminder that battles that did not occur could be significant, the Royalist army did not advance close enough to attack these fortifications, which in effect were protected in 1643 by a larger Parliamentary army in the Thames Valley. However, the fortifications provided a vital advantage of defence in depth and gave Parliamentary forces a greater freedom to manoeuvre. They also indicated the extent to which urban resources provided the potential basis for a major military effort, one also seen with the soldiers provided by the London Trained Bands.

However, when attacks on fortified positions were made by armies larger than those in the defences, and were supported by the heavier pieces of artillery, fortified positions tended to fall. Thus, the gateway of Powis Castle was 'burst quite in pieces' by explosives during the successful Parliamentary attack in 1644, allowing the invaders, 'notwithstanding the many showers of stones', to storm the castle itself. Moreover, to prevent their future use, captured Royalist fortifications were 'slighted' or partly destroyed, as with Corfe, Dunster, Kenilworth and Winchester Castles. 'The stately tower, that looks ore pond and poole' – Raglan in Monmouthshire, had once inspired poets, both in English and Welsh. Charles I had been a guest of the Marquess of Worcester at the castle, which had held out for thirteen weeks against Parliamentary cannon. The demolition of its Great Tower after the castle was taken was a potent symbol of the fall of aristocratic power. The long list of other castles slighted included Abergavenny, Aberystwyth, Caerphilly, Flint, Montgomery, Pembroke, Rhuddlan and Ruthin in Wales alone. The list indicated the extent to which the geography and expression of power was irrevocably changed by the civil wars.

The Restoration of the Stuart dynasty in 1660 in the person of Charles II (r. 1660–85) only resulted in yet more ruthless slighting; now, however, of the defences of major towns that had backed Parliament during the Civil War, towns such as Northampton and Gloucester. When Daniel Defoe visited the latter early the following century, he could only describe it as an 'antient middling city, tolerably built, but not fine' for its 'walls and works', which had successfully resisted a Royalist siege in 1643, were demolished. More generally, castle walls were often key aspects of town defences, so that each was affected by the fate of the other.

A crucial explanatory, as well as comparative, element for the decline in fortifications away from frontiers is offered by the relationship between war, the military and political stability. Threats and conflicts that resulted in stronger cohesion between monarchs and social élites led to greater political stability. This cohesion lessened any need for fortifications within states, such as France in the late seventeenth century. On the whole, domestic opposition, which, across much of Europe, rose to a height in the 1550s and 1560s, and then, after an upsurge in the 1610s, more clearly in the so-called mid-seventeenth-century crisis, became less significant thereafter. This opposition was particularly strong in the British Isles and the Spanish empire, but, in each case, authority was largely maintained. If the Kings of Spain failed to overcome rebellions in the northern part of the Low Countries and in Portugal, they did, between 1560 and 1660, in the southern part of the Low Countries, as well as in Granada, Catalonia and

Spanish Italy. Major rebellions in Naples and Messina were suppressed. These victories, over very different enemies, were crucial to the success of the Spanish empire, as was the total crushing of opposition in Catalonia and Majorca in the last stages of the War of the Spanish Succession (for Spain, 1701–15). The campaigns serve to indicate the extent to which counter-insurgency warfare was an aspect of the period. However, in general, rebellions were led by the local élite and resulted in the fielding of conventional forces.

On the comparative level, similar achievements in strengthening stability can be noted with the Austrian and Spanish Habsburgs, the French Bourbons and with Britain after 1689, but not before. The comparisons reveal the value of contextualizing military success in terms of political circumstances. Internal stability, moreover, was highly significant to external power projection, not only in ensuring sufficient resources, but also in enabling the dispatch of troops. The success of French governments in bringing an end to the Wars of Religion and armed aristocratic opposition in the 1590s, in suppressing Huguenot resistance in the 1620s and in ending the *Frondes* in the early 1650s was crucial to the ability to take a more active international role. However, this success was far from inevitable and the political stability seen in France under Henry II in the 1550s was not really regained until the mid-1660s.

Comparisons, therefore, offer a perspective to correct the all-too-common assumptions about Spanish military redundancy, a redundancy presented as crucial to 'the Decline of Spain', which is one of the building blocks of the historical account when discussing early modern European history. In practice, as well as pursuing its ambitions, the Spanish empire displayed considerable resilience in the face of a host of challenges.

Thus, despite its Iberian and Italian commitments, Spain was able in the 1650s to make a major effort to retain the Spanish Netherlands, one that the French required English assistance to defeat in 1658 at the Battle of the Dunes, a victory followed by peace in 1659. As a reminder of the consequences of multipolarity, Spanish security appeared to depend on French weakness, a situation that in turn encouraged French desires to harm Spain. In the 1520s, and from the 1560s onwards, the Spaniards had been able and willing to encourage disaffection within France, and thus to challenge the power of the Crown, its ability to wage war and the appearance of stability that was so important to a successful foreign policy. Spain's strategy reached a high point, when, in 1585, the Treaty of Joinville brought a formal alliance with the Guise family, the major aristocratic family that were leaders of the Catholic League, and again, from 1648, when Philip IV provided support for those aristocrats led by the Prince of Condé, the victor of Rocroi, who sought to overthrow the government of Cardinal Mazarin. Such sponsorship of aristocratic opposition was both dangerous and humiliating for French monarchs, and only Spain was well placed to do so. Condé became a general fighting the French on behalf of

Philip IV, victoriously so at Valenciennes in 1656. The English repeatedly operated in a similar fashion in Scotland.

This point serves to underline the limitations of thinking in terms of national units and nationalism when discussing this period. The state did not monopolize authority, loyalty or force, and the attitudes of rulers, ministers and nobles were not such that a search for greater central authority appeared normative. The situation with Spain and France pertained more generally and was encouraged by religious factors and by the consequences of multiple kingship: one ruler for many territories, as with Spanish support for Irish opponents of Elizabeth I (r. 1558–1603) and Scottish support for opponents of, first, Charles I (r. 1625–49) and, then, Parliament in the 1640s. An awareness of this element and of Spanish resilience makes French policy in the 1660s and thereafter easier to appreciate. It appeared necessary to take measures to guard France against a revival of the Spanish threat. This was an attitude encapsulated by Louis' frequent references to his grandfather, Henry IV (r. 1589–1610), who had been an active opponent of Spain and had also faced Spanish support for aristocratic opponents. In contrast, Louis saw his father, Louis XIII (r. 1610–43) as a somewhat less impressive figure, although Louis XIII had successfully campaigned against both the Huguenots (French Protestants) and Spain. More generally, and in contrast to Charles Tilly's aphorism, a range of bodies made war, the making of war did not necessarily lead to state formation, and engaging in war undermined the state.

Struggles for security and predominance directly affected third parties, as was clearly seen in the case of Portugal. France had provided aid to the Portuguese who had successfully rebelled in 1640 against the link with Spain, but the Peace of the Pyrenees between France and Spain in 1659 prohibited French assistance and left Portugal to fight alone. When, in 1661, Louis XIV gained direct power on the death of his first minister, Cardinal Mazarin, it was decided that France must help Portugal fight on. This support, as well as military intervention from England, helped win Portugal independence in 1668.

This policy was scarcely new. Henry II of France had successfully supported the German Protestants against Charles V in the 1550s, and to their mutual benefit. In the 1620s and 1630s, Cardinal Richelieu, the leading minister of Louis XIII, sought to weaken Spain and Austria by encouraging opposition, notably among German and Italian rulers, but also from Sweden. Louis XIV was to be a major proponent of such diversionary tactics, which were to be crucial to his diplomatic and military strategies. These tactics, however, entailed commitments as it was necessary to support allies, such as Bavaria, and this increased the risk of conflict. Thus, in 1659, France threatened to invade the nearby Duchy of Cleves in order to persuade its ruler, Frederick William, Elector of Brandenburg-Prussia, the 'Great Elector', to restore gains from France's ally, Charles X of Sweden, a policy repeated in 1679.

Louis XIV has traditionally been criticized for pushing his schemes for territorial expansion too hard, but it is difficult to assess how much expansion is 'enough', a point more generally the case when considering the background to military history. To many Germans, any French expansion was not immutable, but, rather, the product of French strength that could be reversed. Ultimately, French hegemony over the lands between the rivers Saône/Marne and Rhine depended on military strength, for the Dukes of Lorraine were traditional Habsburg allies, in effect heirs to the position of the Dukes of Burgundy, while the Emperor and Empire were keenly concerned to prevent the consolidation of the position France had acquired in Alsace under the Peace of Westphalia of 1648. Indeed, the fate of Alsace repeatedly encapsulated the extent to which Europe's boundaries were set by war. In the case of Alsace, this process continued until 1945 when the Germans, who had held it through conquest in 1870–1918 and from 1940, were finally driven out. Alongside opportunity, the apparent threat from Spain was a factor in encouraging Louis to attack Spain in 1667–8. He won significant gains in that War of Devolution. Louis fought Spain again in 1673–8, 1683–4 and 1689–97.

Spain's achievement in retaining most of its empire in the face of repeated attacks can be more appropriately considered if the significance of the Mediterranean and Latin America is not downplayed. This, however, is apt to happen if a Germanic account of Europe's development, and an Anglophone one of that of the West, is adopted. Thus, in Brendan Simms' much-reviewed 2013 history of Europe, the German question is repeatedly presented as crucial, indeed central to the fundamental issue of whether Europe would be united or dominated by a single force. Similarly, Simms depicts Germany as on the front line of the war with Islam, and as the cockpit of the European ideological struggle created by the Reformation.[13] This is a view that would have surprised Iberian, French or Italian commentators, for all of whom the Mediterranean was the key sphere in the conflict with Islam. This was a conflict that, in the sixteenth century, ranged from Morocco to Cyprus, in the seventeenth from Tangier and Algiers to the Aegean and Crete, and in the eighteenth from Algiers and Oran to Egypt and Palestine. The struggle between Protestantism and Catholicism in the seventeenth century involved Germany, notably with the Thirty Years' War (1618–48), but also Poland, the Low Countries, the British Isles and France. To them, Vienna was distinctly peripheral.

It is not easy to evaluate the respective significance of developments in different parts of Europe, and this makes it difficult to determine what should be the central narrative, both political and military. For example, Louis XIV dominates attention, but his territorial gains in the treaties of 1659, 1668 and 1678 (the Pyrenees, Aix-la-Chapelle and Nijmegen) ending successive wars were less than those of Tsar Alexis of Russia (r. 1645–76) by the Truce of Andrusovo of 1667. Stemming from a conflict that had become a stalemate, this agreement with Poland left Russia with Smolensk,

Kiev and eastern Ukraine, a major extension of dominion, and one that established and re-affirmed (the two linked) Russian territorial norms that are still important to the geopolitics of the present day. In part, this was a matter of the differing nature of the international situation in the two halves of Europe. In Western Europe, where the number of independent states and density of interests were greater, any advance of a certain distance potentially brought more powers into play.

In Eastern Europe, however, there were fewer players. Russian pressure on Poland directly involved, in addition, only Sweden and Turkey. Indeed, Charles X of Sweden both attacked Poland (1655–60) and fought Russia (1656–8) in what was a tripartite struggle. Once differences with Sweden had been accommodated, in an armistice (1658) and then the Treaty of Kardis (1661), Alexis was able to press forward against the Poles with no further bar: the Romanov dynasty had fought them in the 1610s, the 1630s and since 1648. The Turks had many other commitments, notably war with Venice (1645–69) and Austria (1663–4).

Although the infantry techniques of countermarching and volley fire were not without relevance in Eastern Europe, the small number of engagements fought between linear formations and settled by firepower is a reminder that these innovations were not all-powerful and that it is inappropriate to adopt one clear standard for military capability and, therefore, one obvious path for development. In part because he was more concerned about European rivals to the west than the Tatars to the south, infantry firepower was emphasized more by Alexei than his predecessors, but cavalry operations remained very important, not least as raiding could be employed to undermine an opponent's logistics. Sieges also played a role, because control of fortified cities, notably Kiev, Riga and Smolensk, was a key goal.

Alongside the emphasis on the strength and weakness of military factors, Poland was affected by fiscal exhaustion and political discontent, culminating in a civil war in 1665–6. In turn, the Russians had been exhausted by the length of the conflict, and frequent advances had failed to deliver the necessary closure. The conscription of peasants did not yield well-trained or well-motivated troops for Alexei and led towards a major rebellion under Stenka Razin.

In Eastern Europe, there were major opportunities for territorial gain. In the West, in contrast, despite fears, this process appeared far less likely because of the number of second-rank powers willing to combine against any potential hegemon. For example, despite an initially propitious international context, Louis XIV was unable to secure the overthrow of the isolated United Provinces in 1672. Moreover, French success in the Nine Years' War (1688–97) was far more limited than in the Dutch War (1672–8), while France suffered heavily in the subsequent War of the Spanish Succession. While impressive, France's territorial gains in Louis' reign did not lead to a major shift in Western European geopolitics.

Moreover, although emphasized by Louis's opponents, when they sought to encourage opposition, the possibility of French hegemony was unlikely. In the early 1680s, with Austria threatened by a Turkish advance on Vienna in 1683, England affected by serious political contention in the Exclusion Crisis, and Spain under Charles II, a very weak ruler, such dominance appeared possible, but it depended on an international context that Louis could not fix. Moreover, this context did not last. At the same time, military factors proved crucial to its overthrow. The Turks were defeated in 1683. Charles II of England saw off the Exclusion Crisis (1678–81) and his brother, James II, and the Monmouth rebellion of 1685, but James was overthrown by William III in 1688.

The question of relative geographical significance is linked to those of the analysis and narrative of military change that are offered. As Dennis Showalter has cogently argued, military history is the last refuge of the Whig approach, meaning a teleological and progressive account.[14] This is abundantly clear in the treatment of early modern military history, notably, but not only, that of Spain and the Mediterranean. Thus, rethinking the problems of military change and capability offers a fundamental resiting of seventeenth-century Spanish developments, providing an understanding of the context of a military system that in practice was far more impressive than has long been credited. Correspondingly, considering Spain provides a way to assess standard accounts and explanations of military development.

Aside from the question of questioning the standard narrative, and related analysis, of change within and between the parts of Europe, it is also appropriate to emphasize elements of continuity alongside those of development in the practice of war. The splendour of victory was one such element. Indeed, the depiction of war provides one of the fundamental markers of continuity and change. It was through this depiction that war was experienced for the many who did not serve, and was commemorated for all. Whereas the paintings of the nineteenth century, and notably of its second half, were to focus on advancing blocs of soldiers, rather than on their rulers and commanders, and the photographs and film footage of the twentieth century, and (so far) of the twenty-first, were to centre on the individual soldier and his experience; in the seventeenth century, it was very much the ruler as warrior-leader that was the key theme and image. Moreover, this theme and image continued into the eighteenth century, albeit with significant qualifications in its second half.

In his play *Hamlet* (1611), William Shakespeare presented Fortinbras, the fictional nephew of the King of Norway, as a prince 'whose spirit with divine ambition puff'd', and who sought war with Poland in order to 'gain a little patch of ground that hath in it no profit but the name' (Act IV, Scene 4), in other words the prestige of being a ruler as opposed to being landless. Success, more generally, had a highly symbolic value. War was a struggle of will and for prestige, the ends sought being, first, a retention of domestic and international backing that rested on the gaining of *gloire* and, second, persuading other rulers to accept a new configuration of relative *gloire*. This focus led to a concentration of forces on campaigns and sieges made important largely by the presence of the ruler as commander. This was a particularly notable feature of French campaigning in the seventeenth century, as in the campaigns of Louis XIII and Louis XIV. In the case of Louis XV (r. 1715–74), not a martial figure, this feature continued with his campaigning in the 1740s, notably at the siege of Freiburg in 1744 and the Battle of Fontenoy in 1745. Louis XV did not campaign thereafter, nor Louis XVI (r. 1774–92) at all, but royal generalship was to be revived, in a very different form, by Napoleon (r. 1799–1815). He exercised the command Louis XVI did not seek. French monarchs were far from alone in campaigning in person. Most rulers did so in the seventeenth century. Tsar Alexis took a major role at the siege of Smolensk in 1654. Monarchs who were not noted as war leaders still led their forces, as did Philip IV of Spain (r. 1621–65) in 1642, when he joined the army that unsuccessfully sought to suppress the Catalan rising.

The French monarchs proved especially adept at associating themselves with the glory of victory. Moreover, in doing so, they sought a resonance with past glories, the past glories of the dynasty, of the French Crown and of the Classical inheritance. Peter Paul Rubens' painting *The Triumph of Henri IV* (1630) was intended for the gallery devoted to him in the Luxembourg Palace in Paris, but neither painting nor gallery were finished due to the disgracing of Henry's widow, Marie de Medici, that year when she supported opposition to Richelieu. The sketch depicted Henry (r. 1589–1610) entering Paris in a chariot crowned by a winged figure in the manner of a Classical Roman triumph, a frequent and resonant theme, one seen in the iconography surrounding Napoleon and the Italian Fascist dictator Benito Mussolini (r. 1922–43). Henry, indeed, had first entered Paris as king in 1594, and only as a result of military victory and of political success. Rubens also produced paintings depicting the glory of Habsburg victories, including the successful siege of the Dutch fortified city of Breda in 1625 and the Battle of Nördlingen in 1634, and these works cast much light on the preferences of patrons.

Henry IV's elder son, Louis XIII (r. 1610–43), was not an impressive leader, but was nevertheless depicted as a great heroic figure, being compared to Alexander the Great and Hannibal. Engravings were matched by pamphlets emphasizing his successes.[15] Henry IV's elder grandson, Louis XIV (r. 1643–1715), looked back to a childhood in which civil war, in the shape of the Frondes (1648–53), had challenged both the authority and the power of the French Crown. Once the Frondes were overcome, Louis' forces were able to campaign, generally, from 1658, with great success, and he could serve as the focus of triumph, as in Charles Le Brun's *The Second Conquest of the Franche-Comté, 1674*, a painting of 1678–9.

Louis's triumphs, such as the contested crossing of the Rhine in 1672, and the successful sieges of Maastricht (1673), Ghent (1678), Mons (1691) and Namur (1692), were all celebrated with religious services, commemorative displays and paintings. In the *Salon de la Guerre* at the royal palace of Versailles, finished and opened to the public in 1686, Antoine Coysevox presented Louis as a stuccoed Mars, the god of war.

Louis was scarcely alone. His contemporary, Frederick William, the 'Great Elector' of Brandenburg-Prussia (r. 1640–88), commissioned Andreas Schlüter to design an equestrian statue depicting him in armour and holding a field marshal's baton. Another contemporary, Victor Amadeus II of Savoy-Piedmont (r. 1675–1730), was depicted as triumphant in the royal palace at Turin. During the Dutch siege of Maastricht in 1676, William III spent much time in the trenches and was shot in the arm. In 1678, he was described at the Battle of St Denis as armoured with breastplate and helmet 'with thousands of bullets about his ears'.[16] However, some monarchs depicted in martial poses were far from successful, notably Charles I of England (r. 1625–49).

Paintings helped set norms for heroic behaviour. For example, Frederico Bassano's somewhat misleading 1589–90 painting of Charles VIII of France receiving the crown of Naples in 1494, a painting showing him as doing so as the result of a battle that did not in fact occur, was subsequently in the collection of the Duke of Buckingham and then in that of the Austrian Habsburgs.[17]

By the 1690s, over 20,000 French nobles were serving in the army and navy, both then of unprecedented size for France, and this was a bond that testified to aristocratic confidence in Louis. Nobles no longer controlled private armies as during the French Wars of Religion, but their role in the royal army, nevertheless, was one of considerable practised autonomy. Royal splendour thus helped elicit aristocratic co-operation and consent. This was an aspect of the reconceptualization of private–public arrangements that existed as part of what has been termed absolutism, and as an important means of royal power and authority in this system, and yet also a limitation of them. Because the expansion of governmental military strength was a matter largely of co-opting élites, rather than coercing them, it proved difficult to limit unofficial military activity. Military entrepreneurship could be redirected through more regular military channels, notably thanks to the system and ethos of the aristocratic proprietorship of regiments. It proved far harder to suppress feuds, brigandages and duels enjoying élite support, while there were also problems with the co-option of élites. For example, an English memoir on French resources, written in 1678 after a tour of the country, suggested that, although the army had 265,000 troops listed as in pay, at least a fifth 'may be deducted by false musters and other devices of officers, notwithstanding all the great rigour used against those that are found faulty'.[18]

Aristocratic generals played a major role in policy. For example, in going to war with the Dutch in 1672, the key element was Louis' personal support for the war. Of his advisers, Turenne, a leading general, but without any formal competence in the field of foreign policy, was the one with the greatest responsibility for the conflict. Turenne had the crucial track record of success and loyalty. In contrast, Colbert, the finance minister, was opposed to the war, and Lionne, the foreign minister, unenthusiastic.[19]

Royal splendour served, moreover, as the basis of noble splendour. The cult of valorous conflict extolled in works of medieval chivalry[20] was praised in its cultural counterparts of tales and ballads. Honour, fame and shame, individual, family and collective, were defined through accounts of conflict. Violence was celebrated, albeit violence linked with social status. Fame was proclaimed as due to honourable combat by those of inherent status. In addition, the violence depicted was stylized rather than an accurate depiction of combat.

A stress on these themes directs attention away from the idea of bureaucratization. This is particularly significant for the French army as there has been a tendency to present it under Louis XIV as the paradigmatic army of the late seventeenth century. As a result, the army becomes a sort of successor, in the Whiggish account of military history, to the classic 'military revolution' of 1560–1660. Clearly there were changes in the French army, changes, moreover, demonstrating the capacity of conservative societies for reform. However, far from there being a fundamental military problem that required reform, the challenges for Louis and other rulers were far more specific and contingent, namely the tasks of the moment. Thus, there was no dominant teleology forcing or describing the pace of change.

Armies increased in size in part in order to give effect to the aspirations represented by the quest for *gloire*, although limited monarchies and republics could also have increases. The United Provinces developed a major army as well as a large navy. Each was seen as crucial to protection. In Habsburg-ruled Hungary, a reform group of politicians, notably Miklós Esterházy, advocated the establishment of a standing army in the first half of the seventeenth century, in large part in order to drive back the Turks.

Aside from the relationship between rulers and aristocrats, there was an important one with towns. Despite the powerful desire of many cities to run their own affairs as independent entities, territorial states might appear to be more effective providers of protection by ensuring that cities in these states, unless they were in frontier zones, did not require modern (and costly) fortifications or large militias. Care, however, was taken to keep capitals under control, both with fortifications and with garrisons. This was particularly so when attack was a reality. Thus, Maximilian I of Bavaria (r. 1623–51) built a belt of modern fortifications beyond the earlier medieval walls of Munich which had briefly fallen to the Swedes in 1632.

Establishment strengths are unreliable, while effectives are difficult to gauge and there is also the issue of militia. Nevertheless, the number of effectives deployed by the Austrian Habsburgs rose from 33,000 in 1650 to 95,000 in 1695–7, those of Prussia from 700 to 31,000 in the same period, those of other German territories from 15,000 to 150,000, and those of France from 150,000 to 340,000; all figures that should be seen as approximate. Within Germany, the prolonged conflicts against Louis XIV and the Turks from the 1660s encouraged all powers to militarize and to build-up and maintain army size. This emphasis on size, and on permanent forces, reflected not only international competition, but also a desire for control that has been described as absolutism. At the same time, this desire was, in part, a reflection of the fear of disorder. For domestic reasons as well as international, the established means of raising and sustaining forces no longer appeared workable, and notably in crisis environments.[21] In the early 1660s, while at peace, Duke Charles Emmanuel III of Savoy-Piedmont declared six infantry regiments as standing or permanent, thus ensuring that the military establishment created for the wars earlier in the century was sustained. In contrast, in 1617, Charles Emmanuel I had raised an army of 5,000 mercenaries under Ernst von Mansfield, a German prince. Both major and lesser rulers in the second half of the century thus provided a focus for aristocratic loyalty and honourable service.

As this was a period of population stagnation, economic difficulties and climate cooling,[22] and notably so in contrast to the major population growth of the sixteenth century, the increase in army size was very significant in proportionate terms. It pressed hard on government resources and, therefore, on the societies of the period. Grain prices rose and the response could be violent as when the peasants of the Sundgau rose against Swedish forces in 1633. In turn, failure to provide sufficient food both greatly sapped the strength of soldiers, individually and as a group, and seriously affected their morale.

There were clear consequences for campaigning. Larger forces required a system of logistical support that had operational as well as tactical consequences. Assured supply routes meant that it was inadvisable for invading forces to bypass fortified position. This situation was further encouraged by the need to move artillery trains (cannon, their crew, supplies and draft animals). These could not readily go across country, but were generally restricted to roads or rivers. The consequence of the blocking position of fortresses was a focus on sieges. This was further underlined by the need to capture major positions in order to demonstrate control, and thus affect the arithmetic of peacemaking, as territorial possession was the key currency in negotiations. This need helped ensure the significance of capturing cities such as Barcelona, Lille and Prague. French competence in siegecraft was largely due to the work of Sébastien Le Prestre de Vauban, although his ideas and work built on the experience and publications of earlier experts, for example Antoine de Ville, who became Military Engineer to Louis XIII in 1627. His *Les fortifications ... contenans la maniere de fortifier toute sorte de places tant regulierement, qu'irregulierement* (Lyon, 1628) was reprinted in 1640 and 1666, and used by Vauban, which provides an instructive instance of the interrelationship of developments in the two halves of the century. In turn, Vauban's many successes in siegecraft and fortifications led to the publication of his works well into the eighteenth century. An edition of his collected work was published in both Amsterdam and Leipzig in 1771.

The role of logistics also meant that the often costly 'small war' of skirmishes linked in particular to requisitioning were highly important. Ironically, this prefigured the extent of 'small war' in the post-1990 world, notably in former Yugoslavia in the 1990s; although control over land and the ability to drive off ethnic opponents were the key issues then, rather than requisitioning, important as the latter was.

In the early modern period, the problems of supplying forces and supporting military establishments contributed strongly to domestic disaffection, as, with different contexts, in Catalonia in 1640 and England in 1641. In turn, armies were used to contain and suppress such disaffection. Thus, to rephrase Charles Tilly, oppression made armies and the armies made oppression. The absence of police forces meant that troops were frequently employed for policing purposes; but the limited nature of royal control in many, especially frontier, regions was such that the army was the appropriate solution anyway. Troops were employed for a range of activities that today are associated with the police, such as guarding official buildings, figures and prisoners; deploying at public executions; escorting money shipments; keeping an eye on markets; and responding to demonstrations, which could lead to firing on rioting crowds. Troops employed for such purposes were not armed differently to those used for warfare. Major risings were suppressed across Europe, including in Brittany (1675), Bohemia (1680) and south-west England (1685). The Marquise de Sévigné referred to the Breton trees as bowed to one side because of the weight of the peasants hung when the 1675 rising was suppressed. In 1670, the Russian army destroyed the peasant-Cossack army of Stenka Razin, a Don Cossack who had rebelled against the social politics of the Tsarist regime, especially control over the serfs. In 1681, Victor Amadeus II of Savoy-Piedmont used 3,000 troops to suppress resistance in Mondovi to duties on salt, a crucial source of revenue, but also a staple of life.

Urban autonomy was also challenged. When the States of Holland sought to save money by reducing the size of the Dutch army after the Peace of Westphalia, William II of Orange imprisoned eight of its members and sent his cousin, William Frederick of Nassau-Dietz, with a 10,000 strong army, to seize Amsterdam, the leading city, by force. The city had been warned in time to fortify, and bad weather foiled the campaign, but, having seen the seriousness of William II, Amsterdam changed policy. The Bicker faction had been dominant at Amsterdam. Their opponents, the Oetgens faction, manipulated the situation to their advantage. They arranged a compromise with William whereby Amsterdam agreed to support his army (especially through cannon production), the Bickers were forced to resign, and a proper siege was averted.

The *gloire* gained from war between rulers was also at the cost of civilians as well as soldiers. The storming of the city of Magdesburg in 1631 by an Imperial army under Tilly and the subsequent brutalization of the population, as well as the French bombardment of Brussels in 1695, in which there was much devastation of the city, caused major outcries, with news of the devastation spread in the culture of print, notably with vivid woodcuts of the murder of civilians in Magdeburg. The Imperial army was presented by Protestants, as if it were a new instance of the army of Herod carrying out the Massacre of the Innocents in order to kill Christ. A similar comparison with the Spanish army under the Duke of Alba in the Low Countries in the 1560s had already been made by the painter Pieter Bruegel the Elder in his work *Massacre of the Innocents* (c. 1565–7). In practice, although not invariably, brutality on campaign was commonplace. It was exacerbated when troops were unpaid, as in Transylvania in the 1600s, when Michael the Brave of Wallachia was not paid by the Habsburgs. There and elsewhere, devastation disrupted social and economic life and helped to cause famine and epidemics.

The ability of states during sustained conflict, and despite the related logistical problems, to retain their military effectiveness was influenced by factors over which there was limited control. The prime instance was the weather, which could greatly affect the harvest. These, however, were not the sole problems. In May 1677, William Skelton the English envoy in Vienna, noted that Duke Charles V of Lorraine, the Austrian commander in the Rhineland, 'wants ammunition and cannon … besides he will ruin his army if he goes from the Rhine but four days march'. That September, he added, 'where money and bread is wanting, no general can do wonders'.[23] Logistical difficulties encouraged an emphasis on the strategic offensive, because it then became possible to tap the economies of occupied areas, either by pillage or by 'contributions': taxes enforced under the threat of devastation. This system of transferred costs both enhanced the destructiveness of war and made it more important not to lose control of territory. The size of armies and the low (by later standards) agricultural yields combined to make the situation serious. For example, the armies Tsar Alexis of Muskovy (Russia) sent into Polish-ruled Belarus in 1654 were enormous, of unprecedented size in Muscovite history and responsible for a terrible amount of devastation. Religious animosity between Orthodox (Russians) and Catholics (Poles) played a major role in this case. Social animosity could also be an issue, as in 1676 when it was related to the problems created by supporting units during the winter in order to be ready for the following campaigning season:

> The government of Arensberg, a place in the diocese of Cologne, having lately driven out two Osnabruck and one Celle regiment that had taken

quarters in their territory, which they did by six thousand peasants whom they raised upon them on a sudden; an agent from the Duke of Celle tells me that this affront is highly resented by those dukes and that they have given out orders to some new forces to march into the same quarters who it is supposed will severely revenge the disgrace put upon their companions.[24]

Such violence was commonplace. Thus, in September 1676, the French sent out a raiding party from Maastricht, a fortress captured from the Dutch in 1673. This party burned down houses, took prisoners and extorted contributions of supplies to support their garrison. The Dutch, however, forbade their subjects to pay these contributions and, as a result of the non-payment, the French executed the hostages the following May.

The often-brutal support of troops from occupied areas was a practice shared with non-Western states. In contrast, the pattern seen with the raising of navies by the liberal political systems of Britain and the United Provinces (Netherlands) was very different. They were notably successful at eliciting the co-operation of their own and, indeed, other capitalists. This co-operation produced a symbiosis of government and the private sector that proved effective. Moreover, this sector extended across society. Thus, in the summer of 1676, John Ellis, visiting William III's forces besieging Maastricht, noted peasants bringing in forage and wood 'as to a mart'.[25] Fiscal crises could be handled by creative credit mechanisms, including the issue of paper notes by the Bank of England, an institution, established in 1694, that was important in successive conflicts with France.[26] The significance of oceanic trade engaged a major commitment by the private sector to developing naval strength. Unlike the British army, the navy was an institution answerable to Parliament more than to the ruler.[27]

Moreover, the Western industrial system was well adapted to producing a large number of warships and their cannon. The force-number ratio at sea was very different to that on land, and increasingly so as the force-projection (and cost) of each warship increased from the sixteenth century with successive advances in gunpowder-weapons technology. Individual warships could deploy greater artillery power than entire field armies, a situation that remained the case into the early nineteenth century). Indeed, the chronology of naval organizational development was different to that for armies in the West.[28] Professionalization, specialization, machinization and state control all became more evident in Western navies in the sixteenth and seventeenth centuries. The technical specialization that was to be so significant for modern Western armies began earlier at sea. Cohesion and state direction of the officer class were greater at sea than on land. In large part, this was because greater entrepreneurship was expected there and was, indeed, necessary. This was true of sailing skills, fire control, logistics and the maintenance of fighting quality and unit cohesion.

Numerous large three-deckers were built from the 1660s. Like the line-ahead tactics that they helped make possible, this building reflected the ability of naval systems to develop a capability in which resources, organization and the pressure of conflict combined. Naval strength was also underwritten by large-scale work in developing an infrastructure of bases.

In the early 1690s, Britain replaced France as the leading naval power in the world, a position it was to sustain until passed by the Americans in the early 1940s. The British naval position was enhanced by alliance with the Dutch in successive conflicts between 1689 and 1748. Navies, notably the support of their construction, maintenance and operations, focused the extent to which war and military capability in Europe increasingly entailed the intersection of capitalism and the state. This intersection was central to the ability to marshal resources, and was focused, and symbolized, in institutions such as the Bank of England, as well as in international patterns of credit and investment. The institutions, indeed, were highly dependent on these networks, not least in ensuring that Britain could draw on Dutch and Swiss capital. This military–financial combination preceded[29], and helped finance, the military–industrial complexes of the nineteenth and twentieth centuries. An economic system stressing values of labour, thrift, efficiency and accumulation contributed to military capability. There were also requirements for bureaucratic regularity and for more general literacy and numeracy, requirements which had clear organizational and social consequences.

This system – and the ethos linked to it – were very different to those associated with the armies of the period. This difference can be related to the extent to which trade competition was a dimension of rivalry in which the norms of dynasticism played only a limited role.[30] At the same time, the social typology of conflict has to be handled with care. For example, the consequences of social hierarchy and aristocratic factionalism were scarcely absent from these navies. Forcible enlistment was common to both, while there was no role for operational consent on the part of sailors in state forces, no more than there was for soldiers.

This was very different to the situation in a range of independent or autonomous forces within the European system, such as mercenaries, irregular troops, privateers and pirates. A gap between those groups and those of regular, or more regular, forces developed as contractualism declined. This decline reflected the definition and development of the nature and power of the state as feudal practices declined. Indeed, although their power has been exaggerated, the 'Enlightened' Despots of the eighteenth century, such as Frederick II, 'the Great', of Prussia (r. 1740–86) and Joseph II of Austria (r. 1780–90), wielded more control over their armies, both soldiers and officers, than their sixteenth- or seventeenth-century predecessors had done.

As a reminder that other perspectives are pertinent, it is necessary to note that nothing in Europe compared in scale or drama to the conquest of Ming China by the Manchu in the mid-seventeenth century. Indeed, there is something strange not only about the standard account of military history, with its heavy emphasis on the Thirty Years' War and its near total avoidance of the contemporaneous conquest of China. There is also something troubling about accounts of Western military history that do not devote sufficient attention to the possible implications of non-Western developments. The Manchu triumph was a victory for cavalry over the then military system of China, with its emphasis on positional warfare, and was also a victory in which political factors were important, notably the lack of Chinese unity and the incorporating ability of the Manchu.[31] It is all-too-easy to dismiss the Manchu success as another triumph for 'barbarians', and, thus, as an anachronistic development that does not deserve scholarly focus, but there is no unitary model of military effectiveness in any given period nor any pattern of linear development.

As a result, the discerning of pattern and relative significance amongst developments in the West itself should be handled with considerable care, alongside comparisons of relative significance at the global scale. Yet, on balance, the social, economic, governmental and cultural differences, in Europe and more widely, between land and naval power deserve attention. In the case of 'modern', i.e. specialized, navies, the appropriate model is state-driven and centred, to a degree that was only later true for armies. A focus on navies has a more general relevance in emphasizing the need to downplay in the discussion of Western developments, the period of 1560–1660, the classic period of supposed military revolution, and, instead, to devote more attention to the following century. In addition, naval strength and its use contributed greatly to Western exceptionalism.

CHAPTER FOUR

The Aristocratic Order and the
Pressures on it, 1700–1800

Domestic consolidation followed by external strength was again, as in the seventeenth century, a key element in European politics. This was an element that very much linked internal developments with the international dimension. This process was widely seen as states responded to, and recovered from, the major strains arising from bitter division and lengthy warfare in the early years of the eighteenth century. This could be observed, for example, in the response of Peter the Great of Russia (r. 1689–1725) to the Great Northern War of 1700–21 with Sweden. It was also the case for Spain once the destructive civil war of the War of the Spanish Succession had been brought to a close in 1715, for Hungary after the 1703 rebellion was brought to a negotiated close in 1711, and for Britain in overcoming the Jacobite rebellions of 1715, 1719 and 1745.

In some respects, indeed, there was an action–reaction, even rhythmic, character to the period. Thus, large-scale warfare in the 1690s–1710s was followed by far less in the 1720s and, to a degree, 1730s, before a resumption of large-scale conflict in the early 1740s. After the varied conflicts were brought to a negotiated end in 1748, there was a period of peace. However, large-scale war resumed in 1756, lasting until 1763. Then, mostly, there was peace in Western and Central Europe until 1792, albeit significant warfare in Eastern Europe in 1768–74 and 1787–92. The general pattern, a pattern in which resources, as well as issues, played a role, was clear.

However, aside from the issues involved in arguing from outcomes to causes, a frequent problem, the detailed pattern, as so often, was far more complex. This complexity needs to be considered in order to understand how warfare and preparations for conflict were experienced. For example, 1736–9 were peaceful years in Western Europe, but not further east as, first, Russia and, then, its ally Austria attacked the Turkish empire, beginning a war in which the Russians did well, but the Austrians very badly. As a result, Austria in 1739 had to return gains, principally Belgrade, made in the previous war with the Turks, that of 1716–18. Belgrade had already been captured and lost during the war of 1683–99.

In detail, the situation could be far more complex. Thus, 1787 was not a year of war in Western Europe, but it could have been one of major conflict. In the context of violent political division within the United Provinces between the House of Orange and their republican opponents, a longstanding division, notably in the province of Holland, that had led to coups on earlier occasions, particularly in 1672 and 1747, the Dutch Crisis of that year entailed a Prussian invasion of the United Provinces and a supporting British naval mobilization on behalf of the Orangeist faction, as well as preparations for a rival French intervention that did not take effect. The successful Prussian siege of Amsterdam brought to an end a campaign that represented the most successful assault on the Dutch Republic, albeit one benefiting from internal conflict. This success contrasted with the Spanish failure to subjugate the Dutch Revolt, as well as with the eventual failure of the French attack in 1672. Amsterdam had also been threatened by William II of Orange in 1650.

Wars that did not take place are an instructive aspect of this period as of others. They underline the extent to which the prospect of war was a key element of the international situation, the military system and the political culture of the period. For example, in 1723, a major Russian attack on Sweden was feared, while, in 1725–31, war involving Austria, Britain, France, Prussia, Russia and Spain repeatedly appeared likely. In the event, full-scale conflict was avoided in each case, although there was an unsuccessful Spanish siege of Gibraltar in 1727, as well as the surrogate conflict represented by such operations as naval blockades and the movement of threatening armies. These helped keep tension high and thus encouraged a search for military capability, both by means of the improvement of the military and in terms of foreign alliances. The prospect of war ensured that governments were kept in a constant state of unease. This was the case even for states such as Denmark and Portugal that largely avoided war. However, in the case of each of these powers, there were not only wars, but also war panics, as for Denmark in 1716–20, 1749 and 1790, and for Portugal in 1735–7. In the case of Denmark, these panics related to the prospect of war involving Russia, a more formidable power than the traditional enemy, Sweden. In addition, major states involved in numerous wars could have fought more. Thus, Britain and Russia did not go to war, but they came very close in 1720 and 1791 and less close in 1726–7 and 1773.

Focusing on individual states can capture the interaction of general trends with specific developments. Spain provides a good instance, and not least of rapid change in its military and the difficulties of thinking in linear terms. Furthermore, Spain is instructive because there is a general tendency to write it off as part of the wider thesis of a transformative 'Decline of Spain'. Having triumphed in a difficult and lengthy civil war, Philip V of Spain (r. 1700–46), the second grandson of Louis XIV of France, was then able to pursue ambitious policies in Italy from 1717, a process involving conflict in 1717–20, 1733–5 and 1741–8. A key objective was that of regaining territories lost in the partition of the Spanish empire, a partition that was one of the key themes of the War of Spanish Succession and the subsequent Peace of Utrecht (1713). In a separate conflict, Philip also regained Oran in North Africa in 1732. Spain's achievement becomes clearer in a comparative context. In contrast, the Maratha rebellion proved too difficult for the Mughals in India. Moreover, in 1722–3 the Safavids of Persia succumbed to an Afghan rising against a background of a more general failure to dominate the borderlands.

The re-creation of the Spanish army and navy under Philip is a notable feature in Spanish military history. It also proved highly significant in European history given the success of Spanish expansionism under Philip, but was less so on the world scale precisely because he devoted his efforts to European goals. Outside Europe, there was no comparable commitment. The invasion of British-held Georgia from the Spanish colony of Florida in 1742 involved only local forces and failed. With space at a premium in books, Spanish developments in this period are commonly obscured by those of Russia, Prussia and Britain, which underlines both the role of later authorital choice and, somewhat differently, the extent to which conflict was indeed a key feature of the eighteenth century, as was the prospect of conflict.

The strengthening of the Spanish army had a number of roots. An element frequently underplayed in military history is that of experience. The Spanish army benefited from the high tempo of campaigning during the War of the Spanish Succession (for Spain 1701–15), a campaigning that was very different in the experience offered to that between the 1660s and 1690s when the Spaniards had essentially been on the defensive, in Italy, the Low Countries and northern Spain, against repeated French attacks. There was also the benefit derived from a co-operation with France during the War of the Spanish Succession, for the French army offered an effective 'modern' model: Louis XIV sent forces into the Spanish empire to help Philip V. Moreover, the new Bourbon dynasty and civil war that the War of the Spanish Succession entailed for Spain provided both need and opportunity to remake patronage networks in the army and to rethink best practice, as had also happened with the Vasa in Sweden in the 1590s.

This embrace of novelty was further encouraged because the 1690s and 1700s, as mentioned in the last chapter, saw a transformation in weaponry and tactics in Christian Europe, as the pike was replaced by the bayonet, with infantry firepower thus enhanced. This more effective infantry encouraged a shift in the composition of the Spanish army. Although there were significant variations in figures during the period, the size of the cavalry, and the percentage of the Spanish army it represented, both fell from 1714 to 1748. Conversely, the infantry rose under both criteria.[1] The same happened elsewhere, for example in the Turkish empire.[2] The emphasis on infantry was especially appropriate for expeditionary warfare involving transport by sea, as such transport was often very damaging to horses. Transportation by sea was not an element that changed prior to the development of steam in the nineteenth century.

Prior to that, the vulnerability to the elements greatly affected not only the safety, but also the predictability of voyages. It was an aspect of the powerful role of environmental parameters, not least in encouraging voyages in certain seasons. This was the counterpart of the place of the climate in determining the growing season of crops, and thus the availability of fodder, which was necessary both for cavalry and for draught animals. Indeed, grass growing at the side of roads was a crucial resource and a comment on the logistical capability of the period. While this factor did not prevent winter campaigns, such as that of French and Sardinian forces against Austrian-held Lombardy in the winter of 1733–4, or that of the Austrians in Bavaria in the winter of 1741–2, both of which were successful, it made these operations more difficult, and thus discouraged them. The springtime beginning of most campaigns had a purpose, not only in terms of grass growing, but also as the ground was no longer frozen while river levels fell when snowmelt ceased.

So also with naval blockade. Thus, in September 1756, the First Lord of the British Admiralty drew the attention of his ministerial colleagues to the dire consequences of maintaining the blockade of Brest, France's major Atlantic naval base into the winter: 'that the crews of the ships are very sickly, that the ships must necessarily return in order to be refitted, and that, upon the whole, the fleet would run the utmost hazard, were it to continue cruising off Brest, beyond the middle of the next month'.[3] Wooden ships dependent on the wind were highly vulnerable to storms. The problems posed by the weather helped make the concept of control of the sea inappropriate. It was possible to evade blockades as in 1708, 1719 and 1745 when invasion attempts were launched on Britain. This problem was accentuated by the absence of reliable surveillance: this was limited to the telescope, while messages were passed from ship to ship by flags flying at mastheads. In 1719, the main Spanish invasion attempt on Britain was defeated by the weather, but a subsidiary invasion attempt reached Scotland.

Spanish military effectiveness, and political control over the military, the latter a crucial element in military history, then and on other occasions, both increased because, in 1734, Philip V ordered the establishment of thirty-three new provincial militia regiments, to provide a reserve of 23,000 men. This militia, which, however, did not cover the Aragonese realms or Navarre, important regions of Spain with strong traditions of autonomy, freed Spanish regular troops for service in Italy, and subsequently served, in the 1740s, to recruit for the army in Italy. Its campaigning then has attracted insufficient scholarly attention.

As a result of this availability, there was less of a need to rely on hiring foreigners to serve in the army, which had been a major, and expensive, strand in the seventeenth century. This change affected issues of cost and reliability, as foreigners often presented more conditional military service. The new system represented a total revitalization of the Spanish militia, and also a specialization of the military resources of the state. This transformation was comparable (although not in scale) to the banner system of the Chinese military; and also to the less well-defined differentiation seen with Turkish forces.

In addition, under Philip V, there was a new and more effective administrative structure for the army, one that matched the major changes seen in the rest of Spanish government, and notably in the navy, which was comprehensively reorganized in the 1720s and 1730s. In part, these changes were an attempt at revival after civil war, a theme seen on other occasions, but there was also a drive for more central direction. This was a common feature in the period, one that preceded the efforts associated with the Western rulers of the second half of the century who are described as Enlightened Despots. On the French model, the Spanish army under Philip V benefited from a network of *intendentes* of the army (officials in the regions), who were answerable to a Secretary of State for War, and thus responsible for implementing his instructions. For the navy, there were *intendentes de marina* and a Secretary of State for the Navy. This process was as one with that of the bureaucratization in Russia represented in particular by the War College created in 1718–19 by Peter the Great (r. 1689–1725), as well as his establishment of the Russian navy, with St Petersburg founded by Peter in 1703 as a fortified naval base from which to challenge Sweden. This new city very much represented state direction in the military sphere.

At the same time, the role of success or failure in battle in affecting the consequences of administrative changes was readily seen with the contrasting cases of Spain and Russia. Philip's achievement with the navy was seriously compromised in 1718 as a result of heavy losses at the hands of the British in the Battle of Cape Passaro. This peacetime attack was a response to the earlier Spanish invasion of Sicily in defiance of the Peace of Utrecht of 1713, which had been a key element of the peacemaking ending the War of the Spanish Succession. The Spanish navy was rebuilt after its defeat in 1718, but remained in the shadows of British naval power. However, there is a tendency to underplay the role of navies other than the leading one. This is less the case with the treatment of armies. The tendency to underplay the Spanish navy is linked to the relative neglect of the Mediterranean compared to Atlantic waters. Britain, France and Spain were naval powers in both.

In control of Gibraltar from 1704 and of the island of Minorca in 1708–56, 1763–82 and 1783–98, the British had bases in the Mediterranean where their deployment of warships dramatically demonstrated a linkage between different parts of Europe, as well as the ability of credit networks to move funds and to finance the purchase of supplies. The Russian navy was threatened by British naval deployment to the Baltic, but, in the context of multiple British naval commitments, there was no Russian defeat to compare to Cape Passaro. Indeed, the threat of the deployment of galley-borne Russian troops became a major aspect of Baltic power politics, and, in particular, a major challenge to Sweden's security. Swedish policy was affected accordingly. After 1719, the two powers only fought three wars: in 1741–3, 1788–90 and 1808–9; but the threat of Russian attack was far more frequent, for example in 1749 and 1772. In each case, Russian governments sought to affect the direction of Swedish policy. The ability of hostile military capability to affect or seek to affect policy by means of intimidation, indeed, was a central feature both of international relations and of domestic politics. This capability gave a point to military prepar-edness and also helped ensure that war was not necessarily the leading issue in assessing military capability.

The institutional structure of the military is an element that it is too easy to underplay when considering eighteenth-century Europe. Indeed, admin-istrative form and bureaucratic regularity, despite their many deficiencies in practice, were an important element in the ability to organize and sustain both mass and activity. Without them, standing forces were difficult to maintain other than by adopting ad hoc remedies to ensure support.

As a result of the Spanish revival, Spain's potential and Philip V's inten-tions were serious issues for other states. This was clearly shown in 1732, when there was significant anxiety about Spanish plans for the major expedition being prepared in Catalonia. In the event, Oran in modern Algeria was the destination, but there had been concern about the target being Italy, Britain or the British colony of Minorca. While there was anxiety among the potential targets, the knock-on effects in European power politics were such that other governments registered strong interest. Such anxiety and interest was also an issue on other occasions, notably, with Spain, in 1741. In 1753, rumours of apparently imminent attacks included those of a Prussian attack on Hanover and of an Anglo–Russian negotiation to transport Russian troops to Holstein, which was to be part of a wide-ranging assault on Prussia.[4] In addition, Britain and Prussia came close to going to war with Russia. In the event, there were no such attacks in 1753 and, when war broke out in 1756, it took a different form.

Such concerns emphasized the degree of unpredictability in international relations and strategy that led to questions about how best to prepare for conflict[5], and to manage risk. What might be called 'anti-strategy', or preventative strategy, is a key aspect of military activity and development. The same is true for procurement, tactics and weaponry. The easiest forms of prevention were military strength and deterrent alliances.

Returning to Spain in the early eighteenth century, weaknesses did not end. Thus, the Spanish army in Lombardy in January 1734 suffered from serious supply problems, which, in part, were due to operating in the winter. Due to a shortage of money, the Spanish army destined for Italy in 1741 faced multiple difficulties, including with the readiness of the artillery.

Nevertheless, in each case, armies operated, and with success. More generally, there was an important and notable increase in overall effectiveness. This was seen, in particular, in successful Spanish campaigning in Italy in 1717–18 and 1734–5.

This campaigning demonstrated the way in which the course of conflict within Europe again served to prevent the emergence of a hegemonic power. By 1735, Don Carlos, Philip's elder son by his second marriage (later Charles III of Spain), was established in Naples and Sicily after a decisive victory over the Austrians the previous year at Bitonto. The Austrian hegemony in Italy created by victories in the 1700s and affirmed in the peace settlement of 1713–14 had been overthrown in southern Italy. This was important in the challenging of the Austrian reach for more general predominance, and prefigured the Prussian success in doing the same against the Austrians in Germany and East-Central Europe in the 1740s and 1750s. Thus, the absence of a European hegemony was related to the failure of hegemonic ambitions in particular regions of Europe. The interaction of the latter involved rival coalitions, military prioritization and diplomatic strategy, each of which was to remain a key element of European power politics. The overthrow of the Austrian position in southern Italy was an aspect of the failure of such a regional ambition. In this case, the ambition had been enshrined in the 1713 Utrecht peace settlement, which had reflected the success of the wartime Anglo-Austrian alliance and notably of the Austrian conquest of the area, a conquest generally ignored in histories of the war.[6]

The campaigns of the early decades of the eighteenth century saw a working through of the political, governmental, organizational and tactical developments of the late seventeenth century. In the case of the last, the bayonet–flintlock musket combination helped to lessen the role of cavalry and ensured that casualty rates in battle could be high. This was especially so as a result of the exchange of fire at close quarters and between lines of closely-packed troops, which was the formation chosen to maximize firepower. Soldiers fired by volley, rather than employing individually aimed shot. Despite the bayonets, hand-to-hand fighting on the battlefield was relatively uncommon, and most casualties were caused by shot. The accuracy of muskets was limited, and training, therefore, emphasized rapidity of fire. Drill and discipline accordingly focused on this. Limited accuracy was exacerbated by the clouds of smoke that arose from the use of black powder and the extent to which it was not fully combusted. These clouds made it difficult to breathe and see during the battle. Limited accuracy encouraged remaining in position and firing at a close range that ensured that it was possible to hit the other side.

For infantry, cavalry and siegecraft, there was a consistent tension between firepower and shock tactics. The different choices made reflected circumstances, experience, the views of particular generals and wider assumptions in military society. These choices were not dictated by technology. In one light, the focus on attack represented a cultural imperative in the face of the growing strength of firepower, but, in practice, this strength did not preclude advantages for attacking forces. The prestige of the attack, rather than a reliance on ideas and practices of deliberate siegecraft, could encourage attempts to storm fortresses, but so could a need for speed, both in order to press on to achieve results and so as to deal with logistical problems.[7]

Eugene of Savoy (1663–1736), one of the foremost generals of the age, successfully served the Austrians against the Turks and the French. Although he deployed his troops in the conventional manner, Eugene placed a greater premium on manoeuvre in campaign, and attack in battle, than did his unsuccessful French rivals. In northern Italy, in the 1700s, during the War of the Spanish Succession, Eugene did not allow the French emphasis on the defence of river lines and fortified positions to thwart his drive for battle and victory, notably at Carpi in 1701. In part, this was a consequence of Eugene's personality: the preference for excitement and acceptance of risk that took him into the thick of the battle. In turn, this brought him fame and glory and took glory from his opponents, as with Jan Smeltzing's medal, *Louis is ejected from the Sun's Chariot after the Battle of Turin* (1706), a victory by Eugene over the French army. Eugene's recently restored Winter Palace in Vienna included a hall with paintings of battle scenes, as well as stucco reliefs with military themes.[8]

Eugene also took the lessons of his campaigning against the Turks, over whom he had won a major victory at Zenta in Hungary in 1697, into the world of campaigning against Western rivals. The extent to which this transition occurred in Western military history varied by general, unit and army; and all within the context of the interplay of circumstances with the ability to detect opportunities. The transition, which was most apparent with Austria and, even more, Russia, is underplayed if the emphasis is solely on developments within the West.

The British general, John Churchill, 1st Duke of Marlborough, was another keen attacking commander, although his Dutch allies were far more reluctant to risk battle.[9] Marlborough and Eugene co-operated to defeat a Franco–Bavarian army at Blenheim in Bavaria next to the River Danube on 13 August 1704, thus thwarting an attempt to overthrow Austrian power that would very much have left France dominant in Europe, and certainly in Western Europe. Allied to Hungarian rebels against Austrian Habsburg rule, the French were able to hope for a major change in the European system; although coherent planning was far more elusive. This victory was largely due to Marlborough's tactical flexibility, in particular to his ability to retain control and manoeuvrability, an ability that contrasted with the failure of his opponents. The decisive factors were mastery of the terrain; the retention and management of reserves; and the timing of the heavy strike in the centre where the opposing line was broken. Such tactics were to enable Marlborough to win similar victories over the French at Ramillies (1706) and Oudenaarde (1708).

Tactics alone, however, did not suffice. Marlborough benefited from the extensive experience the Anglo–Dutch forces had gained from campaigning in the area in the 1690s, as well as from impressive staff work, and a logistical strength based on good public finances and the capacity of the mercantile economy.[10] At Malplaquet (1709), Marlborough again won, but at a great cost as the French had learned how to oppose his tactics, thus lessening their effectiveness and the resulting capability gap. The same was to be the case repeatedly with the eroding of short-term advantages and successes, as with those of Frederick the Great of Prussia, Napoleon (Bonaparte), Napoleon III, German warmaking in the late nineteenth century and Hitler's *blitzkrieg* approach.

Austrian and British victories undermined Louis XIV's diplomatic strategy, leading allies to change sides or be overrun. In 1703, Louis was deserted by both Pedro II of Portugal and Victor Amadeus II of Savoy-Piedmont, each being offered support and territorial gains by the Grand Alliance. Louis had been unable to provide Pedro with naval protection against the threat of Anglo–Dutch naval attack. A similar process was seen in both world wars. Moreover, in 1702–3, the territories of two of Louis's German allies, the Elector of Cologne and the Duke of Brunswick-Wolfenbüttel, were overrun. To retain the support of the third, Elector Max Emmanuel of Bavaria, Louis promised to support his acquisition of the Lower Palatinate and the Spanish Netherlands (Belgium). By 1703, the objectives of both alliances had increased greatly, which helped make compromise difficult.

Blenheim itself was followed by the overrunning of Bavaria, which was a verdict that was not to be militarily challenged during the war. Instead, other than in Spain, French strategy became mostly a matter of frontier defence, as was to happen again in 1743, after defeat at Dettingen, and in 1813, after defeat in Leipzig, each French defeats in Germany. Frontier defence, however, was a course of action that made it difficult to retain and gain allies, that posed a serious logistical strain on supporting French armies, and which made victory impossible. Moreover, Louis believed his honour was involved in supporting Max Emmanuel, a key consideration. Supporting allies was also necessary in order to prevent a rallying to Louis' opponents. In November 1704, a Franco–Bavarian treaty committed Louis to continue the war until Bavaria was retaken and enlarged.

In a pattern common with most wars, diplomacy continued during the conflict itself. Thus, in 1706, defeat by Marlborough at Ramillies and the expulsion of the French from the Spanish Netherlands led Louis XIV to try peace proposals. Again, Marlborough's victory over the French at Oudenaarde in 1708 and his capture of the major fortress of Lille later that year, made Louis more eager to settle, but defeat also affected the room available for manoeuvre. In turn, Marlborough's pyrrhic victory at Malplaquet, followed by only slow progress in capturing French fortresses, helped move the political dynamic more towards a position conducive to the French. In Germany, the Imperial Diet at Regensburg declared in July 1713 that the French proposals would 'tarnish the glory of the German nation'. However, outnumbered and pushed back by the French, who captured the fortresses of Freiburg, Kehl and Landau in 1713, the Emperor Charles VI was forced to negotiate.

As with Marlborough, Marshal Saxe, the leading French general of the 1740s (who had served under Marlborough and Eugene), and Frederick II, the Great, King of Prussia (r. 1740–86) were also skilled in attack. In 1745, against the Austrians, Frederick developed the attack in oblique order, so as to be able to concentrate overwhelming strength against a portion of the linear formation of the opposing army. Frederick devised a series of methods for strengthening one end of his line and attacking with it, while minimizing the exposure of the weaker end. This method depended on the speedy execution of complex manoeuvres, for which well-drilled and well-disciplined troops were essential. It was essential to move more rapidly than the opposing side in order to maintain the advantage of deployment. The oblique attack was used to great effect, most notably in defeating the Austrians at Leuthen in 1757, and the Prussian army enjoyed the highest reputation in Europe until the triumphs of the forces of Revolutionary France from 1792.

As a more general indication of the problems of military operations, it is instructive to consider why Frederick II's major victories during the Seven Years' War were not more decisive. There were strategic, organizational and operational reasons. Frederick could not spare the time for a lengthy pursuit of a single enemy, given the number of other enemies who threatened him. In addition, not yet organized in divisions or corps, the armies of the time were clumsy instruments, while there were few commanders of detached armies or forces who were psychologically prepared for independent decision-making. That Frederick frequently lost more men than his enemies, even in his victories, compounded another organizational issue, namely that his tightly disciplined troops could not be unleashed in a headlong pursuit without the danger of the units becoming less coherent or even disintegrating because of desertion as soon as they were out of sight of their officers. In operational terms, the Prussians were poor in siegework and often lost momentum by getting stuck in front of fortresses and fortress-cities.

Furthermore, the Austrians had soon developed effective counter-tactics, retaining in battle reserves that could be moved to meet the Prussian attack. As a result, Frederick encountered greater difficulties against Austrian forces both in the latter stages of the Seven Years' War (1756–63) and in the subsequent War of the Bavarian Succession (1778–9). In the latter, Frederick won no victories in a conflict in which blocking positions, not battle, predominated. In face of a more complex situation and changing circumstances, Prussia's reputation was overrated, rather as that of Germany was to be after Prussian successes in the 1864–71 Wars of German Unification. On the other hand, that was an understandable response to successive victories.

An emphasis on the attack, moreover, was seen in the eighteenth century in the case of Gaelic, Polish, Russian and Swedish forces. Thus, the enhancement of firepower from the 1690s, with the widespread addition of socket bayonets to flintlock muskets, had not banished the strategic, operational and tactical offensive in the West, nor its cultural significance. French writers stressed the shock and weight of forces attacking in columns. In addition, shock won over firepower in the case of cavalry tactics. The seizure of the initiative also repeatedly played a role in Austrian and Russian victories over the Turks, and notably in Russian attacks in the 1768–74 conflict, in which Russian forces successfully advanced south of the River Danube, despite the impressive Turkish fortresses along the river. These victories helped ensure that Russian power increased in Europe as a whole, notably at the expense of what France tried to create in Eastern Europe, a *barrière de l'est* of Sweden, Poland and the Turks directed against the Russians. As a result of Russia's successes, the balance between Austria and Russia moved towards the latter, while the position of French predominance created by Louis XIV was lost anew as it had been initially by defeat during the War of the Spanish Succession. Russia was to beat the Turks anew in 1787–92 and 1806–12, ensuring that the fate of the Turkish empire became an important issue in Western power politics.

An emphasis on shock did not necessarily lessen the value of firepower, especially because the latter could be used to prepare for the assault. However, a teleology focused on rising firepower is inappropriate. Moreover, any account that approaches tactical success in terms of the technological (weaponry) and organizational (tactics, drill, discipline) factors that maximized firepower is a limited one. In practice, the real point of drill and discipline was defensive: to prepare a unit to remain in action in the face of death, regardless of casualties. The psychological pressure of resolve was highly significant. The issue of shock versus firepower – of offensive efficacy or effectiveness in causing casualties – were not as important as a unit remaining able to act, and tractable to its commander, while receiving casualties. This is a continual theme in military history. Moreover, linear tactics in practice were a general concept including a substantial variety of precepts among which line formations were only one. Therefore, formations in column were not in themselves in existential opposition to linear tactics as a whole, as long as their deployment was not intended to break up the close-knit network of tactical rules and customs, and mechanistic creeds that informed the ideas behind linear tactics.

Firepower played a major role in sieges, in the shape of siege artillery, and the movement of these heavy cannon was important in the planning of operations. Nevertheless, many fortresses, often major ones, such as Prague in 1741 and Bergen-op-Zoom in 1747, fell to assault. The speed with which Austrian forts in modern Belgium fell to French attack in 1744–6 became a convenient explanation of failure in the War of the Austrian Succession; but this explanation in practice exaggerated their significance in the campaigning, and notably, at the expense of battles. Victories at Fontenoy (1745), Roucoux (1746) and Laffeldt (1747) enabled the French to take the initiative in the struggles for fortresses. Moreover, while the defence and siege of fortifications were to play an important role in the Seven Years' War in Europe (1756–63), this was less so than in the conflicts of 1688–1748. In part, this situation reflected the absence of campaigning in the Low Countries during the Seven Years' War, but, alongside the extent to which fortifications continued to represent an important force multiplier and proof of control, there had also been a shift towards a greater significance for battle which seemed better able to convey control.

An aspect of the improvability of Western military practice was that this issue was widely debated. Much of this debate was taken forward through publications. Aside from the debate of shock versus firepower that attracted great attention from the 1720s, with Jean-Charles Folard drawing on his experience of the War of the Spanish Succession to emphasize the former, there was printed discussion over a range of topics including best practice in fortification and whether pikes should be reintroduced. As an instructive comment on the modern tendency to adopt a teleological account, part of these debates involved a consideration of precedents from Antiquity, notably Macedonian and Roman warfare. This was seen, for example, in Saxe's *Rêveries* (1757). A society heavily influenced by the Classics encompassed warfare in this influence. Saxe criticized reliance on firepower alone and, instead, advocated a combination of individually aimed fire and shock attacks with bayonets, each of which were linked to his stress on morale. Saxe's work encouraged fresh thought.

The battles in which he was involved in 1745–7 involved large numbers of men: 200,000 at Roucoux and 215,000 at Lawfeldt. This, the fluidity of the fighting and the extent to which each battle was a combination of a number of distinct, but related, struggles all anticipated aspects of Napoleonic warfare. Saxe's generalship was instructive not only because of his battlefield ability to control large numbers effectively in both attack and defence, but also because of his determined espousal of a war of manoeuvre with an emphasis on gaining and holding the initiative.

Western armies and navies were 'standing' (permanent) forces under the direct control of the rulers. The spread of conscription greatly altered the social politics of military service and war, although it was not universal. In Britain, where there was a hostility to military power, conscription was restricted to the navy where it operated in wartime by means of the forcible seizure seen with press gangs. Attitudes were different as far as the army was concerned. For example, the newspaper *Old England*, on 25 November 1752, warned about the danger of Britain becoming a military power, a reference to persistent opposition distrust of William, Duke of Cumberland, Captain General, who was the surviving son of George II. George himself had earned fame by commanding during the Battle of Dettingen in 1743, a victory over the French. Victor at Culloden in 1746, Cumberland commanded British forces in the Low Countries in 1745–8, but without much success. More seriously, as commander of a Hanoverian army in Germany in 1757, Cumberland was defeated by the French under the Duke of Richelieu at Hastenbeck, and negotiated the surrender of his forces and a neutrality for Hanover. This led to Cumberland being disgraced by his father.

As a means to raise manpower, systems of conscription were less effective than they were to be in the twentieth century, not least because of the limited amount of information at the disposal of the state, notably over population size and location, as well as the weakness of its policing power. Nevertheless, the ambition to create and sustain large armies ensured a reliance on conscription, and notably as a result of the shortage of manpower during the seventeenth and early eighteenth centuries. In 1693, each Prussian province was ordered to provide a certain number of recruits, a number that was achieved by conscription. The same year, French militia were sent to fight in war zones; from 1688, they had been raised by conscription among unmarried peasants. Conscription systems spread rapidly. They were introduced in Denmark in 1701, Spain in 1704 and Russia in 1705: each of these powers was then at war. In Prussia, a cantonal system was established between 1727 and 1735. In this, every regiment was assigned a permanent catchment area around its peacetime garrison town, from where it drew its draftees for lifelong service. Such systems increased control over the peasantry, who were less able than mercenaries to adopt a contractual approach towards military service and less likely than urban workers to enjoy exemptions from service. In the face of concern about Prussia and Russia, conscription was imposed in Austria and Bohemia in 1771.

Alongside recruits, peasants had to support the military, which was a major burden. The lack of barracks ensured that troops were frequently quartered in the homes of peasants, who also had to provide food. Peasants also provided free labour on fortifications and for military logistics. This contributed to peasant discontent, not least in Hungary in 1735.

Recruitment practices were as important an aspect of rising state military power as the number of troops in armies, the latter being a criterion which is sometimes employed in a somewhat crude fashion as the sole indicator of such power. New recruitment systems were mediated by aristocratic officers, and in France and Prussia the dominance of the officer corps by the nobility greatly increased. These systems reflected an enhanced control on the part of government, as well as an aspiration to control. Indeed, there was no longer a figure equivalent to Wallenstein, the independent entre-preneur who raised and commanded armies for the Emperor Ferdinand II in the 1620s and early 1630s (deploying possibly as many as 150,000 troops), before being assassinated in 1634 when his loyalty became suspect. Thanks to his efforts, Wallenstein had acquired major estates and become Duke of Friedland.

At sea, a parallel was offered by the role of prominent Genoese figures in Spanish naval strength in the Mediterranean in the sixteenth century, notably members of the Doria family. In the eighteenth century, the equivalent figures were usually within states, but naval strength did require far-flung networks able to procure supplies and support operations. These networks were more significant than the crude number of warships. The availability of experienced sailors was also important for, to be effective, warships required sailors able to operate the ships and also to fire the cannon at a rapid rate.

By the late eighteenth century, military entrepreneurship was not as independent as it had been in the late seventeenth, let alone in the early seventeenth. As a result, the system did not sap governmental control, both politically and operationally, to the degree that had occurred earlier. This change was crucial to the ability to think and act effectively in strategic terms and to operational ends. This ability was not new, but the increase in discipline, planning and organizational regularity and predictability, that characterized Western armies and navies, made it less difficult to implement strategic conceptions. As a result, Western powers could now match the Chinese ability to plan and implement. The greater effectiveness of military forces was demonstrated by Russia under Peter the Great (r. 1689–1725) and by Prussia from 1740. France was able to deploy and sustain significant forces on more than one front in the 1670, 1690s, 1700s, 1730s, 1740s and 1750s, which greatly increased the military and political challenge it posed to opposing coalitions. In the case of France, such activity had been seen in the 1550s, 1630s, 1640s and 1650s, but less successfully so, in large part due to supply and financial issues. However, while this change can indeed be seen, it is important to note the problems produced by supporting armies and navies of this scale, as well as the extent to which entrepreneurship had provided an ability readily to deploy experienced forces and to achieve goals accordingly.

The ability to sustain forces on more than one front repeatedly ensured that prioritization between them was a key strategic issue and means. In operational terms, the pressures of prioritization also opened up the prospect for diversionary attacks. Thus, in November 1746, Austrian forces invaded Provence in southern France from Italy. Encouraged by the British and supported by their navy, the invasion was in part mounted to divert French efforts from the Low Countries. However, both sides encountered supply problems in the winter campaign, and the Austrians were greatly distracted by a rising in their rear in Genoa. The French successfully counter-attacked in January 1747 and the Austrians were driven out of Provence.

Enhanced Western organizational capability and political control over the military in the eighteenth century were not simply a matter of financing, supplying or moving armies and navies, but also improved the organizational and operational effectiveness of individual units. On the global scale, Western armies moved most towards a large-scale rationalization of such units: they were to have uniform sizes, armaments, clothing, command practices etc. Such developments made it easier both to exercise command and to implement drill techniques that maximized firepower. Allied and subsidized units could be expected to fight in an identical fashion with 'national' units, which was a marked contrast to the situation in the Asiatic empires, where there were major differences between core and ancillary troops.

More generally, far from being rigid or anachronistic, pre-revolutionary (i.e. pre-1789) Western warfare was dynamic and flexible. It could also deliver decisive results in both battle and war, as the loss to Russia of Sweden's empire in modern Estonia and Latvia demonstrated. Peter the Great's total victory over the outnumbered Charles XII of Sweden at Poltava in Ukraine in 1709 was followed by the rapid conquest of Estonia and Livonia in 1710, and then by the conquest of Finland and the projection of Russian power westward into modern Germany.

The War of the Polish Succession (1733–5) is not generally seen as particularly significant. However, it displayed decisiveness, not only in enabling the Bourbons to establish themselves in southern Italy, but also in ensuring that Russia determined the election of the new King of Poland. The Russian protégé, the Elector of Saxony, defeated the Polish choice, who was the father-in-law of Louis XV and who, being Charles XII's choice for the Polish throne, had unsuccessfully opposed Peter the Great. In 1733–4, the Russians successfully supported the new king against Polish opposition. A small French expeditionary force that intervened failed to raise the Russian siege of Danzig (Gdansk) in 1734. At the same time, decisiveness was not only a matter of such sweeping successes, successes that, in part, prefigured later concepts of decisiveness, indeed total war. The French advances in the Moselle and Rhineland in 1733–4 and, with greater territorial gains, in northern Italy in 1733–5, were also 'decisive' in that they established that France could successfully exert pressure on Austria and in the face of major Austrian efforts. In 1734, the French beat off Austrian attempts to reconquer northern Italy. The Austrians were not distracted by war with the Turks, as they had been in the 1690s, nor by a Hungarian rebellion, as in the 1700s. This French capability underlined the vulnerability of the Austrian Netherlands (Belgium), which was not invaded but, instead, protected by a neutrality convention accepted by the United Provinces (Dutch Republic).

The war ended with an armistice (1735) and later a peace treaty (1738) in which the major powers secured outcomes: Russia a client in Poland; Spain the establishment of a Bourbon branch in Naples and Sicily; France the future acquisition of Lorraine; and Austria a more compact position in Italy and a French guarantee for the Austrian succession. This outcome, alongside the lack of drama in the campaigns in the Rhineland in 1733, 1734 and 1735, and the fact that Britain did not intervene, unlike in the Nine Years' War, and the Wars of the Spanish and Austrian Succession, has led to a tendency to underplay the significance of the war and, more generally, the extent to which conflict was seen as a means to secure major changes in the international system.

The ambition represented by the latter reflected the extent to which armies were regarded as the enablers of international transformations. In 1733–5, transformations that were considered, included a new order in Eastern Europe in which Russia was not only thwarted in Poland but also restrained by a French-supported league of Poland, Sweden and Turkey. Such a league would see Sweden seek to regain its Baltic losses and the Turks do the same over Azov. Within Central Europe, negotiations between France and Bavaria were designed to challenge Austria, as was France's unsuccessful attempt to recruit Frederick William I of Prussia. In the event, despite concerns in 1735, there was no French movement into Bavaria, which remained neutral. French interest in supporting opposition circles in Britain was also significant as being designed to thwart any entry of Britain into the war on the Austrian side. So also was the earlier interest in backing a Jacobite rebellion. These interests did not result in action.

Conversely, Austria and Britain supported the westward move of Russian troops into the Empire (Germany) in 1735, a move designed to counteract France's position and prospects there. This demonstrated the way in which the deployment of force was a key element: it was to be repeated when Britain in 1748 subsidized the westward movement of Russian troops in order to affect the outcome of the War of the Austrian Succession. This policy represented an alignment of the profits of an oceanic commercial system with the manpower and industrial resources of a land power. Repeatedly during the French Revolutionary and Napoleonic Wars, the British were to support such a movement.

The deployment of a large British fleet to the Tagus estuary in 1735 in order to thwart a threatened Spanish invasion of Portugal, a fleet that remained there until 1737, was another instance of force projection. At the same time, this deployment was very different to that of the Russians, a difference that in large part reflected the contrasts between the means and impact of land and naval power. More generally, comparisons between the two repeatedly encounter difficulties, which, thereby, serve to underline the problems involved in proposing models for military history; notably discussion about capability, change and significance, each of which are capable of many definitions.

In all cases, the use of force was related to a political jockeying for position. For example, France had many problems with her allies. Charles Emmanuel III of Savoy-Piedmont spent much of the War of the Polish Succession manoeuvring for diplomatic advantage and entered into secret negotiations for a unilateral peace, as he was to do again, this time when allied with Austria and Britain, during the subsequent War of the Austrian Succession. Underlying the tension over strategy during the War of the Polish Succession, with France opposed to Spain's plan to conquer Naples and Sicily and leave the defence of northern Italy to the French, was an unsuccessful Spanish determination to hold the diplomatic initiative.

For Britain, alongside major differences, notably in exceptional trans-oceanic imperial expansion, there was a parallel trajectory to that of other European states, with the subjugation of regional opposition, as in Spain, again a factor, the key region being Highland Scotland. To turn to the image of anachronism, castles, by the eighteenth century, were very much an echo of the past in Britain. Whereas, during the Middle Ages, defensibility and the grand house were combined in the form of the castle, after that time the two elements were separated. On the one hand, there were the undefended grand houses of society, such as Blenheim, the palace built for the victorious Duke of Marlborough in the 1710s, and named as a continual reminder of his prowess at the battle in 1704. This was a reminder taken further in such decorations as the tapestries that were commissioned and still hang there. On the other, there were the defended installations of the state, such as the naval dockyards.

At the time of the Jacobite risings in 1715–16 and 1745–6, aristocrats temporarily regretted their defencelessness. Lord Glenorchy wrote to this daughter in April 1746, the day before the Jacobites were crushed at the Battle of Culloden: 'I have often repented taking out the iron bars from the windows and sashing them, and taking away a great iron door, and weakening the house as to resistance by adding modern wings to it. If it had remained in the old castle way as it was before, I might have slept very sound in it, for their whole army could not have taken it without cannon.'[11] However, this view was restricted to that emergency. The declining signifi-cance of walls was also seen with cities. Karlsruhe, begun by Karl Wilhelm of Baden-Durlach in 1715, was wall-less, although most German cities did not lose their walls until the nineteenth century.

The Jacobites, whose strength centred in the Scottish Highlands, were led in 1746 by Charles Edward Stuart, Bonnie Prince Charlie, the elder son of the Jacobite claimant to the throne. Their victorious opponents were commanded by William, Duke of Cumberland, the younger (and young) son of George II. This struggle between princes scarcely matched ideas of bureaucratic state direction: appointment through talent would have left neither man in charge. Similarly, although Charles XII and Frederick the Great were talented generals, that was not why they gained their positions.

As in North Wales after conquering it in the late thirteenth century, the British government built forts to overawe the Scottish Highlands so as to prevent a recurrence of the Jacobite risings. However, these forts were different to the form of traditional castles, and none was in private hands. The wide distribution of the castle throughout the British Isles, from the Norman Conquest in the eleventh century onwards, had been the remarkable result of a partnership between public and private power. But, from the mid-seventeenth century onwards, the role of providing defensive fortifications would be replaced by a state monopoly. From then on, the government would invest in only a very few strong buildings, and would place much greater trust in the protection offered by the Royal Navy. Aristocrats might have unprecedented wealth, and might live in castles, such as Alnwick (Duke of Northumberland) and Powderham (Earl of Devon), that had become stately homes; but, now, aristocrats were to be part of the state and did not have the military means to oppose it.

The same bringing of aristocrats within the state was true in other European states. Thus, in Hungary, the Habsburgs used the army to suppress aristocratic and peasant opposition, notably the Rákóczi rising in 1703–11. This rising exposed the contradictions within rebellions, notably the tension between nobles and serfs. Rákóczi's willingness to promise freedom to the serfs in arms and their descendants was unacceptable to the lords. This, however, did not mean the end of the aristocratic military system for, instead, it was transformed as an aspect of the major changes in the European political and governmental situation from the seventeenth century. Also in the 1700s, there was an insurrection in the Cévennes mountains in France as Protestants responded to forcible conversion with violence, and, in turn, their interpretation of God's will led to local Catholic action and subsequently to brutal repression by royal troops.[12]

The French government claimed in 1749 to be in a position to put 150,000 troops into the field. That France had been heavily defeated at sea by Britain in 1747 in two battles off Cape Finisterre was far less significant for potential allies than its repeated victories on land in 1745–8: victories over British, Dutch and Austrian forces at Fontenoy (1745), Roucoux (1746) and Lawfeldt (1747), each of which established and registered the then state of military capability and affected the fate of fortified positions. The danger that the United Provinces would be overrun by the French led to peace, but in a context that was very different to that of the conquest by French Revolutionary forces in 1795, a conquest that was followed by the overthrow of the established system of government.

In *ancien régime* France and elsewhere, there were functional, social and ideological dimensions to the union between Crown and aristocracy manifested in the shape of greater military deployments. As in the late seventeenth century, it proved possible, as a consequence, to increase army numbers, and both on a permanent basis and if required for particular conflicts. The French army, which, under Louis XIV (r. 1643–1715), set the model for the rest of Europe, rose to wartime peaks of 340,000 in 1695–7, 300,000 in 1710, 303,000 in 1735, 345,000 in 1745 and 347,000 in 1760–1; although all figures have to be handled with some care. In addition, its peacetime strength, at 150,000 in 1714, 160,000 in 1735, 201,000 in 1740 and 160,000 in 1770, was considerable and far greater than had been the case in the sixteenth century. The scale of military activity was further impressive because France, consistently, had the second largest navy in the world, after that of Britain, and an extensive system of fortifications to protect its frontiers and ports, as well as fortified positions in its colonies, notably Louisbourg and Quebec, which finally fell to Britain respectively in 1758 and 1759.

Union between Crown and aristocracy in France was helped by shared prestige. In 1734, Louis XIV's surviving grandson, Philip V, told the French envoy that war was necessary for the political stability of the French monarchy.[13] He meant that serving the Crown gave the aristocracy something appropriate to do and was also a source of prestige. Indeed, Louis XV benefited from his association with Saxe's victories. Having followed Louis on his 1745 campaign, Charles Parrocel exhibited ten paintings of Louis' victories the following year. There was a general air of heroism, one in which Louis was able to share. In contrast, a humiliating defeat by the Prussians at Rossbach in 1757, followed by repeated disasters at the hands of the British in 1758–62, seriously compromised the prestige of the French monarchy. This prefigured the more extreme contrast between the prestige of the victorious Napoleon III in 1859 and his total humiliation in 1870.

France was the dynamic military power on land in Western Europe in the 1740s. In 1741, against Austria, and 1744 and 1745–6, when threatening an invasion of Britain, France had a chance to knock out one of its leading opponents, indeed the best chance until the Napoleonic invasion of Austria in 1805. Such opportunities were rare in *ancien régime* warfare, not because goals were limited, but due to the combination of the constraints of distance and the nature of symmetrical warfare. France herself benefited from this situation, as when defeated and/or invaded in 1636, 1675, 1708, 1709, 1743, 1744 and 1792, because her centre of power, Paris, was far removed from the frontier. In contrast, French governments fell as a result of invasion in 1814, 1815, 1870 and 1940. In each case, the attacking force had a greater operational dynamic and tempo than during the *ancien régime*. This, rather than the technology of transport, was the key element.

In 1745–8, France enjoyed a military position and run of successes that was not to be matched and bettered in Europe until 1795–7. She was in a position to make territorial demands, but, however desirable these might have been for domestic reasons, they had less happy international consequences, not least by helping to keep alive the hostile wartime opposition coalition. Having failed to recast Europe by partitioning the Habsburg inheritance in the early 1740s or by installing a client regime in Britain in 1744–6, the French had to work with a less welcoming European system, and this was best exploited by not presenting French policy as dominated by territorial aggrandizement. Alliance with Austria from 1756 to 1792 was both cause and consequence of this stance. It was crucially displayed in the prioritization that led France to go to war with Britain in 1778 in support of the American 'Patriots' while refusing, that year, to support Austria against Prussia in the War of Bavarian Succession.

French territorial gains came from inheritance (Lorraine, 1766) or purchase (Corsica from Genoa, 1768), although, in the face of popular opposition, the island had to be conquered in 1768–9. This conflict illustrated the variety of *ancien régime* warfare. Initial French failure in 1768 was followed in 1769 by success by the much reinforced French forces. That campaign showed, like the overcoming of the Jacobites in Scotland in 1746, that irregular forces could be defeated by superior firepower, especially if they attacked prepared opponents. The campaign also indicated the potential of coordinated independent forces operating against irregulars, as well as the strength of major states. France was able to sustain a considerable force where provisions were in short supply, to overcome defeat and to return to the attack, proceeding systematically to obtain a planned military outcome. In response to the continuance of guerrilla opposition in 1769–70, the French used devastation, terror and the road construction that enhanced mobility and extended the range of routine authority. Those found carrying arms were killed, and by the spring of 1770 Corsica had been subdued.

The French were not alone in having a large army. Directed by the Imperial Council of War, the Austrian army (the army of the Austrian Habsburgs) rose to wartime peaks of 137,000 in 1714, 205,700 in 1735, 203,600 in 1745, 201,300 in 1760–1 and 497,700 in 1789–90. These and similar rates of increase elsewhere were the product of two related, but different, socio-political currents. The first was the Crown–aristocracy realignment of the late seventeenth century in Europe, a factor that demonstrated the significance of social underpinning and the politics bound up in that. This realignment was, simultaneously, the foundation of the *ancien régime* military and the factor that kept it working. In Hungary, where wars had revealed the inadequacy of traditional means of raising and organizing armies, notably the general levy of the nobility, the basis of its tax exemption, the Diet of 1715 saw the King and the Estates co-operate to establish a permanent army. This was to be paid for by taxes, while the obligation on the nobility to obey the ruler's call for a general levy continued. In 1741, the Estates promised Maria Theresa, the embattled new ruler, four million guilders in war taxes, as well as the nobility's general levy, 60,000 recruits and food and forage for the army, in return for promises of autonomy. The Hungarian forces served to help overrun Bavaria in 1741–2, and, in particular, offered a cavalry that Austria could not provide. Such variations are worthy of note alongside the more general tendency to present the regular military as similar in force structure and, therefore, in symmetrical terms. Maria Theresa enunciated a clear and consistent strategy with her focus, as in May 1756, on the defence of the Habsburg hereditary lands, notably Austria, and not on what she termed the 'remote parts of her dominions' such as the Austrian Netherlands (Belgium).[14]

Secondly, and as an aspect of the Crown–aristocracy alignment, but one with the potential for a very different outcome, came, as discussed earlier, the development of conscription systems by a number of states, notably Russia and Prussia. These systems rested on, and represented, the realignment of Crown and aristocracy, and a related model of state-army identity, as well as the raising of information about numbers and location of people. Conscription and censuses were a government project that proved less effective than in the twentieth century, but more so than the means of raising troops in the early seventeenth.

The process, however, was unpopular, as in Hungary where, in 1784, Maria Theresa's son and successor, Joseph II, proposed a reliance on German troops in order to introduce a census that would forward conscription, a conscription that would encompass the nobility. From 1786, the army was also used to carry out a land survey in Hungary. Royal authority in defiance of established constitutional ideas and political practices was also seen in 1787–90 in recruitment for war with the Turks, and in raising supplies without co-operating with the Estates. Encouraged by Prussia, opposition rose in Hungary in 1789, and, in 1790, Joseph II stepped back, abandoning his policies. Crown and nobility in Hungary (as elsewhere) came to co-operate against Revolutionary France, the fear of social revolution leading the Diets of 1790 and 1792 to vote additional help. Hungary tends not to feature in general histories of Western warfare, which underlines the need to ask critical questions about the issue of relevance, the nature of coverage and its distorting consequences. The relationship in Hungary between the domestic willingness to support military preparedness and the international conjuncture, including foreign intervention in domestic politics, is striking. It could also be seen elsewhere, for example in the United Provinces.

Effectiveness was a matter not only of raising large numbers of troops, but also of ensuring that it continued to be possible to do so despite the high rate of losses of men when campaigning. In part, this rate reflected the casualties of conflict, casualties heightened by the difficulties of treating the wounded. However, losses due to disease (which was exacerbated by shortages of food and clean water and a lack of cover) were usually more serious. Infectious diseases were particularly grave. There was a lack of understanding of disease and of its vectors. In general, losses to disease, notably if, but not only, operating in tropical climes, were higher than those to battle until the end of the nineteenth century. There was also persistent desertion, particularly of troops, but also of sailors. As a result, just as individual units had to retain the ability to take casualties and to go on fighting, so the same was true for armies as a whole. Wastage rates, in both peacetime and war, were higher than for modern European armies.

Conscription systems and military professionalism were not co-terminous, but the former encouraged an emphasis on the directing role of the state. This emphasis challenged the implicit, but often uneasy, partnership between Crown and aristocracy. So also, to a degree, did professionalism, for, while many aristocrats sought the prestige of command, not all of them wanted the chore of service, and notably so in Western Europe. Hierarchies in command that did not match the hierarchy of social rank were potentially highly disruptive. While much of this challenge was latent, nevertheless there was already an important change in tone. Knowledge was applied at the operational level, while there was a proliferation of textbooks and military academies that schooled cadets in military engineering. An emphasis on commanders with planning skills encouraged a demand for intellectual accomplishment and technical skill. The latter was particularly significant for the command of ships, as navigation required a knowledge of astronomy and calculation. Technical skill was also important for artillery officers, such as Napoleon.

At the same time, the model and practice of state control and direction had to face the reality of what has been termed the contractor state. These delegated military systems saw many functions in effect sub-contracted. This was done in a variety of ways, but the overall effect both increased the number of stakeholders in the state and yet also weakened what was to be understood, in the prism of later utilitarian bureaucracy, as control and direction. The *ancien régime* military, and the system it rested on, were therefore affected by a range of internal tensions, tensions which led to difficulties, discontent and even peasant insurrections, as in Transylvania in 1784. That was a major rebellion crushed by the army.

From a very different direction, the military was also to be challenged by intellectual speculation and radical politics. The first, associated in particular with the influential intellectual movement of the mid and late eighteenth century known as the Enlightenment, but, in practice, far more widespread in its causes and course, asked questions about practicality and challenged established forms of prestige. This was a matter not only of fame derived from war but also of the automatic reverence for social rank. Enlightenment tendencies were potentially subversive in that they raised important questions about professionalism. Enlightenment writers also made highly critical remarks about the value of war. This was particularly apparent with the *philosophes* in France, and was an important aspect of their mid-century criticism of Louis XV. Voltaire proved an especially sardonic critic of war as pointless and destructive, and notably of the Seven Years' War (1756–63). War, indeed, wore down both civilians and military. In 1761, Major-General George Townshend reported on British operations in Germany:

> this exhausted, pillaged, infected country where nothing but chicanes in war, and misery and despair to the inhabitants remains. Our army is really a scene of indiscipline, weakness and almost despondency. I never saw so much pillage and desertion; it is general.[15]

In a different light, the questioning associated with the Enlightenment gave renewed energy to the discussion about methods of conflict that became more active from the 1720s. This discussion was notably apparent in France, but was also seen more widely, including in the German lands and in Britain. As a result, military development from the eighteenth century, and particularly from the 1760s, very much took place in a context of public debate, a situation that continues to the present. This debate was different in scale and character to the more episodic discussion in print that had been seen from the Renaissance. Military history was an important aspect of this discussion, and took on relevance in this context. This discussion went back to the Classics, but there was also consideration of recent and current conflicts. Thus, the supposed lessons of the American War of Independence (1775–83) were debated.

Radical politics, some of which developed in the shadow of the Enlightenment, posed a more acute challenge to the *ancien régime* military and to the society it represented and protected. These politics began first in a marginal part of the Western world: thirteen rebellious colonies of British North America. However, the idea there of a citizens' militia in practice drew on deep roots in Western Culture, notably that of the Classical world, of medieval and early-modern republics and of more recent British history. Thus, in the mid-1750s, an argument for a revived British nation, including a robust and purposeful masculinity, was linked to calls for a militia to protect Britain against invasion. The alternatives presented were of a militia 'all interested in the general weal, rather than ... a rabble of mercenaries, either natives or foreigners'.[16] These ideas were brought to fruition in North America. In practice, the challenge posed to the established social politics was scarcely truly radical: no women or African Americans were made officers. Nevertheless, in terms of the Western values of the age, including those of relatively enlightened Britain, the appointment as officers of men of humble background represented a dramatic instance of a 'levelling spirit'.[17]

This process was to be taken further with the armies of revolutionary France. In 1792, they began a period of war that was to last, with only brief intervals, until the final defeat of Napoleon at Waterloo in 1815. In part, it was the very logic of a military that served a radical republic that was the key element, for the republic created in France in September 1792 with the overthrow of the Bourbon dynasty was more radical in intention, rhetoric and practice than the then current European republics in Italy, the Netherlands and Switzerland, let alone far more radical than had been envisaged by most of those who pressed for change when the French 'Revolution' began in 1789. Pressure for a more rigorous warfare, indeed a contemporary form of total war, developed in response to what was seen as the ideological threat from the French. In August 1792, William, Lord Auckland, a senior British diplomat, pressed that war not be conducted:

> with the courtesies of the age ... the French troops, however despicable they may be in point of discipline and command, are earnest in the

support of the wicked and calamitous cause in which they are engaged
... I sincerely hope that it may be a plan rigorously observed, to disarm
every place and district through which the troops may pass, to destroy
the arms, to dismantle the fortresses, to demolish the cannon, powder
mills etc, and all forges for arms etc, and to issue a notice that any
place or district found a second time in arms shall be subject to military
execution ... if neglected, there is reason to believe that the impression
of the interference will at best be transitory.[18]

That this change occurred in what was widely seen as the leading
monarchy in Europe underlined the shock for the remainder of Europe.
So, even more, did the pace of French success. By the time the republic's
government was overthrown in a military coup headed by Napoleon in
November 1799, its forces had defeated the other powers of Western
Europe and had achieved a rate of conquest, notably in late 1792, that
was totally different to the *ancien régime* norm. It had taken France several
years of campaigning to conquer much of the Spanish, later Austrian,
Netherlands (Belgium) in the 1670s, 1690s, 1700s and 1740s. In contrast,
after failed offensives in April and June 1792, the French, helped greatly
by a weak Austrian response, conquered the region in November 1792.
The 'Western Question', that of France's expansion, ambition and role in
Western Europe, a question to the fore from the 1660s to the 1740s, and
then shelved by France's alliance with Austria negotiated in 1756, was now
revived and made more urgent

Whereas, in 1787, the Prussians had successively invaded the United
Provinces (modern Netherlands), in 1792 their invasion of France was
a failure, being stopped at Valmy, east of Paris, by firm resistance from
a larger army and, in particular, its cannon. The Prussians had already
encountered serious problems with the intractable terrain of the Argonne,
logistics, the effects of rain on the roads and sickness, especially dysentery.
Unlike in 1870, they were not prepared for a major campaign, and a
numerous, well-prepared French army was sufficient to check them without
a large-scale battle. There was no full-scale engagement at Valmy. The
French artillery decided the day against the heavily outnumbered Prussians
who did not press home the attack with great vigour.

In the British Parliament in April 1797, Richard Brinsley Sheridan, an
opposition spokesman as well as a playwright, mocked government assur-
ances about the ease with which the French would be destroyed by the
armies of Britain and its allies:

I will not remind those gentlemen of their declaration, so often made,
that the French must fly before troops well disciplined and regularly
paid. We have fatal experience of the folly of those declarations; we have
seen soldiers frequently without pay, and without sufficient provision,
put to rout the best-paid armies in Europe.[19]

Indeed, the French enjoyed operational and organizational advantages over their opponents from the outbreak of war, advantages that were later to benefit Napoleon; while the commitment of the political system of the Revolution to war by August 1792 and thereafter was also significant. The *levée en masse*, a general conscription ordered in 1793, raised large forces, and these were used for offensive operations to a degree that the *ancien régime* French militia had not been. Ideas of valour, indeed masculinity, were presented in terms of such action. After the arbitrary chaos of the initial years of the Revolution, there were also improvements in military organization, with conscription formally introduced in 1798. French armies were able to operate effectively on several fronts at once to match the opposing forces of much of Europe, to take heavy casualties, and to continue fighting. Although there were major difficulties, notably in logistics, the French army was moulded and sustained as a war-winning force, being more successful than Louis XIV had been in his multi-front campaigning in the 1700s.

The aggressive style of revolutionary French war-making, in strategy, operations, tactics and seizing supplies from the areas in which they campaigned, was matched by a battlefield deployment in independent attack columns. Preceded by skirmishers who disrupted the close-packed lines of opponents, and supported by massed cannon, these columns proved effective. This was notably so against a static linear defence in the Battle of Jemappes on 6 November 1792, after which Austrian-ruled Belgium was speedily conquered. Brussels fell on 13 November, Ostend on 16 November, Liège on 27 November, Antwerp on 29 November and Namur on 2 December. Further south, French troops captured Speyer on 30 September, Worms on 4 October, Mainz on 21 October and Frankfurt on 22 October. Most cities were no longer in a position to mount resistance.

On 16 November 1792, the Executive Council decreed that the Austrians should be pursued wherever they retreated, a threat to neutrals. Moreover, on 19 November, in response to appeals from foreign radicals, the National Convention passed a decree that the French people would extend fraternity and assistance to all peoples seeking to regain their liberty. As a general principle, this was subversive of all international order. On 1 February 1793, the National Convention decided unanimously to declare war on Britain and the Dutch, making novel use of the notion that war was declared on sovereigns, and, thus, that aggression was not being committed against other peoples.

The French went on to drive their opponents in 1794 from Belgium, where the Austrians had regained control, and then from the Netherlands (Holland). Amsterdam fell in 1795. The conquered Dutch on 16 May 1795 accepted satellite status as the Batavian Republic, a massive indemnity, major territorial cessions, a French army of occupation until a general peace was negotiated, and a loss of control over the navy, the last a key issue as France struggled to offset Britain's naval power and to be able to mount an amphibious intervention in Ireland as was done, without success, in 1798.

The creation of a total of six dependent republics on the Dutch pattern epitomized the use of power to make revolutionary changes elsewhere in Europe. In 1797, the opposing First Coalition collapsed as a result of Austrian defeat. That year, Napoleon, having conquered northern Italy, advanced towards Vienna to extort favourable terms in a way that had not been sought in 1735, although, in 1741, French and Bavarian forces had advanced towards Vienna and in 1704 they had threatened to do so.

Although revolutionary radicalism was not sustained in the late 1790s, the French regime remained bellicose. The government of the Directory (1795–9) believed war necessary in order to support the army, to please its generals, and, for these and other reasons, to control discontent in France, not least by providing occupation for the volatile commanders, the views and ambitions of many of whom were not limited to the conduct of war. In northern Italy, initial French victories by Napoleon in 1795–6 had led to pressure for further conquest, in order to satisfy political and military ambitions and exigencies. However, in the 1790s, as in the 1700s and 1740s, French methods did not guarantee success, and there were setbacks, as in early 1792, and defeats, as at Neerwinden in 1793 and Amberg in 1796. In addition, it proved difficult to fix success. Thus, the brutal exploitation of northern Italy in 1796 led to a popular uprising that was harshly repressed. On the pattern of the suppression of royalist opposition in the Vendée region of France, the destruction of the revolt entailed summary executions and the burning of villages. The French were not alone. Russia suppressed a rising in Poland in 1794 and Britain one in Ireland in 1798. On the other hand, the French claimed to be advancing the cause of peoples.

Force increasingly defined France's response with other powers, leading Russia into hostilities with her. France was still at war when Napoleon seized power in November 1799. An artillery officer by background, and thus more technically proficient than most officers, he crushed a royalist rising in Paris in 1795 with a 'whiff of grapeshot' – the use of artillery against demonstrators, and made his name in 1795–7 with a campaign in northern Italy characterized by swift decision-making and rapid mobility. His siting of artillery was particularly important to his repeated success in battle. Napoleon's generalship was characterized by self-confidence, swift decision-making, rapid mobility, the concentration of strength at what was made the decisive point and, where possible, the exploitation of interior lines. Keen to keep his army in being after peace was negotiated with Austria in 1797, Napoleon had then successfully invaded Egypt in 1798, rather as, victorious in Gaul (France), Julius Caesar had then invaded Britain in 55 and 54 BCE. Initially victorious, Napoleon found campaigning in Palestine in 1799 more difficult. Nevertheless, he was able to benefit in 1799, both by misrepresenting his operations and from a sense that the Directory needed replacement.

In an action–reaction model of military history, it might be concluded that French success also set a new military norm for other powers. However, aside from the problems posed to other states by the social politics of Revolutionary France, it was not the case that the latter was so universally successful military as to discourage attempts to maintain existing systems. Moreover, these systems could be highly effective, or, at least, sufficiently so to adapt to a degree of change. Whereas the hitherto high reputation of the Prussian army was superseded by, and then succumbed to, that of France, notably as a result of Napoleon's victory at Jena in 1806, the Russians continued to demonstrate flexibility and success. In the 1790s, they defeated the Turks, the Poles and the French, and, in 1806–14, the Turks, the Swedes and the French.

The defeat in 1794 of the Polish rising against the second partition of Poland by Prussia and Russia in 1793 demonstrated anew that revolutionary forces were not always successful, a point that was to be valid anew, albeit in different political and military contexts, for such forces in the nineteenth and twentieth centuries. In 1795, in the third partition (the first was in 1772), Poland was partitioned out of existence by Austria, Prussia and Russia. It was not recreated until late 1918 when the defeat of all three powers in the First World War created new opportunities for Polish nationalists. In 1939, Poland was to be partitioned anew by Germany (which then included Austria) and the Soviet Union. This pattern demonstrated both geopolitical continuities and the decisiveness of war.

Alongside ideology and politics as dynamics and forms of change, it is appropriate to consider the role of science and technology. These were significant not so much in specifics but in the broadest sense. Indeed, over a longer timescale, the potential of Western warfare changed as a result. This, indeed, was a key reason for governmental support of what has been termed the Scientific Revolution, and, indeed, for the logic of Enlightened Despotism, the dominant form of government in the Western world from about 1740 to about 1790. Improvements in government were very much directed to achieving more resources for the military and, more generally, to supporting war. The scale of war was an issue. In 1760, Dresden was unsuccessfully besieged by the Prussians from 13 to 30 July, during which time the 14,943 strong defenders fired 26,266 shot and 326 mortar bombs from their 193 pieces of artillery, 1,583 grenades and 386,684 gunshots.

The eighteenth century witnessed the linkage of Newtonian science to military engineering, artillery and military thought. In particular, ballistics was revolutionized in mid-century, notably by Benjamin Robins and Leonhard Euler. Theoretical and empirical advances greatly increased the predictive power of ballistics, and helped turn gunnery from a craft into a science that could, and should, be formally taught. These developments both greatly affected the use of artillery and encouraged the growth of military education. Rulers established military academies. Much effort was also devoted to improving artillery, notably by Austria in the 1750s and by France from the late 1760s. Increased standardization was important, and notably with the French artillery. Such standardization increased predictability in use, and thus enhanced tactical regularity. The artillery was to be used to great affect by the French revolutionaries, including Napoleon.

All major states were able to share in these changes, or aspects of them, or, at least, to do so eventually. As a result, the change did not cause any fundamental transformation in the Western system, at least in the long-term. Nevertheless, the caveats (about aspects and concerning the long-term) are very important. Partly as a result, if France reverted to Bourbon rule in 1815, the Europe in which Louis XVIII gained power was different to that in which his older brother, Louis XVI, lost it in 1792, albeit not to the extent that was to be apparent by the revolutions in 1830 and, even more, 1848. Moreover, the aggregate potential of this system against both non-Western opponents and internal rebels increased. Potential, however, did not dictate outcomes, as the course of the warfare in 1792–1815 fully demonstrated.

CHAPTER FIVE

The Rise of the Bureaucratic State and of Mass Society, 1800–1900

Each of the subjects outlined in the first paragraph of the Preface was very much obvious in this period. Long-term military developments, notably in the way war was waged, were linked to the major changes, indeed transformations, in the European international system, as well as in Europe's position in the world, as the leading European empires each became more powerful than any earlier empire. The multi-polarity of the European system was writ large on the world scale, with Britain the largest empire in the world and France the second largest, while the global position of the European empires and economies helped provide resources that permitted fresh investment in military capability. These developments created military and political requirements that were of significance for both governments and societies, requirements that were framed and perceived in what was seen as an intensely competitive international environment, notably in the latter half of the century.

In response to these requirements, the experience of military service became widespread, indeed, in most states, normative, with conscription. That Britain did not rely on conscription became an aspect of what the British saw as their country's exceptional character and, thus, as the undesirable quality of conscription. Military service by conscription was supported by reserve systems in which those men who were not, usually because no longer, conscripts retained the obligation to serve in the military. This reserve status entailed a preparedness that included several weeks' annual full-time training and manoeuvres. That troops were speeded to these manoeuvres by rail exemplified the interaction of military practice, technological advance and the economic growth and organization, including financial resources, which led to the development of railways. As a result of this and other practices, the linkage of nation, army and state became more potent. In turn, this linkage affected the presentation of military history and, indeed, national culture as a whole. An exemplary military past for the nation was increasingly seen as a key element in national identity, and as one that anticipated the future.

This history was in part separate to the emphasis on the military as a means of dynasticism; but the two were repeatedly closely linked. The republican future envisaged with the French Revolution, where a republic was declared in 1792, had proven short lived. Most European states were monarchies. Moreover, this was also true of newly created states in Napoleonic Europe in the 1800s, and remained the case after the fall of the Napoleonic empire in 1814, and, again, in 1815: he had crowned himself Emperor in 1804, a dramatic display of the benefits of being a successful warlord. Napoleon was a monarch with his origins and career in the military. At his coronation, there had been generals and uniforms aplenty, for Napoleon had turned his generals into a new aristocracy. One, Bernadotte, became King of Sweden; another, Murat, King of Naples.

Due to the end of the republics of Genoa, Venice and Netherlands, each conquered by the French, more of Europe in 1815 was ruled by monarchies than had been the case in 1789. In addition, rebelling from the Netherlands and Turkey respectively, both Belgium and Greece became monarchies in the 1830s. This process continued into the early years of the twentieth century, including with Norway in 1905. However, a republican trend replaced it from the late 1910s.

Dynasticism can be seen as redundant and anachronistic, but the views of rulers, for example of Napoleon III of France (r. 1852–70), remained very important, notably in international politics and military patronage. This was also true of the new Balkan monarchies, such as Romania and Bulgaria. Dynasticism, therefore, was still a major factor, and dynasties, new and old, could trace their position to success in war, and very much sought to do so. Rulers served. Charles, Duke of Brunswick, the Prussian commander in the successful invasion of the Netherlands in 1787 and the unsuccessful invasion of France in 1792, was mortally wounded fighting the French at the Battle of Auerstadt in 1806. Again fighting the French, his son, Duke Frederick, was mortally wounded at the Battle of Quatre Bras in 1815. Frederick's cousin, Frederick, Duke of York, the second son of George III, commanded the British armies sent to Belgium in 1793 and to the Netherlands in 1799.

The changes referred to in the first paragraph were mutually reinforcing, and it is very easy, and on a familiar pattern, to make the entire process appear not only inevitable, but also clear-cut. Moreover, that was an analysis that appeared appropriate to contemporaries. This was not least because the process matched evolutionary ideas about the development of species, ideas that became important in the second half of the century. These ideas were readily transferred to the very different case of human society. The key common element was that of conflict. If conflict between species was apparently instrumental in determining not only their adaptability, but also the success of this adaptability, then conflict presumably played the same role in human society. It was inherent and natural, and the agency through which this conflict would be conducted was society in its political form, the state. Conflict was presented as conferring and confirming manliness, and in a culture and society where that relationship was regarded as important and exemplary.

An international system with competing states was not only regarded as appropriate but also as necessary. The undesirable alternatives appeared to be either an over-mighty imperial power that would be destructive of liberty within Europe, a form of Napoleon redux, or the chaos of individual or non-state violence. The former was referred to by Karl Marx, the formulator of Communism, as 'Bonapartism'. This was Marx's critical response to the military adventurism of Napoleon III and the Emperor's use of war in order to acquire a prestige that would help express and sustain his domestic political position, and his role in history. Before becoming Emperor, he was President of the French Second Republic from 1848 to 1852. In one respect, Napoleon III's position and policies were a variant on Charles Tilly's adage, but there was also, with Napoleon III, an echo of very old patterns of rule and authority, ones that predated any concept of modern statehood. Indeed, this continued role for warleaders, monarchical *gloire* and dynasticism needs to be considered alongside the standard narrative of state development. This role looks towards the bellicose role of some monarchs at the start of the First World War.

Alongside that role, it is appropriate to ask whether it became less the case in the last decades of the nineteenth century. In addition to the continued role of monarchs and dynasties, not least with the ruling houses of Prussia and Britain gaining imperial status, for Germany and India respectively, as those of France and Austria had already claimed, monarchs were increasingly absorbed within the scale and complexity of the governments and states they ruled or presided over, while dynasties had to adapt or respond to nationalism. This caused them much difficulty.

State development was closely linked to the greater availability and improved application of resources. Unprecedented population growth and industrialization were important but so, even more, were their utilization through effective systems of conscription, taxation and borrowing. As a consequence, resources could be deployed and anticipated with unprecedented precision, and thus military planning was enhanced. These developments ensured that technological advances could be readily applied. In turn, the pace of the latter reflected the availability and use of resources, as well as the skills available through unprecedented industrial growth and educational provision. Coal-based ironworking combined with machine tools to produce a metallurgical capacity able to meet the hopes and then demands of war-makers.

As a key instance of technological development, land warfare was transformed by the continued incremental changes in firearms, such as the introduction of the percussion rifle and the Minié bullet, both in the 1840s and, subsequently, of breech-loading cartridge rifles. The net effect, for both handheld firearms and artillery, was very substantial changes in precision, range, speed of use, rate and ease of fire, and the mobility of troops and, to a degree, artillery. Moreover, in the century after Napoleon's final defeat at Waterloo in 1815, greater and more predictable production of munitions flowed from a more streamlined and systematized manufacturing process. This process was better able to give effect to requirements for the planned production of standardized weapons, and of their parts and ammunition. The overall result was a degree of change in weaponry far greater in pace and scope than over the eighteenth century.

The extent of change was even more the case if logistics, command and control, and naval warfare are considered. Steamships, the railway and the telegraph made a major and increasing difference, as well as creating antici-pations of further change, and imminently. They did so both to nearby operations, such as the Franco–Prussian War (1870–1), and to those waged at a greater distance, such as the Crimean War (1854–6). The combination of steamships, railways and telegraphs made it possible to apply and direct greater resources, and in a more sustained fashion than hitherto. This enhanced capability did not necessarily determine the course of conflict, but it did make it far easier to organize war. The potential value of change in creating a capability gap between states was lessened by this change being rapidly disseminated, and thus general within the European system, albeit with significant variations, and, moreover, variations that helped define relative capability. Alongside this, aggregate military capability increased and the latter both enhanced Europe's global position and transformed the potential character of war within Europe.

Yet, the mechanization of European warfare should not be exaggerated, by 1900, let alone 1870, and on land as well as at sea. When the First World War broke out in 1914, there was an average among the European combatants of only one machine-gun per thousand troops, and some armies, such as the Austrian, were in a poor state. Moreover, although the French Revolutionary and Napoleonic Wars (1792–1815) saw experiments with submarine warfare, as well as the first use in Europe of the air for conflict (reconnaissance balloons for artillery spotting in 1794), and the first use in the West of rockets, none of these made any real impact in the nineteenth century. In addition, investment in all of them combined was very small. It was not until the twentieth century that the actual dimen-sions of conflict expanded with effective air, submarine and rocket warfare. Furthermore, it was only then that the chemistry of war acquired the tool of modern poison gas, and thus introduced a potent new form of conflict. Looked at differently, steamships, railways and telegraphs represented more significant developments. The first transformed naval warfare, and the first two the character of logistics. As a result, and through these means, strategic and operational potential altered as they had not hitherto done, as did the potential of war.

Napoleonic warfare in 1799–1815 established expectations and set the tone for conflict in Europe over the subsequent century. Napoleon I's rapid and victorious offensives provided a pattern for emulation. Most particularly, Napoleon III's image owed much to his attempt to annex this legacy; but it was not only pursued by the French. Moreover, the key texts on war during the century, those by Clausewitz, a Prussian, and Jomini, a Swiss who had served in the French and Russian armies, were very much written in the shadow of Napoleon I's successes and, to a far lesser extent, eventual failure; as was teaching in the military academies.[1]

Napoleon I's command of the *Grand Armée* against Austrian and Russian forces in 1805, and against the Prussians in 1806, proved particularly influential in setting a model for pace, organization and outcome. The link between tempo and outcome appeared clear. British efforts, not least the payment of subsidies made possible by the system of public finance and by dominance of oceanic trade, helped lead to the creation of the Third Coalition against France, although British funds were not what kept the allies in the war, and the extent of these in comparison to resources raised by the allies themselves has been greatly exaggerated by British scholars. The coalition was a formidable international combination, but suffered from a lack of organizational cohesion or unity. In secure control of France and the Low Countries, and with a well-prepared army, neither of which were to be the case in 1815, it proved easier for Napoleon in 1805 to respond rapidly to circumstances. He proved a master not only of gaining the initiative through rapid campaigning, but also of moving large forces on the battlefield. In 1805, an Austrian army was outmanoeuvred and forced to surrender at Ulm, before Napoleon pressed on eastward to occupy Vienna and then, in an even more spectacular victory, to defeat an Austro-Russian army at Austerlitz on 2 December. He benefited from the overconfidence of Tsar Alexander I of Russia, the nominal commander of the Austro–Russian forces. A strong Russian attack on Napoleon's right was held in marshy terrain by French infantry, and the French then turned the weak flank of this attacking force to crush the Russians. In 1806, the Prussians were rapidly overthrown, with a major victory at Jena on 14 October leading to the destruction of Prussia's military reputation and being followed by the capture of Berlin. Napoleon had used massed artillery and substantial numbers of skirmishers at Jena. The Prussians suffered from deficient training and organization, poor command, lack of recent war experience and difficult strategic circumstances.

These were impressive eastward projections of French strength, far surpassing anything achieved under the *ancien régime* prior to the French Revolution. It was necessary to go back to Charlemagne (r. 771–814) to see such range on the part of a French ruler, but the context was very different not least as the density of population was far greater by the 1800s while political entities were less amorphous than had been the case during the Middle Ages. Moreover, Napoleon exceeded Charlemagne's range with his operations against the Russians in Poland in 1807, albeit encountering a tougher resistance than those mounted by the Austrians and Prussians, notably at the Battle of Eylau. Napoleon's operations in 1805–7 were very different from those of the French Revolutionary forces. There was no equivalent in the 1790s to Napoleon's successful advance into Central Europe, nor to the defeat, in 1806–7, of the main Prussian and Russian armies. Napoleon benefited in 1806 from being able to fight the Prussians before Russian reinforcements could arrive, while the Prussians suffered from deficient training and organization, poor command, lack of recent war experience and difficult strategic circumstances.[2]

At Eylau on 8 February 1807, battle with the Russians revealed the degree to which French success was dependent on opposing weaknesses, a situation that was also to be true of the Germans in the Second World War. Russian attacks pressed the French hard, and repeated French attacks failed to break the Russians, who withdrew during the night. French casualties were heavy and, although Napoleon had gained possession of the battlefield and Russian losses were heavier, he had not triumphed tactically or operationally. However, at nearby Friedland on 14 June, the Russians attacked with an inferior force and with their back to a river and lost heavily. These casualties left the Russians so battered that they needed time to recuperate and to rebuild their army. The peace with Russia reflected, in part, the exhaustion of both sides.

When Napoleon and Alexander I signed the Treaty of Tilsit on 7 July 1807, Russia abandoned its ally Prussia to Napoleonic terms, while Napoleon was able to recreate a diminished Poland as a client state, undoing the earlier partitions of 1772–95. In the Treaty of Paris, which followed in 1808, the size of the Prussian army was restricted and a heavy indemnity specified. In effect, the European mainland west of Russia was under Napoleon's control. This process was furthered with his defeat of Austria in a renewed war in 1809, notably thanks to victory at Wagram (5–6 July), and by his overthrow of the Spanish monarchy in 1808, although French forces were challenged in Spain by a serious rebellion that proved impossible to suppress. Whereas Austria had been part of potent alliances against France between 1792 and 1805, this was not the case in 1809. Napoleon had won quiescence or even support, and thus lessened the options for his opponents.

Napoleon reconceptualized military rule by focusing it on army as well as ruler. In place of dynasticism, his military dictatorship emphasized the honour of dedication and professionalism, both of which were focused on Napoleon and defined by him. The army represented this process and was the vital means to disseminate the relevant values. In 1804, 80,000 troops witnessed Napoleon handing out medals to almost 2,000 troops, in an elaborate spectacle staged on the cliffs at Boulogne. He encouraged soldiers to defend their reputation and the honour of the French name.[3] Although French propaganda presented Napoleon as always in favour of peace, the regime, in practice, celebrated power, not least the power of victory, in its iconography and commemorations. This was a repeated characteristic of the Napoleonic regime. Moreover, the increase in the tendency to employ soldiers in diplomatic roles markedly contributed to a growing militarization of the conduct of French policy. This was an important aspect of a failure to appreciate that an effective diplomatic service must produce reports and ideas that might be challenging. The Napoleonic system and psyche required force. Napoleon did not understand compromise, and rejected the excellent advice he received. However, even without these character flaws, he faced formidable obstacles.

At the same time, Napoleon's trajectory reflected the degree to which Europe was still inherently a multi-polar system. Indeed, the intensely political nature of war was shown with the difficulties of obtaining lasting peace. These difficulties reflected not only Napoleon's commitment to war as a form of destiny and glory, but also the problems others found in accepting his methods and position. Napoleon was gravely weakened by the precarious nature of his new imperial system and the limited support it enjoyed across much of the continent that he could otherwise dominate militarily. Napoleon's failure to bring lasting peace was in part a testimony to his unwillingness to compromise, but was also the product of a widespread reluctance to accept his perspective, a reluctance that reflected the strength of political identities. Charles V and Hitler faced similar situations, although, in each case, there were specific contexts and issues in military and political history. In the case of the French Revolutionaries and Napoleon, the limited purchase of radicalism, reform and liberalism, and the degree to which conservatism rested on popular support, repeatedly emerged.[4] That the New World followed another course was partly due to the play of circumstances, but also reflected and strengthened important differences in political culture between the Americas and Europe.

The politics of the Napoleonic Wars were very much seen in the strains of alliances, and, moreover, in the response of occupied peoples, for example to French conduct in Spain.[5] Napoleon himself observed in 1808, 'Three-quarters of war is about moral factors; the balance of real forces only accounts for one quarter'.[6] The political side affected war-making in a number of additional ways. A practical, as well as psychological, ability to make work combined armies, in the sense of armies from a number of national sources, was important, as was the experience of fighting in a number of different environments. The British were impressive in the former, and they and the Russians were both effective in the latter.[7] Moreover, whereas Napoleon initially benefited from the operational and organizational advantages that the French enjoyed over their opponents in the 1790s, these relative advantages were eroded in the 1800s as other states absorbed many of France's developments.

As before, multi-polarity had military as well as political dimensions. Victories in 1805–6 created a misleading context. In contrast, Napoleon found it impossible to secure decisive victory over the Austrians in 1809, and over the Russians in 1807 and, more obviously and seriously, 1812. The British forces sent to Portugal and Spain to help resistance to French rule won a series of major victories, including Salamanca (1812), Vitoria (1813) and Toulouse (1814). The first two led to the French being driven out of Spain, after which the British invaded France itself. In more significant engagements in which Napoleon was personally in charge, the slogging match of the Battle of Borodino (1812), seen in France as a victory over the Russians, was followed by similar slogging battles at Leipzig (1813) and Waterloo (1815) that were clearly total French defeats.

In the 1800s, Napoleon had built both on changes in the French army in the last decades of the *ancien régime*, notably improved artillery, and on those of the French Revolutionary armies. In some respects, he joined together the advantages of both and created an effective synthesis that was more than a sum of the parts. Moreover, he pushed through an important reordering of the military administration between 1800 and 1802. The conscription system, which had become less effective in the late 1790s, was strengthened, providing Napoleon with a key capability. He benefited from the peace on the Continent in 1802–4 to train his force and produce better balanced corps, with increased artillery and cavalry. Napoleon developed the corps as a level above that of the division. Both could include all the arms (infantry, cavalry and artillery), and be large enough to operate effectively, to which end both were given effective staff structures. The corps added, to the flexibility of the earlier divisional system, the strength necessary both for Napoleon's campaigns of strategically applied force and for the grinding, if not attritional, battles of the period where opposing forces would not collapse as a result of well-planned battlefield moves. This situation looked towards battles in the 1850s and 1860s, and to the later development of armies and army groups for similar reasons in the two world wars. At the same time, albeit at a smaller scale, elements of the same factors had been present in the combined arms forces of the medieval and early modern period.

For Napoleon, corps operated effectively, both as individual units, as against the Prussians at the Battle of Auerstädt (1806), and in concert. Able to act independently, corps helped make what is now referred to as operational warfare more feasible. It is important, both for the Napoleonic period and for all others, not to idealize organizational units and developments. For there was always considerable variety in practice, a point also true for tactical methods and for doctrine. Nevertheless, the corps system enhanced military strength, not least by enabling combined arms to be used more effectively. In the 1790s, the French division had been a force of all arms, typically two brigades of infantry, one of cavalry and a battery of guns. However, this force structure meant that the artillery and cavalry were split up into small units, which deprived them of much of their striking power. Under the corps system, by contrast, both cavalry and infantry tended to be controlled at a higher level. Moreover, they could be grouped into separate formations. This separation and concentration posed fresh issues for generalship and underlined the continued problem of organization.

Skilled staff work was important to Napoleon. The French organizational and command structures, energized and articulated by skilful staff work, were vital to Napoleon's characteristic rapidity of movement. Putting aside the almost mystical readings of his generalship, such as those advanced by many French writers later in the nineteenth century, Napoleon was good, sometimes very good, at working within the constraints of the weapons and forces available. He also proved adept at relaxing these constraints, not least by taking pains to understand the theorists of the previous generation, by developing appropriate tactics to maximize potential (especially the firepower of massed artillery), by making a major effort to train his troops, and by developing a staff to increase operational potential. Napoleon concentrated his resources and attention on a single front, seeking, in each conflict, to identify the crucial opposing force and to destroy it rapidly. Indeed, the preference for rapid results prefigured that of German planning in 1914 and 1939–41.

In systematizing earlier developments, Napoleon proved a particularly strong believer in the value of artillery, organized into strong batteries. Napoleon increased the number of field guns and the ratio of guns to infantry, and replaced eight-pounders by the heavier twelve-pounders. The increase in the amount of shot available per cannon helped make continuous fire possible. Napoleon used his cannons as an offensive force. This looked towards the heavy use of artillery in subsequent Western warfare. In turn, sheltering troops on reverse slopes to shield them from direct French fire, as the British did at Waterloo, looked towards first the 'empty battlefield' of dispersed units and then to troops seeking the shelter of trenches.

However, the relative military advantages that France had enjoyed in the 1790s and early 1800s were eroded thereafter, particularly in the early 1810s, and, in practice, from 1808. As a result, France lacked a lead comparable to that enjoyed (although not without anxiety) at sea by the British after Horatio Nelson's shattering victory over a Franco–Spanish fleet at Trafalgar in 1805. As so frequently in Western military history, a capability gap on land had been swiftly closed.

Combined with the widespread reluctance within Europe to accept Napoleonic views, this closure ensured the end of his drive for hegemonic power and its replacement by a relatively rapid overthrow of his position. Widespread opposition to French dominance required a skilful response, both military and political, but Napoleon could not provide this. This situation anticipated Hitler's failure in the Second World War. Napoleon's retreat from Moscow at the end of the 1812 campaign, with his army ebbing away into the snows, was a fitting symbol of the folly of his attempt to dominate all of Europe. On this retreat, the unprepared French lost heavily to privation as well as to the pursuing Russians. Logistics, politics and combat all played a major role in the failure.

Moreover, the 1813 campaign indicated that symmetry had revived in Western warfare, at least on land. It proved possible, at Leipzig, after smaller-scale French victories over Austrian, Prussian and Russian forces earlier in the year, to inflict a major defeat on the main French field army, and without the benefit to his opponents of the distances and climate of Russia. Aside from a more general response against French hegemony, there were also more specific developments that affected the French position. The aura of Napoleonic invincibility had been wrecked by the Russia campaign, and Alexander I was determined to overthrow Napoleon. Russia's victory over France in 1812–13 was, at one level, also simply the culmination of a triumphant overcoming of the *barrière de l'est* seen in successes at the expense of Sweden (1808–9) and the Turks (1806–12), with victories resulting in treaties in which Russia's position was accepted.

In addition, the Austrians had now learned to counter the French corps system by using one of their own, and the Prussians had improved their army, not least by developing a more coherent and comprehensive staff system. They had also tapped into a widespread popular rejection of Napoleon. In 1813, Frederick William III summoned the Prussian people to fight for their king, fatherland, freedom and honour.

At Leipzig, the 'Battle of the Nations' (16–19 October 1813), the three nations and their Swedish ally deployed 365,000 men as their forces converged on the battlefield. The outnumbered Napoleon, who had about 195,000 men present, was outmanoeuvred, losing control of the tempo of the battle. This contrasted with his skill in dominating the dynamic of struggle, both operationally and tactically, in his campaigns and battles in 1795–1806. The greater complexity of battle owed much to its new scale, and this challenged earlier systems of command and control. At Leipzig, Napoleon failed to use the advantage of the central position. There had been developments in the nature of war, particularly its greater scale, which made Napoleon's task more difficult from the late 1800s, not least by widening the gap between means and end. In the Waterloo campaign in 1815, Napoleon suffered much from poor staff work. In part, this confusion reflected the difficulty of grounding a new system in a hurry, without the continuities present prior to Napoleon's abdication in 1814.

Yet, there was also a contrast between Napoleon's methods and the new Prussian general staff system, which provided both coherent central direction and an effective system of links between the centre and individual units, a system designed to ensure unity in command. Each Prussian corps and division contained a group of staff officers headed by a chief who was responsible both for advising the commander and for maintaining links with the centre. This was a corporate system unlike the essentially personal command one used by Napoleon. Other difficulties were posed by the major increase in the resources, including manpower, used for war from the

1790s and the significant problems these posed for command-and-control. Moreover, there was a marked deterioration in French tactics in the latter period of Napoleon's reign, with no equivalent to the improvement seen during the First World War with both the British and the Germans.

In early 1814, France itself was invaded; indeed, the centre of French power was attacked, as it had not been since 1792. Moreover, this invasion was more successful than that in 1792 had been. After initial successes against the more exposed units of his opponents, the greatly outnumbered Napoleon was outmanoeuvred and outnumbered by invading Austrian, Prussia and Russian forces that fought their way to Paris, ignoring his position on their flank. Paris was occupied on 31 March. Abandoned by many of his generals, Napoleon was obliged to abdicate unconditionally on 6 April. Although he had fought a number of successful battles, France was demoralized and the state was collapsing. A combination of heavy taxes, unwelcome demands for conscripts shooting up, the heavy casualties of 1813, and a sense of failure, destroyed Napoleonic rule even while the fighting went on. Ready to pile up the bodies, Napoleon had refused to face reality; but the Senate had deposed him on 2 April, and his remaining generals then insisted on his abdicating.

Evading capture, he returned from exile on the island of Elba in March 1815, rapidly regaining power from the weak and unpopular Louis XVIII. Landing in Provence on 1 March, Napoleon was welcomed in Paris on 20 March. This was one of the most successful campaigns of the century, and one that demonstrated the importance of political context: there was neither battle nor siege in this campaign. Instead, Louis' system disintegrated as his forces, despite the promises of commanders, proved unwilling to mount resistance. Alongside the uncertain response of the French military in March, there was Napoleon's drive, his ability to grasp the initiative and his rapid advance.

As is so often, a struggle within one state led to a broader war, however. In this case, the European powers that had defeated Napoleon in 1814 were absolutely determined to prevent his return which they saw as likely to create fresh instability, a correct view despite Napoleon's claims that he wanted peace. Distrust of Napoleon took precedence over tension between the allies. Meeting already at Vienna to negotiate a comprehensive peace treaty, Austria, Prussia, Russia and Britain each promised on 25 March to field 150,000 troops, the British contingent in part to be raised by paying for allied units. The scale was different from that of the challenge faced by Frederick the Great during the Seven Years' War; as was the 'miracle' required.

Napoleon found little enthusiasm in France for a new struggle, and conscription, which had been increasingly gruelling in Napoleon's last years, was particularly unwelcome. Conscription had been abolished, and the Legislative Chamber was unwilling to recall the class of 1815. Napoleon responded by seeking to circumvent the situation and the Chamber, which he correctly identified as a source of élite opposition. To do so, Napoleon classified the class of 1815 as discharged soldiers who had to serve, and he was able to raise about 46,000 men, but none reached his army in the field. However, Napoleon could call on veterans whose experience was essentially one of war and most of whom saw few opportunities under Louis XVIII. Moreover, repatriated prisoners and soldiers recalled from half-pay, as well as sailors from the navy, all served to build up the army.

Napoleon, in turn, invaded Belgium on 15 June 1815, aiming to inflict sequential defeats on his opponents, and thus to peel away the resolve of the opposition coalition. Napoleon had to prevent the impact of the resource gap by disrupting the operations of the coalition forces, using location on interior lines to split the opposing forces, even the odds and win successive victories. Moreover, such success would disrupt the coalition, provide supplies for the French army from conquered territory and secure support within France. He attacked British and Prussian forces in Belgium because they were closer than advancing Austrian and Russian armies. There was also the hope that the Whig opposition would gain power and change British policy if Napoleon succeeded. This, however, was a strategy of gambling against ferocious odds.

Napoleon's key force was *l'Armée du Nord*, comprising 123,000 troops and 358 cannon, as other units had to be deployed to protect France's other frontiers and to resist possible rebellion, notably in the Vendée. There was also a serious problem in providing the necessary equipment. This problem reflected the degree to which the army had been neglected under Louis XVIII, with a particular failure to maintain the necessary *matériel*. As a result, once back in Paris, Napoleon had to devote a major effort to secure sufficient weaponry and horses.

At the same time, war is a matter of relative risk, advantages and capabilities. The poor state of the Duke of Wellington's army was in part a reflection of the rapidity with which Britain and the Netherlands had pushed to take a peace dividend. The British army had been cut with large-scale discharges, while other units had been sent to North America to take the offensive in the war of 1812–15 with the United States, or were deployed to deal with disaffection in Britain, notably from the Luddites, who violently opposed new industrial technology, or to garrison Ireland. After indecisive battles at Ligny and Quatre Bras on 16 June with Prussian and Anglo–Dutch–German forces respectively, battles that reflected the difficulties of obtaining victory, Napoleon was defeated at Waterloo on 18 June as defensive British (and allied) firepower beat off successive, poorly coordinated French frontal attacks. The French army was not at its peak, but nor was it well commanded. The individual arms, infantry, cavalry and artillery, were not combined ably, and there was a failure on Napoleon's part to grasp tactical control. This was initially another version of Borodino. The opening French attempt to break through the opposing centre failed. Subsequent attacks were no more successful, although they

placed a strain on the defence. Colonel James Stanhope of the First Foot
Guards reported next day:

> When the French cavalry attacked us in our squares (which they did
> with the most persevering gallantry, never retiring above 100 or 150
> paces and charging again) our men behaved as if they were at a field day,
> firing by ranks and with the best possible aim. Under a most destructive
> cannonade and having several shells burst in the middle of us, not a man
> moved from his place ... At the last we became exposed to the united
> efforts of all their arms and changed from line to squares and from
> squares to lines, as the circumstances of the case required ... There was
> a moment peculiarly critical and where nothing but the extraordinary
> steadiness of the troops saved the day.[8]

Napoleon had already failed by the time Prussian forces arrived to assist the
British, leading to the last stage of the battle in which a general attack was
launched on the French who were routed and driven from the battlefield.
A total victory had been obtained. The Prussians drove it home by 'killing
with rare abandon, bayoneting the wounded and cutting down stragglers',
although such conduct was more common than is often appreciated[9], and
was to continue to be so in the twentieth century.

After the battle, France was easily invaded. British and Prussian forces
advanced on Paris, while Austrian and allied armies invaded eastern France,
and a fleeing Napoleon surrendered to a blockading British warship. This
blockade was an important aspect of the strategy of the 1815 campaign,
for it enabled the British to provide support and encouragement to French
opponents of Napoleon as well as to enforce political and economic
isolation on the regime. Napoleon not only coped far worse militarily with
failure than Louis XIV (in 1673 and 1708–9) or Louis XV (in 1742–3
and 1757–9) had done, but also faced very different political consequences. This point underlines the importance of a grounding of rulership
in legitimacy as well as success. The lack of any sustained opposition to
the invaders reflected the collapse in Napoleon's popularity and the sense
that Waterloo represented a decisive victory. Napoleon had exhausted his
strategic options and his political point, rather as Hitler was to have done
by the late summer of 1944, but there was no fanatical resistance, unlike
in Germany in 1944–5. France, in 1815, fell the same way Prussia had in
1806. Napoleon's regime was dependent on his main battle army and on his
prestige. Resting on these fragile and now weakened foundations, it rapidly
collapsed. Thus, the character of politics gave a result to the events of war.

Louis XVIII was restored. Waterloo had determined, not only the
struggle between Napoleon and his international opponents, but also that
with counter-revolutionaries, notably in southern France and the Vendée.
The battle led to the revival of royalist militias and their activities captured
the extent to which civil conflict was part of warfare. In a 'White Terror', the

targets of the militias were people identified as opponents of the royalists, but the violence also had a religious complexion, with Catholics attacking Protestants, who were portrayed as disloyal. Paris itself and much of France were placed under Allied occupation as a guarantee both of Louis' position and of the payment of French reparations. Wellington, victor at Waterloo, was head of the occupation forces. One hundred and fifty thousand strong, they remained in place until the reparations were paid off in 1818. A new geopolitics was dramatically displayed with this occupation, which had no precedents. Napoleon himself was taken to distant St Helena, a British island colony in the South Atlantic, where he remained until he died. That he was held there was a demonstration of British power as well as a guarantee of the position of the restored Bourbons in France.

In 1815, on the third anniversary of Borodino, Alexander I, accompanied by Francis I of Austria and Frederick William III of Prussia, each dressed in Russian uniform, reviewed 150,000 Russian troops at Chalons to the east of Paris. Russian success was a key cause of Napoleon's failure.[10] This success, alongside that of the British, demonstrated the effectiveness of *ancien régime* militaries as opposed to the Napoleonic system. At the same time, the result was more complex, not least in terms of the need to consider military and political factors, as well as short-term and structural ones.

The end result of Napoleon's efforts in 1815 was to enhance British maritime and Russian land power. Both states were on the edge of Europe, and thus more able to protect their home bases than other European countries (which was also true of the United States), and yet were also capable of playing major roles in European politics. Thus, the tactical and operational proficiency of their forces was matched by a strategic advantage stemming from their ability to deploy considerable resources and from a base that it was difficult to conquer. The extent of these resources was important, because the scale of warfare, and the simultaneity of commitments, and of operations on many fronts, were such that war posed formidable demands on the countries and states involved. The response to these demands required not simply resources in aggregate, but also organizational developments and co-operation between governments and political élites. While this was not new, the scale of warfare was. The Russian army may have received as many as two million recruits between 1802 and 1812. In 1812, 420,000 regulars were recruited, as were 200,000 militia, while 110,000 muskets were made.

Britain and Russia represented extensive economic systems. Britain drew not only on its own resources, which had been greatly enhanced by population growth and agricultural, industrial and transport improvements, but also on the global trading system that it was best placed to direct and exploit thanks to naval strength and maritime resources, not least in grain production and metallurgy, although administrative sophistication and fiscal capability were less in evidence than in Britain. The success of Britain and Russia defined Europe and the postwar world, notably in ensuring that Europe reverted from Napoleonic hegemony to the multiple statehood that distinguished it from so many of the other heavily populated regions of the world. This was as much a consequence of Napoleon's fundamental political failure as of the absence of a lasting military capability gap in favour of France.

An account of conflict, whether of the Napoleonic Wars or other ones, from the perspective of commanders, risks ignoring the human experience. The casualties of war were plentiful in this period. Wellington remarked that, next to a battle lost, the greatest misery was a battle gained. Combat certainly required a disciplined willingness to accept hazardous exposure. Captain John Hill wrote to his brother-in-law after Waterloo, 'The front wound still continues to discharge very much. He is a most confounded ugly fellow … as big as a tea-cup … I got the grape shot in my shoulder and five other wounds in my face… Honesty [his horse] got three shot.… He bled to death',[11] a reminder of the very many animals that died.

Casualties included not only the large number of soldiers and sailors killed, wounded or captured, but also the many civilians who suffered. They were frequently brutalized. In addition to killings and woundings, there were also numerous rapes.[12] War was punishment. In 1815, Major William Turner, part of the British army advancing after Waterloo, wrote from near Paris: 'Every town and village is completely ransacked and pillaged by the Prussians and neither wine, spirits or bread are to be found. The whole country from the frontier to Paris laid waste.'[13] This was seen as a response to the harsh treatment of Germany by French forces from 1792, and notably the humiliation and seizures Prussia had suffered in 1806.

Aside from the numerous casualties among soldiers and sailors, and medical care was limited, as was pain-relief, there was also the harsh nature of military service. Food and water were often in short supply, and the quality of both was frequently poor. This contributed to the frequency of intestinal diseases, which were particularly serious due to the already often-weakened nature of the troops, notably thanks to a lack of adequate nourishment. In addition, soldiers usually lacked cover, conspicuously so on the night before Waterloo, their loads were heavy and their clothes were generally dirty and uncomfortable, and often wet. There was scant rest and marching was frequently arduous. Pay was low and the care of veterans poor. Sickness was persistent. Russia suffered possibly 660,000 military casualties between 1789 and 1814, many due to disease and poor diet. Thanks to cholera, the Russian army that invaded Hungary in 1849 lost 11,028 men, compared to only 543 in battle.

Given this background, the extent to which the governments of the period were able to sustain large forces appears impressive. Despite serious logistical strains, strains left in the increasingly numerous accounts of participants, armies were able to go on operating; and breakdowns, such as seriously affected the French in Russia in 1812, were exceptional. In many respects, the dire conditions and problems of soldiers and sailors matched those suffered by much of the general workforce, especially the unskilled, which, indeed, helps explain why it was possible to recruit soldiers and sailors, and why mutinies were few.

Much that Napoleonic warfare is noted for had been anticipated in earlier conflicts. This is the case with large armies, a strategy of movement, a preference for battles over sieges, a greater emphasis on artillery and light infantry. In this context, Napoleon was more of a consolidator than an innovator. However, the political and social contexts and their consequences for military activity were arresting. Large conscript armies, organized into corps, were a new development in Western Europe, although the situation looks somewhat different from a Chinese perspective. The key development was that of scale, and the resulting organizational, operational and logistical challenges and solutions bound up with the issue of scale at this juncture. The military effectiveness, in the widest sense, of Western states, increased as formidable resources were devoted to warfare. As a consequence, the practice of the mobilization of a large proportion of national manpower and resources became more insistent. By 1813, the Prussians had 100,000 regulars and a 120,000-strong militia, the *Landwehr*.

As a prime instance of the primacy of political factors in military organization and goals, there was a preference, for several decades after the Napoleonic Wars, for long-service regulars, rather than for raising large numbers of conscripts. Experienced troops were seen as more valuable, both in battle and for irregular operations, as well as, crucially, being more politically reliable and able to repress revolution, which remained an ever present fear.[14] The introduction of limited conscription in France by Louis XVIII in 1818 was preceded by heated debates in which concern about the revolutionary potential of the 'nation in arms' was expressed. This stress on obedience was linked to a growing conservatism in the military establishment, one, in part, reflected in opposition to liberal aspects of society. The net effect was to compromise military possibilities for the future, not least in terms of failing to create a trained national reserve.[15] There were similar tensions elsewhere and, indeed, across the century.

The continuum in European warfare, from rapid offensives to slogging matches, which had been seen in the French Revolutionary and Napoleonic Wars, remained the case throughout the nineteenth century. In the case of the first, the Austrians, who in 1815 had swiftly defeated Murat's attempt to support Napoleon by driving them from Italy, rapidly crushed liberal uprisings in Naples and Piedmont in 1821, and in central Italy in 1830. The French did likewise in Spain in 1823, and the Russians in Poland in 1831. However, the Dutch failed to do the same in Belgium in 1830–1, and French intervention against them ensured that their initial failing proved lasting. Nationalism was an important element in these conflicts, creating a destabilizing ideological component in power politics. The French success in 1823 contrasted with that in 1808–13, in large part because the French benefited from taking part on behalf of King Ferdinand VII in what was a civil war. The opposing liberal Spanish army, unpaid and short of supplies, mounted little opposition. The Austrian operations in 1821 and those of the French in 1823 indicated the value of having professional forces able to fight limited wars for particular ends. There was no need for a *levée en masse*.

The 1823 campaign was a successful example of how foreign intervention could tip the balance in a domestically divided state. French action was accepted by the Holy Alliance of leading European conservative states, although Britain was opposed to the step and Austria uneasy about it. A comparison with French failure in Spain in 1808–13 would have repaid the attention of military commentators in subsequent decades, but warfare, such as that in 1823, was not regarded by them as exemplary and there were no battles to command attention. The 1823 campaign also did not satisfy the interest, seen in particular with the writings of Jomini, in producing formulaic guidance to operational effectiveness.

In Belgium, the Dutch army failed in 1830 to suppress a rebellion in Brussels against rule by the Dutch William I and independence was declared. In 1831, when the Dutch invaded in greater strength, led by the heir, William, Prince of Orange, a veteran of Waterloo, they met weaker, poorly organized and inexperienced opponents. However, having driven them back, the Dutch stopped their advance in the face of Anglo–French pressure that, crucially, included a French army. Different politics thus led to very contrasting outcomes. Napoleon had been the problem in 1815, but, once he was gone, it was possible, in co-operation with leading European powers, for France to take a more assertive role in international relations. Moreover, the army was intended as a support for political order and social stability within France.

The most sustained conflict of this period occurred in Spain. It is largely ignored in standard works on military history, which is a mistake because the conflict highlights the significance of civil wars. In the First Carlist War of 1833–40, Don Carlos, 'Carlos V', resisted the bequest of the Spanish throne to his niece, Isabel II, by her father, Ferdinand VII. Opposition to a female monarch was combined with hostility to the constitutional reform promoted by Isabel's supporters and, more generally, to liberalism. Dynastic and political considerations were impacted in specific social and regional contexts. Like the Miguelism in Portugal that had led to civil war over the royal succession from 1828 to 1834, Carlism was a conservative movement that drew on peasant anger against liberal government, and thus reflected internal tensions that looked back not only to the Napoleonic period but also to opposition to the Enlightenment reforms of the late eighteenth century.

As an instance of the varied legacy of Napoleonic-era warfare, the key Carlist commander until his death in 1835, Tomás Zumalacárregui, was a veteran of the struggle against Napoleon, a struggle that served as an important model for the Carlists as the army had stayed loyal to Isabel. Zumalacárregui brought coherence to Carlist operations and created a successful guerrilla army. However, its success, in overrunning the mountainous north, was not matched by an ability to capture cities, win international support or make a successful transition to conventional warfare. Carlist divisions played a key role in ending the war, one in which strategy, morale and generalship were shot through with political considerations.

In mid-century, there was the swift and comprehensive Austro–Russian defeat of a Hungarian rising in 1849, a conflict that receives insufficient attention other than in Hungary where it served to affirm nationalism and later, during the Cold War, provided a way to express hostility to the Soviet Union. This was a large-scale war with the Russians deploying about 200,000 troops and the Austrians 175,000. The outnumbered Hungarians deployed 170,000 troops and were also outgunned. Defeated, many of the Hungarians returned home while the remaining forces surrendered. Some of the commanders were executed. Earlier, the rising in 1848 had seen the creation of a new, national Hungarian army, based on a special force of *Honvéd* (Defenders of the Fatherland), originally formed from within the National Guard. Looking towards later ethnic conflict in the Balkans, notably in the 1910s, 1940s and 1990s, the crisis led to the slaughter of peasants by others of different ethnic and religious background, notably in the Banat (Vojvodina): thousands were killed in 1848. This was an element of the military and political history of the century that is largely forgotten outside the region.

As an instance of the variety of conflict, there was also the long siege of the Black Sea naval base of Sevastopol (1854–5) during the Crimean War between Russia and a coalition, eventually, of Britain, France, Sardinia and the Turks, a conflict, in contrast, that is much discussed. The war, the largest-scale conflict between European powers in the century prior to the outbreak of the First World War, demonstrated serious problems in utilizing military capacity and became a slogging match. Indeed, the Anglo–French effort has been frequently criticized. In contrast to Prussian leadership in 1864–71, there was a lack of purposeful planning and of command coherence. The Allies surrendered the mobility obtained in launching an amphibious invasion of Crimea by besieging Sevastopol. The city was well-defended, and initial attacks failed. The attackers lacked adequate experience in siegecraft, and had to face a type of trench warfare that was different to earlier sieges. The Allies also had to confront both particularly bad weather, which hit supply links across the Black Sea, and repeated attempts by the Russian army in Crimea to disrupt the siege. The latter led to a series of battles.

This conflict, nevertheless, indicated the ability to deploy large forces at a considerable distance. Indeed, the powers allied against Russia did so until they had secured their means and achieved their task, goals that had eluded Napoleon I and were to elude Hitler. Limited war worked in 1854–6. The siege also provided an indication of the growing scale of combat made possible by industrialization: the Russians were supported by over 1,000 cannon while the Allies fired 1,350,000 rounds of artillery ammunition. The scale of demand was to increase. In thirty-six hours at the Battle of Sedan in 1870, the Prussians fired 35,000 shells.

Searching for a conflict to award the title the first industrial war may not be a helpful task, but the Crimean War merits consideration under this head. One British officer wrote to his beloved, 'now I am so accustomed to the noise that I believe I could go to sleep in a battery when the enemy were firing at it'.[16] Both Britain and Russia had advanced metallurgical industries. Moreover, the Allies benefited from steamships in transporting and supporting their forces. In contrast, Russia lacked rail links to Crimea.

Similarly, in 1859, during the Franco–Austrian war in Italy, both sides employed railways in the mobilization and deployment of their forces. The French moved 50,000 men to Italy by rail, a movement that made an impression by suggesting modernity. The transition from the introduction of viable steam locomotives to the large-scale movement of troops by rail had taken less than thirty-five years. Railways were to be used even more successfully by the Prussians, and as an integral part of their planning. Telegraphs, another new technology, were also utilized in 1859, while the French used steamships to deploy troops to Italy. The international context was important. Far from a new Napoleon focusing and dominating the anxieties of Europe, Napoleon III was able to find allies: Britain and Piedmont in the Crimean War, and Piedmont and the liberal cause of Italian unification against Austria.

The Crimean War also demonstrated the increased lethality of infantry firepower. The Anglo–French forces were fortunate that the Russians were still reliant on smooth-bore muskets and lacked modern rifles and artillery. In contrast, the British had adopted the Enfield rifle in 1853. This percussion-lock rifle was more accurate and effective than the musket. The rifled barrel gave bullets a spin, which led to a more stable, and thus reliable, trajectory. The percussion cap, coated with fulminate of mercury, produced a reliable, all-weather, ignition system. Positioned over the fire hole, it ignited the main charge, replacing the flintlock as a firing mechanism; the flintlock had replaced the matchlock in the late seventeenth century. Meanwhile, in place of the spherical musket ball, came the Minié bullet. Developed by Captain Claude-Etienne Minié, this easily loaded, cylindro–conoidal lead bullet expanded when fired to create a tight seal within the rifle, obtaining a high muzzle velocity. It was aerodynamically more efficient than the musket ball.

These and other innovations increased the effective range of deadly infantry firepower, while the casualty rates inflicted on close-packed infantry rose dramatically. At the Battle of Inkerman on 5 November 1854, attacking Russian columns, seeking to close to bayonet point, took heavy casualties from the Enfield rifles of the British, and were defeated. This attack was regarded by some as akin, in part, to a second Waterloo, when the French had been defeated by British firepower, although, ironically, Britain's French ally in 1854 helped save the day.

Heavy casualties were also seen in the 1859 Franco–Austrian war in Italy, with the French and their Piedmontese ally attacking poorly commanded Austrian armies and winning a series of victories, notably Magenta and Solferino. As so often, both modernity and continuity can be discerned. The new French rifled cannon were superior to their Austrian smooth-bore counterparts and destroyed most of them with accurate counter-battery fire, before being turned on the Austrian infantry. The latter were unable to draw much benefit from their technically advanced (although still muzzle-loading) Minié-style rifles. The Austrians had not been adequately trained in range-finding and fighting and, as a consequence, the French were able to close and use their bayonets. In consequence, tactics were similar to those under Napoleon I with dense deployments and column formations. The heavy casualties from these battles helped inspire the establishment of the Red Cross.[17] These victories did not prepare the French for war with the Prussians in 1870–1, not least because the Prussians were able to gain and use the initiative.

Machine guns, automatic repeating weapons, followed. In 1863, Joseph Montigny introduced a 37-barrel *mitrailleuse* and in 1866 the French army developed an adapted 25-barrel variant. In 1870, the British began testing Gatlings, American machine guns, which, indeed, Napoleon III had attended firing trials of in France in 1867. In Britain, in a process of careful trial that became increasingly common, these guns were examined by a Special Committee on Mitrailleurs, and, in 1871, it recommended their use. Similarly, the Enfield and Martini-Henry rifles were selected in Britain as a result of the trials of prototypes. As weapons became more complex, so the military-industrial complex became more intertwined, with governments investing in private-sector technology during the experimental phase as part of a broader collaboration on research and development.[18] Moreover, exports enhanced the influence of these procedures. Britain, France and Germany were the major exporters of armaments. The most successful German exporter, Krupp, benefited from the high reputation of its artillery. Belgium, Bulgaria, Italy, the Netherlands and Romania were among the regular and major customers for the guns.[19]

The greater deadliness of firepower resulted in a need for larger armies in order to sustain operations. The extent to which battles were fought over a broad front further encouraged the quest for numbers. The broad-front battle had been dramatically seen at Leipzig (1813). It was characterized by independently advancing forces that converged on the opponents, a process aided by the organization of armies into corps, which provided independently operating mixed arms forces. The same was to be very much seen at Sadowa (Königgratz, 1866). The quest for numbers was eased by the extent to which lengthy training was not necessary in order to ensure that rifles were used in a lethal fashion.

These factors contributed to the noticeable increase in the size of armed forces in the second half of the century. The context of demographic growth, industrialization, global trade in food and the rising power of government was also significant. Each of these elements increased greatly. This serves as a reminder about the difficulties of isolating particular factors. In response to the rise in systems of conscription, there was an emphasis on recruiting nationals, rather than on hiring transnationals motivated by pay or ideological considerations. Indeed, the mercenary became a far less common figure in European warfare, and those unable or unwilling to serve in the military of their own state generally fought outside Europe, for example in Latin America.[20]

The potential of war appeared to have been greatly expanded. Sweeping Prussian successes against Denmark (1864), Austria and its German allies (1866) and France (1870–1), the second of which was particularly swift, led to the conclusion that offensive operations, carefully planned by an effective and professional general staff, that drew on the transport and logistical possibilities provided by railways, would rapidly lead to decisive victories, such as at Sadowa in 1866 in which each side deployed a quarter of a million men. Field Marshal Moltke (Moltke the Elder, in contrast to his nephew, Moltke the Younger, in 1914) adapted Napoleonic ideas of the continuous offensive to the practicalities of the industrial age, including railways. He successfully sought to destroy the cohesion of the enemy army and to envelop opposing forces; rather than relying on frontal attack. Whereas Napoleon had used separately operating corps within his army, Moltke employed independently operating armies, which reflected both the opportunities and the problems presented by his larger numbers. Furthermore, unlike Napoleon, who concentrated his forces prior to the battle, Moltke aimed for a concentration of his armies in the battle itself. The Franco–Prussian War saw systematized conflict employed by the Prussians to offer an hitherto unprecedented degree of methodical effectiveness. This was a reflection of the Prussian determination to treat war as a scientific process conducted by highly trained professionals directing affairs in a planned fashion based on systems and processes of training, rationality and communications articulated through an efficient staff system.[21] In contrast, the French had no effective general staff. As a consequence of these command differences, the Prussians managed risk and error whereas the French experienced it, which ensured that they could not maintain effective mobile defence. In 1870, aside from Prussian superiority in command and control, and at both the tactical and the operational levels, there was a clearly planned strategy. Tactical differences were also significant, not least the French preference for tight defensive formations, which increased their vulnerability to firepower, and the Prussian stress on open-order deployment (which reduced vulnerability) and on related small-unit fire tactics.

The defeat of France led to a new political order in both countries. Napoleon III abdicated after defeat and surrender at Sedan led to a revolution in Paris in which he was replaced by a Government of National Defence and what became the Third Republic. The forces of the new republic suppressed the radical Paris Commune in May 1871 with over 10,000 Parisians killed in extensive street fighting. About the same number who had been captured were promptly shot.[22]

The King of Prussia had been declared Emperor of Germany, an empire proclaimed at Versailles on 18 January 1871, in what was a major humiliation for the French. Thus, Prussia became the basis for a new German state, in which the Prussian dynasty presided over the other German dynasties, a state that was made more prominent and powerful by the annexation of Alsace and of part of Lorraine from defeated France. Reparations were also enforced, as they had been after Napoleon's defeat in 1815, as was an occupation until they were paid off in 1873. The memorialization of victory became a key component in what was a militarized society. Columns of victory, triumphal arches and celebratory statues were erected in German cities, and celebrations were held accordingly. Sedan Day was celebrated annually. The war was presented as a unifying experience and as a proof of German capacity. The increased prestige of military service helped lead German cities to vie for garrisons.

Successive victories in 1864–71 also led to a rise in the prestige of German war-making, and these victories provided a ready subject for military education, as well as in war games. The French staff college, reformed in 1876–8, was modelled on Berlin's *Kriegsakademie*. This prestige led to an increased interest in Clausewitz. German prestige was also displayed in uniforms. Whereas, in the 1850s, the uniforms of many armies had been modelled on those of France, from the 1870s the Prussian uniform became the norm.

Moltke, the architect of the campaigns, however, himself warned of the hazards of extrapolating a general principle of war from them, and was increasingly sceptical about the potential of the offensive. Indeed, prefiguring the situation the Germans were to encounter in 1914 and 1939–41, and indicating what Clausewitz termed the friction of war, Prussian skill, at the operational and tactical levels, had not prevented many difficulties from arising. This was, in part, a matter of Prussian deficiencies. For example, there were serious logistical problems in 1870, with confusion on the railways and, ironically, a return to dependence on horses; the Germans were also to be heavily dependent on horses during the two world wars. In addition, there were the problems posed by opposing capabilities, notably Austrian artillery in 1866 and French rifles in 1870–1.

Furthermore, deficiencies in leadership and strategy on the part of Austria and France played into Prussian hands, enabling them to outmanoeuvre their opponents. In 1866 and 1870, as for the Germans in 1939–40, Moltke won victories of manoeuvre (although attritional pounding in the actual battles also played a role), in which he was fortunate in the folly of his opponents. Napoleon III proved a particularly maladroit leader for the French, but the calibre of his generals was also poor and that despite the high level of recent French experience of war, in Algeria, Crimea, Italy and Mexico. French generals proved unable to match Prussian tempo, in part because they were less able to handle the potential of rail, but also because they mishandled the attempt to gain the strategic advantage by taking the first step. Instead, the French failed to sustain the initiative and fell back. Subsequently, the outnumbered French, who adopted a generally defensive posture, were repeatedly outmanoeuvred by more adept Prussian commanders. The two main French armies were defeated separately. In 1866 and 1870, as more generally, for example with German successes in 1939 and 1940, it is necessary to focus on relative capability, and on the extent to which offensives were (or were not) countered by defensive skill, not least by the availability and use of reserves. The Austrians demonstrated the role of particular conjunctures in 1866: beaten at Sadowa, they had earlier defeated Prussia's ally Italy at Custozza.

There were also the many problems posed by conscript armies. Raising large forces created or exacerbated serious issues of supply, training and command. Numbers alone could not suffice: it was the way in which men were trained and integrated into existing military structures that was crucial, as the Prussians showed. Problems were not readily apparent in peacetime, but conflict exposed the military's inability to operate as envisaged. In practice, bulk did not equal mass, nor movement manoeuvre. Logistical support was frequently inadequate. This was/is frequently the case, but the necessary improvisation was lacking. These problems encouraged an emphasis on attack, in order to obtain a quick decision, contributing to the high-tempo warfare of the period.

Prussian successes led to a degree of delusion, and the problems of effectively directing and maintaining large armies were not fully appreciated, in Germany or elsewhere, until the First World War (1914–18). In particular, there was a failure to assess adequately the second stage of the Franco–Prussian War and a preference, instead, for a focus on the rapidly successful offensive and battles of the first stage, culminating with the surrender of the defeated Napoleon III at Sedan on 2 September 1870. In the second stage, in contrast, the Prussians had been faced, as they advanced into the French interior, by a more disparate opposition, with newly raised forces. These were generally easy to defeat in battle but their resistance prevented the Prussians from gaining the closure they required, not least due to logistical issues. In addition, the Prussians responded to *francs-tireurs* (irregulars) with harsh action including shooting prisoners and burning down settlements. Their army lacked a political remedy to the resistance and relied on terror to achieve its goals, prefiguring German policy during the world wars. Fortunately for Prussia, France accepted terms in March 1871. Indeed, the Germans agreed a truce earlier in January 1871 in order to ensure elections that would establish legitimate French government able to negotiate.

The wars waged by the major powers between 1871 and 1914 did not challenge contemporary military assumptions about the effectiveness of the offensive. For example, by putting the stress on success rather than heavy casualties, observers saw the Russo–Turkish War of 1877–8 as demonstrating the necessary triumph of the attacking power, Russia. However, the successive Russian attempts to storm the fortress of Plevna (in modern Bulgaria) in 1877 before it surrendered that December prefigured aspects of the First World War, including the difficulties of destroying trenches by artillery fire, the employment of machine guns and the heavy use of munitions, both rifle rounds and shells; in other words, the increasing dominance of firepower on the battlefield, with the logistical strains these posed. In the second assault, Russian casualties amounted to 23 per cent of their rank and file. Similarly, the Turks lost heavily in their unsuccessful assault on Russian positions in the Shipka Pass in 1877, covered as these were by integrated fire zones.

This conflict was certainly significant in developing the international links of nationalism. In particular, Bulgarian independence from Turkish rule was essentially the consequence of Russian victory; after the capture of Plevna, the Russians advanced to within fifteen miles of Constantinople and dictated peace terms. The link between Russia and Bulgaria was to be important to the revitalization of Russian support for Slav nationalism, and this support, and the nationalism, were to be translated to serve against Austria as well as the Turks.

The Turks also fought weaker powers, defeating Serbia and Montenegro in 1876 and Greece in 1897. Both of these were rapid successes, with the Turks winning battles at Alexinatz and Djunis in 1876. In addition, however, the Christian Balkan states fought each other. In 1885, the Serbs invaded Bulgaria in the quest for territorial compensation for Bulgarian expansion that year at the expense of the Turks. The Serbs advanced to Slivnitsa, a pass twenty miles from Sofia, the Bulgarian capital, where their attack failed to break the well-located defenders. The Serbs then retreated, being pursued into Serbia by the Bulgarians. This short war is easy to overlook, but it indicates the variety of warfare, a variety also seen in the twentieth century. In 1885, motivation was a key element, with Bulgarian xenophobia proving a major advantage over poorly motivated Serbs. The international dimension was also crucial. Austria was unwilling to see Serbia lose territory, and its pressure led the Bulgarians to desist from their advance on the Serbian capital, Belgrade.

Irregular warfare was also important in the Balkans, notably in Bosnia in 1878 when unsuccessful Muslim attempts to block Austrian occupation led to the deployment of over 100,000 Austrian troops and the large-scale slaughter of Muslim men, women and children. A prime instance of civil warfare was provided by Spain. Queen Isabel was overthrown by an army rebellion in 1868 while opposition came to the fore in 1873. There was a radical and anti-centralist uprising by Cantonalists in a number of cities in

1873, but they suffered from disunity and reliance on the militia and were quickly suppressed everywhere, apart from Cartagena, which fell only in the following year, after being blockaded by land and sea. In 1873, the Second Carlist War also broke out. However, as in the First Carlist War, the Carlists were affected by disunity, the opposition of the major towns and the lack of an adequate supply base or administration, and their last field army was defeated in 1876.

Otto von Bismarck, the German Chancellor from 1862 to 1890 who had been instrumental, with his foreign policy, in Prussian success, had made a major effort to avoid Russian hostility. As a result, Prussia was not faced by Russian armies, as Frederick the Great had been during the Seven Years' War. However, due to a difference over policy, Bismarck resigned after Wilhelm II came to the German throne in 1888. Russia moved into an alliance with France in 1892, exposing Germany to the risk of war on both fronts, a fate avoided by Bismarck, and which Moltke therefore had not had to face. German strategic planning had to respond, but was not to rise adequately to the challenge.

Another aspect of doubt related to the domestic consequences of military service. Moltke opposed the 1889–90 plan of Verdy du Vernois, the Minister of War, to introduce unrestricted conscription because he feared that this would create too many left-wing soldiers and middle-class officers.[23] Moltke voiced his concern about 'people's war' and the social changes it would entail.

Such change was not particularly apparent at the level of officers. In terms of entry to military colleges and subsequent promotion, there was a heavy emphasis on the landed orders, albeit with the caveat that the key element was often family tradition: as under the *ancien régime*, officers were often the sons of officers, and this remained important in Prussia. This pattern could be an aspect of the role of the landed orders, but could also be separate from it. In France, there was a tradition of promotion from the ranks of enlisted men to those of junior officers, but it became much less significant in the 1890s and 1900s, and the officer corps became more socially exclusive. Russia's rulers favoured aristocratic preponderance in the officer corps, and this was still the case in the 1870s, but, afterwards, it became less so, not least because of an expansion of military education.

The naval dimension of military power in the nineteenth century was less a matter of co-operation between the state and the private sector than had been the case in the eighteenth century. That statement, however, can be very differently phrased, and the variations in phrasing capture important nuances. The key difference is that of adding the word 'obviously' after 'less', for that word captures elements both of reality and of perception. In the case of the former, there is the contrast in the nineteenth century between policy that was very much state-directed and in practice led through public institutions, with the reality that the private sector was highly important. Indeed, in many respects, this was more the case than when considering the eighteenth century when the private sector had been particularly significant in logistics, for the capacity of state naval facilities to build cutting-edge warships diminished. The introduction of steam power, iron plating and breech-loading artillery each represented paradigm shifts in production requirements, and also in maintenance. Moreover, for each, there was a lesser tolerance of variations, let alone mistakes, in both the production process and the use of the subsequent systems. Weapons and other aspects of warships became precision machines. Advances, later in the century, in metallurgy, marine engine design and the use of torpedoes were particularly significant.[24]

There were also other important developments. For example, the search for a new propellant that gave increased velocity and range, greatly reduced the volume of smoke and was safer as well as more powerful than gunpowder, not being as susceptible either to temperature changes or to handling dangers. Successive explosive compounds were tried. The British navy turned to cordite, a powder made from a blend of nitroglycerine and gun cotton mixed with acetone. In a classic instance of technological advances requiring a number of steps, cordite was adapted to meet the ballistic requirements of the larger steel guns that the navy had deployed. Initially remade into tubes in order to produce an even burn rate, cordite was modified by adding indentations along the tubes so as to increase the combustion rate and thereby maintain gas pressure as a shell shot down the barrel, ensuring that a shell travelled at an increased rate as it cleared the bore.[25] There were similar changes with other technologies. For example, the effective range and warhead, and speed of torpedoes increased, while gyroscopes were installed in the late 1890s. As with improvements with guns, this enabled naval combatants to stand off more effectively.

As a result of these and other advances, there was not only an increased need for specific production skills, but also for linked management ability on the part of navies. In practice, this meant that navies required engineering knowledge and skills that were very different to those previously enjoyed by naval officers. The technological and technical expertise were part of the naval hierarchy, but they overlapped with similar qualities and characteristics in civil society and, more particularly, with those shown by the employees of companies building warships and producing their components. Moreover, navies took pains to give senior officers experience of the manufacturing process, as with the British navy and the Armstrong Vickers company. Component manufacture became a key element in the construction of warships. It had long been an element, but the element became more significant as the complexity of warships rose. Partly as a result, the extension of military production across the economy increased. This extension reflected the impact of the military, but also its dependence on co-operation.

Perception was also a key factor. Governments did not tend to dwell on the role of the private sector, still less its autonomous, not to say independent, character. The directions of public discussions and memorialization were similar. There was also scant political consideration of what would later be termed the military–industrial complex. As a result, its role was underplayed. In practice, the major transformation of military technology from the 1860s owed much to private-sector enterprise, not least with the design and funding of new weapons. At the 1867 Paris Exhibition, a Krupp steel cannon, capable of firing 1,000-pound shells, was displayed.[26]

Europe's navies saw only limited conflict in European waters in the years between 1815 and 1914. There were occasional battles, such as Cape Navarino in 1827, when British, French and Russian squadrons defeated Turkish and Egyptian opponents, and Lissa in 1866, when the Austrians beat the Italians; but there were far fewer naval battles than during the previous century. In large part, this was because the wars of the period were settled on land, generally rapidly, while British naval power was such as to deter other navies. Thus, in the Crimean War, the Russians kept their fleets in harbour, much to the frustration of the British. Competition encouraged investment. Thus, British fears of invasion from France in the late 1850s and early 1860s led to a naval race and to the construction of expensive defensive positions on the south coast of England. A response to the French development of ironclads, the naval race led the First Secretary to the Admiralty to tell the Commons in July 1861 that he sought 'to engender a proper confidence that we are determined to maintain our maritime position in its integrity'.[27]

Investment in new technology led to an unwelcome degree of uncertainty. This was also seen on land. A letter signed 'Colonel' published in the *Times* on 27 December 1899, noted:

> The modern method of fortifications, introduced with the breech-loading rifle, is based upon the practical indestructibility by modern artillery fire of properly designed earthworks, and the improbability of an attacking force being able to rush a properly prepared position defended by a sufficient number of troops armed with the breech-loading rifle. This improbability became impossibility, now that the magazine rifle is substituted for the breechloader, until the defences shall have been seriously injured by artillery fire.

Single-shot breech-loaders, such as the French Gras and the British Martini-Henry, had been replaced by more effective magazine rifles such as the model 1886 Lebel, the Lee-Metford and the Kropatschek. Approved in 1888, the Lee-Metford was a small-bore magazine rifle fired by smokeless powder, sending a bullet at a muzzle velocity of 2,000 feet per second over a range of 3,000 yards. The small bore meant lighter ammunition and therefore an ability to carry more rounds.

In the meanwhile, in the late nineteenth century, the increase in the size of armies and the development of powerful nationalistic states joined through alliances into antagonistic blocs, underlined the possibility, indeed probability, that conflict might lead to a large-scale war. So also did the bellicose public politics of the period, a public politics linked to a reliance on reservists to make up army numbers. Whereas the widespread opposition to French Revolutionary and Napoleonic forces had, to a considerable extent, reflected local factors, religious anger and xenophobia, nationalism, in the sense of a socially comprehensive and insistent expression of national sentiment was particularly significant by mid-century. National consciousness became nationalism, and it had a symbolic weight as the ritual aspects of community were channelled and, in part, fulfilled. Conscription accentuated the process, as young men were exposed to state-directed military organization and discipline, at an impressionable age and in patriarchal societies where it was easier for authority figures to impose discipline. Military organization, moreover, served to integrate the nation. Stationing troops away from their places of birth and upbringing helped encourage an awareness of the nation.

Conscription, however, was not necessarily popular, and unsurprisingly so given the poor circumstances of military service, including very low pay, inadequate accommodation and, frequently, a lack of food and uniforms. Disease was also a serious issue in garrison towns, featuring prominently alongside brutality and prostitution, in *Sous-Offs: Roman Militaire* (Paris, 1889), a novel by Lucien Descaves based on his military service. In France, where political and social divisions were potent, these extended to the army and the military demands of the state: the military, and the conservatives, wanted a longer term of service for conscripts, whereas the Left wanted broader, but short-term military service. In 1913, when conscription was increased from two to three years, there were riots in garrison towns.

The military also served to maintain domestic order. Organized labour proved a particular target, as in France and Spain in the 1890s. This use of the military underlined its social positioning. Nationalism, the state and the military were not politically neutral. The military acted in support of established order, as in Lyon in 1831 and 1834 and Paris in 1848 and 1871. In 1891, French troops fired on demonstrating textile workers at Fourmies.

The military could also be an element of change. This reflected the varieties, tensions and transformation of conservatism. In particular, the combination of the demands of international competition, with the pressures and opportunities created by large-scale social change, encouraged the embrace of nationalism, while much nationalism, in turn, became more conducive to conservative goals. Change and order could be part of the same process. Thus, in southern Italy, where it had extended its rule in 1860, the new Italian state faced armed opposition, notably to taxation and to military service, with a full-scale rebellion in Palermo in 1866.

In the international arena, nationalism was presented in a highly competitive form, and military service, heroism and self-sacrifice were extolled. Whatever the significance of warfare for states, it was certainly crucial for nations. The honour that had been so central to dynasties now contributed to the identity and bellicosity of nations. Emotions, imagination and interests were all involved and expressed. Commentators claimed that patriotism and war would ease the burden of domestic tensions. In France, the *Ligue des Patriotes* founded in 1882 staged regular pilgrimages to battle sites from the siege of Paris.

The urban geography of the greatly expanded cities encapsulated the memorialization of war. The naming of streets, bridges, public buildings such as railways stations and pubs presented victories. Paris thus honoured Austerlitz, Jena, Wagram, Alma and Solferino. London had Trafalgar Square, Waterloo Place and Waterloo Station. Waterloo was also celebrated by panoramas, theatrical entertainments and the 1816 competition launched by the British Institution for Promoting the Fine Arts. The 360-degree panorama painting of Waterloo exhibited in 1826 in a rotunda by Henry Aston Barker made him a profit of £10,000 in modern-day terms and toured throughout Britain. Philip Astley staged *The Battle of Waterloo* in his hippodrome with 144 consecutive performances on its first run in 1824. The show was revived annually for several decades. Later in the century, there was a significant increase in the number of battle paintings displayed in British public exhibitions and in 1876 50,000 people came to see Lady Butler's *Balaclava* when it was displayed at the Fine Art Society.[28] War news proved particularly popular in the press. War correspondents and war illustrators became established features.[29] Weapons tests were reported by many newspapers and fiction and non-fiction books on military themes became very popular. *The Battle of Dorking: Reminiscences of a Volunteer*, an 1871 account of a fictional successful German invasion, had a second run of 80,000 copies and led to a tranche of such literature.

In Britain, generals such as Roberts and Kitchener were commemorated in the crowded terraced streets of Victorian slums, while the new Houses of Parliament were decorated with paintings and statues of victory, notably paintings of the recent victories at Trafalgar and Waterloo. Military parades were an important aspect of civic life and ritual. Military uniforms, titles and medals and veteran organizations reached deep into what was very much a male-dominated civil society. This was true for empires, such as Austria (the Austro–Hungarian empire) and Britain, as well as for nation-states. The definition, classification and assertion of masculinity owed much to such military themes, themes which bridged different generations of men.

France looked back to Napoleon I's battles as a source of national pride. The fall of Napoleon III ensured that these battles could work for national pride without risking political partisanship. Although a defeat, Waterloo played a role in the French depiction of a glorious military past because it was interpreted in terms of fortitude and heroism. The bravery of men advancing under heavy fire, especially the cavalry and the Guard was played up, while the French superiority in artillery was ignored, as were Napoleon's command failures. Paintings, such as Joseph-Louis-Hippolyte Bellangé's *La Garde Meurt et ne se rend pas* (first exhibited in 1866), of the last stand of the Imperial Guard around their Eagle, depicted heroic resolution. The return of Napoleon's remains to France from St Helena in 1840 proved a festival of national commemoration. While Leo Tolstoy wrote his Russian national epic *War and Peace* (1869) about the Napoleonic invasion of 1812, Victor Hugo lived on the battlefield to write his masterpiece *Les Misérables* (1860) in which Waterloo was described, while Napoleon was presented as a man of destiny and soul brought down by a methodical Gradgrind. The novel had a great impact on contemporaries. Four years later, the poet Charles Baudelaire visited Waterloo, slept in the hotel used by Hugo and asked to be served Hugo's preferred dishes. Fascination with military leadership helped ensure that the anti-German General Georges Boulanger appeared in 1888–9, a strongman who could transform France. He did not rise to the challenge.

In Austria, the nature of civilian–military relations was pushed to the fore during the 1848–9 revolutions. The 1850s was affected by a closer interpenetration between society and the military, a process aided by Emperor Franz Joseph's close personal identification with the army. The legacy of the wars of 1848–9 was seen not only in the Emperor's attitudes, but also in the hero cult centred on Field Marshal Josef Radetzky (1766–1858). A veteran of the French Revolutionary and Napoleonic Wars, and victor, by means of column attacks and bayonet tactics, over the Piedmontese at Custozza (1848) and Novara (1849), he served as the incarnation of the Habsburg military myth, and was celebrated in a Strauss waltz. Radetzky's fame extended across the empire and was particularly propagated by military veterans' associations. Although very much an initiative from below, they served government purposes, not least being seen as a means of bolstering the army's reserve forces. Moreover, the popularity of the veterans' movement coalesced with the emergence of a forceful political Catholicism. The patriotic activities promoted by the veterans confirmed the centrality of the dynasty, while also having consequences in terms of practical politics.[30]

War was proclaimed as a good. Albrecht von Stosch, a Prussian general, referring to war with Denmark in 1864, claimed: 'After 50 years of peace the Prussian state needs a good baptism by fire … much blood will be shed, but so it is with the history of man as with the land we toil over: only by our blood is it nourished.' Outnumbered and out-generalled, the Danes lost heavily to the attacking Prussians with their superior firearms. This was one of the more decisive wars of the period.[31]

The military presence, however, changed. Notably, in 1857, Franz Joseph decided to raze Vienna's defensive walls. Similarly, Copenhagen's moats were turned into parks. In 1859, the walls of Barcelona were demolished to enable the city to expand into the hinterland.

In the Austrian empire, as elsewhere, military service served to reflect and sustain regional and social identities and hierarchies. Religious and ethnic minorities, such as Jews, could suffer harsh treatment. Traditional concepts about the inherent suitability for command of the landed orders, i.e. those with landed property remained strong, as did their converse – the view that townspeople and the middle class inherently lacked the necessary character and qualities, let alone peasants and workers. These social pressures countered the idea of a value-free professionalism. Indeed, professionalism was essentially conceived of in particular social terms. The net effect was to limit efficiency and excellence, as even more did the exclusion of women from combat and command. The social hierarchy was clearly seen at play in the entry to military colleges and in subsequent promotion, and many militaries suffered from a lack of combat experience; in the case of Austria between 1866 and 1914.[32]

Armies faced a volatile social environment in which the large-scale movement of people from countryside to cities was accompanied by growing individualism, not least as a consequence of increased literacy. Thus, the social factors, which had made commanders after 1815 wary of massed forces and feel, instead, more favourably inclined towards trusted units of long-service regulars, were still pertinent at a time when such massed forces were regarded as necessary. The social politics of the military was enforced by the emphasis on drill and discipline. By current Western standards, initiative at the level of individual soldiers was not encouraged.

If most of Europe was at peace after 1871 until 1914, and this was more the case if the Balkans and war outside Europe were excluded, this did not mean that civil society had a degree of passivity and an absence of bellicosity comparable to the situation since 1990, let alone criticism of the value and values of war. Bellicosity was enhanced by the generally highly positive public response to colonial campaigns and by the nature of public history, for the latter very much focused on an exemplary account of conflict. This was also seen in the popular culture of the period, a culture developed as a result of the literacy encouraged by the spread of state education systems, as well as by the interaction of a growing prosperity with entrepreneurial activities, for example by publishers, booksellers and theatrical promoters. In 1882, the British comic operetta *Iolanthe* claimed that 'every child can tell' that Wellington had thrashed Napoleon.

There was very much a public–private partnership of patriotism. As a result, adventure stories for boys, such as the British novels of G. A. Henty, which invited readers to look back to compatriot youths who had served in war, were produced in cheap copies and in large editions. Henty was also a war correspondent. Theatre audiences applauded patriotic tableaux and joined enthusiastically in the choruses of songs that acclaimed martial exploits. The jingoism sung from the popular music-hall stage in Britain in 1878, as it prepared for war with Russia (a war that was averted by the Russians backing down), was matched elsewhere.

Across Europe, nationalism was a central aspect of the process by which the expression and manipulation of public opinion came to play a greater role in political culture. Public scrutiny was part of the process. It was encouraged by the rise of the press and the spread of the franchise. In this period, each was conducive to bellicosity, as war became an expression of nationalism rather than of dynasticism. The cult of decisive victory gained a new social purchase, one in which willpower was presented as crucial. This culture helped explain the willingness of so many to serve enthusiastically when a major war, one unprecedented in their lifetime, broke out in 1914.

CHAPTER SIX

The Challenges of Total War and Ideology, 1900–50

No matter how accustomed we were to the cannonade's rumble, a storm like this rattled our brains, burrowed into our skulls, pressed down upon our chests with a pervasive anguish ... more cannon shots were fired in one night than in a whole campaign of Napoleon's.

CORPORAL LOUIS BARTHAS, NIGHT OF 31 OCTOBER–1 NOVEMBER 1916 ABOUT
ANGLO–FRENCH BOMBARDMENT ON THE SOMME.[1]

The world wars, in both their course and their consequences, led to a massive strengthening of the practical and ideological dimensions of state military systems. There was a fundamental extension of the power of states, an unprecedented mobilization of national resources and the development and application of the all-encompassing idea of the Home Front. Focused on present needs and on future challenges, these processes also entailed a presentation of the past. Alongside the cult of the nation in history, the concept of military history as inevitably leading towards total war was pushed hard. Nationalism and total war were seen as mutually supporting.

The change in this period in the international situation within Europe, and in Europe's place in the world, were both readily apparent. Each issue involved a great power, which underlined the extent to which European military history always involved an interaction with non-European powers, however difficult the definition of Europe might be. The First World War (1914–18) began with the European powers in control, not only of their own continent but also, through formal or informal empire, of much of the world. Russia was one of these major powers. In contrast, by the end of the war in 1918, Russia had ceased to be a major power, had lost much territory and was moving into a traumatic civil war; while the United States, neutral in 1914 and until 1917, was a key member of the victorious coalition. Indeed, a key reason for the German determination to attack on the Western Front in 1918 was a determination to win there before the Americans moved more troops across the Atlantic. As a lesser point, one that captures anew the problem of changing definitions of Europe, Turkey lost its Asian empire as a result of the war and the peace settlement, and ceased to be a major power, although the attempt, in 1919–23, by Western powers, notably Greece, but also Britain, France and Italy, to carve out zones of control in what became Turkey itself totally failed.

In 1939, the European powers again were responsible for launching what became a world war. However, in 1945, they were exhausted anew, even more than in 1918, and the United States was very much the dominant state among the Western powers, at sea and in the air as well as on land. Russia, now the Soviet Union, was the leading state in Eurasia, with its victorious forces in Berlin, Budapest, Prague, Vienna and Warsaw.

These developments and the broader geopolitics of the period, owed much to the interaction of the course of conflict with the resources available. The wars proved very demanding of human resources, for the military and for the economy, both in the production of raw materials, and in industrial processing.

The wars waged in the first years of the century, prior to the outbreak of the First World War, did not challenge contemporary military assumptions about the effectiveness of the offensive. For example, by putting the stress on success, rather than casualties, observers saw the Balkan Wars of 1912–13 as confirming their faith in the offensive, more specifically in massed infantry assaults. This lesson was taken in particular from the Bulgarian victories over the Turks in 1912, in the First Balkan War, such as Kirkkilese and Lyule Burgas. These victories appeared to show the effectiveness of high morale and of infantry charging in to the attack. In contrast, there was a general failure to consider the degree to which the effectiveness of rapid-firing artillery and machine guns might blunt infantry attacks. Indeed, the power of entrenched positions supported by artillery, when neither had been suppressed by superior offensive gunfire, was shown in the failure of the Bulgarian attack on the Turks at Chataldzha in 1912, a failure that prevented an advance on Constantinople. The Balkan Wars also demonstrated the decisiveness of conflict. The first war led to the rapid conquest of most of the Turkish empire in Europe. The victorious powers fell out and, in the second war, Bulgaria was attacked by its former allies as well as by the Turks. This war led swiftly to a new territorial settlement in which Bulgaria lost much of its conquered territory, including the coastline on the Aegean it sought.

As a result of massacres and expulsions in the Balkans linked to the wars, the relationship between Muslims and Christians was strained at all levels: from the political élites to the ordinary people, polarization sharpened. Indeed, the Balkan Wars anticipated the ethnic conflicts and violence that occurred later during the century, in part because making nations out of a multinational space was a brutal process. The Balkan Wars also saw a ruthless mobilization of armed forces and society, notably in Bulgaria, Serbia and Montenegro. The opportunities the Balkan states grasped to assert their claims transformed the international situation and made it more volatile, accentuating the complexities of threat assessments and the linked encouragement to military action.[2]

Already, in the Russo–Japanese War of 1904–5, the defensive advantages (and resulting costs for attackers) resulting from the new, breech-loading, smokeless, quick-firing firearms were noted, and the benefits of field fortifications had been shown. However, there was a firm conviction within the army General Staffs that, sooner or later, the supply of artillery firing high-explosive shells, combined with the élan of infantry advances, would overcome troops benefiting from trenches, barbed wire and automatic weaponry. In the Balkan and Russo–Japanese Wars, as in the Spanish–American War of 1898, the attacking power had won. Combined with a sense of mission that led to a determination to persist even in the event of repeated and heavy setbacks, this attitude was to result in ferociously heavy casualties on the battlefields of the First World War.

Just as the military mind in 1792 was still overly dominated by the Seven Years' War (1756–63) and insufficient attempt had been made to integrate the experience of intervening conflicts, so the same was true of the period 1871–1914, in part because of a sense that Russia, Japan, Spain, the United States and the Balkan countries were somehow lesser and more primitive military powers with little to teach. In particular, the Germans failed to devote due attention to developments, just as they had earlier underrated the lessons of the American Civil War (1861–5). However, the Balkan Wars confirmed for the Germans the insight, gained in the Russo–Japanese War, that combined arms combat was crucial, notably open-order infantry advances after adequate artillery preparations. Moreover, in France, where the army generally ignored experiences that did not conform to its thinking, the Balkan Wars were deployed to support the established offensive doctrine.

Prior to the outbreak of the First World War, the General Staffs of all the belligerents had pre-planned and executed manoeuvres on a massive scale in war games and staff rides (tours of battlegrounds). With these, staff officers convinced themselves that they could knock out their opponents before their own resources ran out. At the same time, there was a major attempt to increase the latter. Indeed, in the run-up to the war, the arms race escalated, both on land and at sea. For example, in a response to the capabilities of rapid-firing field guns, a major effort was made by all the powers to build up the artillery. In 1900, the Russian army ordered 1,000 quick-firing field guns from the Putilov iron works. The deadly effectiveness of field guns in 1914 was to help lead armies to turn to the relative safety, and certainly lower casualties, of trenches. Munitions production had a major impact in terms of industrial capacity. Workshop space in Krupp's Essen works in Germany grew by an average of 5.2 acres per annum in the five years

to 1908 and thereafter up to 1914 by 6.4 acres per annum. Even before
the outbreak of war, Krupp was producing 150,000 shells of all calibres
monthly.

Troop numbers were also an issue as it was appreciated that a major
war would entail heavy casualties and operations across a broad front or
fronts. In Britain, the established opposition to conscription was challenged
by bodies such as the National Service League that pressed for it against
the background of concern about the international system and increased
calls for a national rearmament that embraced society as a whole. As
part of a general preparedness for war, there were also major naval races,
most particularly between Britain and Germany, but also involving the
Mediterranean naval powers, notably Austria (which then had an Adriatic
coastline), France and Italy. The potential of air power and mechanized
vehicles excited interest alongside some influential scepticism: in 1906,
Emperor Franz-Josef of Austria dismissed the prototype of an armoured
car: 'such a thing would never be of any military value'. However, in 1911,
in Libya, the Italians dropped the first bombs, only eight years after the
beginning of manned powered flight.

The theme of the mobilization of society was one that was to be significant
for much of the twentieth century, although it ebbed in its closing decades
as the Cold War came to lack resonance for much of Europe's population.
In many respects, the theme of mobilization was driven forward by the First
World War, but it was already present. Indeed, the more intense attitude in
the 1900s towards international competition, and what were presented as
the necessary internal consequences of national strengthening, provides a
contrast with the late nineteenth century. Then, both were present, but at
a less intense level.

In 1914, war began in the Balkans with conflict between Austria
and Serbia. The assassination in Sarajevo by Serbian-directed terrorists
of the heir to the Austrian empire, Archduke Franz Ferdinand, both
greatly angered the Austrian government and provided an opportunity
to consolidate Austria's position in Bosnia where it was challenged by
Serb-encouraged South Slavic nationalism. There appeared to be a clear
opportunity to punish Serbia and, in doing so, to establish a dynamic of
success and prestige.

Austria, to thwart international mediation, declared war on Serbia on
28 July and hostilities began there. Nevertheless, the key front in 1914
was to be in France. Rival European alliances, notably that of Austria and
Germany, acted to speed the crisis, and not to restrain it; while the peace
movement totally failed in the latter. The Germans sought to repeat the
successes of Napoleon I in 1799–1809 and of Moltke the Elder in 1864–71
by mounting and winning a war of manoeuvre. However, owing to the
alliance between France and Russia, the latter the supporter of Serbia,
there was now the need for Austria's ally, Germany, to plan for a two-front
conflict as its predecessor, Prussia, had not had to do in 1864–71.

Austria sought to overcome the deterrence of Russia's possible support for Serbia by means of its alliance with Germany. However, Germany believed that the alliance between Russia and France posed such a serious challenge that it was necessary to extend any war to include France. Paris was apparently more vulnerable to German attack than Moscow, not least because, unlike in 1792, 1870 and 1940, Alsace and part of Lorraine were already under German rule and French armies, therefore, had less room for manoeuvre and less defence-in-depth.

The strategy of first strike underlay German planning prior to the First World War. Concerned about the ruinous consequences of a lengthy positional conflict, Count Alfred von Schlieffen, Chief of the German General Staff from 1891 to 1906, developed a plan for an attack on France through neutral Belgium. Seeking to harness the prestige of the example of the crushing Carthaginian victory by Hannibal over the Romans at Cannae in 216 BCE by means of an envelopment, and designed to permit flank attacks on the French, who were configured to fight Germany on their common border, as in 1870, this plan was to be the basis of German strategy in 1914. However, Schlieffen excluded non-military problems from General Staff thinking, ensuring that planning failed to devote due weight to political consequences. Invading through Belgium brought Britain, one of the long-standing guarantors of its neutrality, into the war against Germany, which transformed the strategic task facing Germany, and notably so in the long-term.

Furthermore, Schlieffen failed to adapt his plan to changing circumstances, notably Russian recovery from defeat at the hands of Japan in 1904–5 and her build-up of an army that, despite its limitations, was more powerful than that of Germany's ally, Austria. This build-up reflected the politics of international alignments. French loans, notably that of 1905, gave Russia access to French capital markets, a prime instance of international public–private co-operation. Peacetime expenditure on the military in Russia rose as a percentage of total government expenditure from 23.2 in 1907 to 28.3 in 1913. The failure to give due weight to the politics of strategy was to be a more general issue with German policymaking, and in both world wars. This issue also invites consideration of earlier periods in which the politics of strategy are more obscure.

Schlieffen's successor, Helmuth von Moltke (Moltke the Younger), the nephew of Moltke the Elder, and his colleagues in the General Staff, like their Austrian counterparts under the unstable Conrad von Holzendorf, wanted the challenge of war. They saw it as an opportunity to achieve hegemony and to transform society by overawing the left wing and those tendencies that opposed their political assumptions, for example Slavic nationalists in the Austrian empire. By emphasizing future threats, and stating that victory was still within grasp in 1914, the military leadership helped to push civilian policymakers towards conflict. No alternative scenario to that of an all-out war was offered to the policymakers by the generals. However, although Moltke planned for a short and manageable war, one that could defeat the Franco–Russian alliance and benefit from its fragility, he feared that it could be a long struggle. As in 1870–1, Germany was not prepared for such a struggle, but its demographic and economic growth were such as to ensure that it could be confronted, a situation that was to recur from 1939. Nor, even more, was Austria prepared.

In the event, the 1914 campaign showed that German war-making, with its emphasis on surprise, speed and overwhelming and dynamic force at the chosen point of contact, was not effective against a French defence that, despite heavy casualties, retained the capacity to use reserves by redeploying troops by rail during the course of operations. Rail increased the benefit of the traditional advantage of being on interior lines. After initially mounting an unsuccessful and very costly offensive in Lorraine, the French speedily moved troops by rail from their right flank to their left where they were able to oppose the German forces that had advanced through Belgium. Aside from serious faults in German planning and execution, notably strategic understanding and leadership, there were also problems with German logistics, equipment and discipline that qualify the usual picture of total German competence. Similar points can be made about the other combatants in 1914, which focuses attention on the contingencies and outcomes of conflict.

The French success in stopping the Germans in the Battle of the Marne in September 1914, a counter-offensive made possible by the German failure to prevent a large gap opening up between their advancing forces, ensured that there would be no speedy end to the war. France was saved, and certainly in comparison to the campaigning of 1870. Had Paris fallen, then the Third Republic might have collapsed. Germany, from the Battle of the Marne, was thereafter committed to a two-front war. This made it difficult, as originally planned, to shift forces to the east in order to defeat the Russians rapidly. A two-front war gave the Germans issues of prioritization as a new strategic challenge that posed serious questions had to be confronted. In turn, these issues posed challenges to the Allies. The initial Russian offensive had been defeated in East Prussia, as attacking armies that failed to co-operate were separately defeated with heavy losses by the Germans at the battles of Tannenberg and the Masurian Lakes. This was an example of a more general failure of the offensive that year, one that can also be seen in the Austrian failure in Serbia. The major exception was the Russian offensive into Galicia, Austrian-ruled Poland. Although Germany had failed to knock France out, Germany's extensive territorial gains in Belgium and France in 1914 became a key political and, thereby, strategic fact. As the Germans wished to retain some gains in any peace, so the Allies needed to drive them back in order to ensure that they were not perceived as having failed.

The First World War is generally recalled as a brutal struggle in which millions died in trench warfare with little apparent point. The stress is on impasse and indecisiveness, there are frequent complaints about incompetent commanders and foolish command cultures, and the abiding image, notably in Britain, is of machine guns sweeping away incredibly vulnerable lines of attackers. Battles, most particularly Verdun (1916), the Somme (1916) and Passchendaele (1917), are seen as terrible indictments of a particular way of war, at once costly in lives and remorseless, with valour subordinated to machines. Indeed, the experience of conflict changed, with trench warfare creating new sensations, including of sound.[3] Alongside the churches, and the public as a whole, the arts struggled to give meaning and witness to the conflict, which was possibly best captured in Percy Smith's etching *Death Intoxicated* from his 1919 *The Dance of Death 1914–1918*. In it, a joyous skeleton accompanies the fighting.

There was the particular horror of gas, first used by the Germans in 1915. On 28 April 1915, the *Times* reported of the fighting near Ypres in Belgium:

> The strong northeast wind which was blowing from the enemy lines across the French trenches became charged with a sickening and suffocating odour, which was recognised as proceeding from some form of poisonous gas. The smoke moved like a vivid green wall some 4 feet in height ... Some strange cries were heard, and through the green mist ... there came a mass of dazed and reeling men, who fell as they passed throughout ranks. The greater number were unwounded, but they bore upon their faces the marks of agony. The retiring men were among the finest soldiers of the world, whose sangfroid and courage have been proverbial throughout the war. All were reeling through us and round us like drunken men.

On 7 May 1915, an anonymous correspondent in the paper commented on:

> this diabolical form of torture ... we had no difficulty in finding out in which ward the men were, as the noise of the poor devils trying to get breath was sufficient to direct us ... Their faces, arms, hands were of a shiny grey-black colour, with mouths open and lead-glazed eyes, all swaying slightly backwards and forwards trying to get breath ... The effect the gas has is to fill the lungs with a watery, frothy matter, which gradually increases and rises till it fills up the whole lungs and comes up to the mouth; then they die; it is suffocation; slow drowning, taking in some cases one or two days ... over half the men who reached hospital have died ... It is without doubt the most awful form of scientific torture. Not one of the men I saw in hospital had a scratch or wound. The nurses and doctors are all working their utmost against this terror; but one could see from the tension of their nerves that it was like fighting a hidden danger which was overtaking everyone.

Gas was also used elsewhere, for example by the Austrians against the Italians in the Caporetto offensive in 1917. During the war, 90,000 troops died from the use of gas and 1.29 million soldiers were injured. There were also psychological consequences, notably 'gas fright', as well as civilian casualties. The consequences could also be long-term, with mustard gas eventually causing lung cancer as well as late-onset blindness.

The popular view gives credit to the invention of the tank by the British for helping overcome the impasse on the Western Front in France and Belgium. Moreover, the Germans are presented as succumbing to domestic dissatisfaction and related problems that owed much to the socio-economic and political strains arising from the British naval blockade of Germany, culminating with the overthrow of Kaiser Wilhelm II and the old ruling order in late 1918.

In fact, although there were attritional aspects to specific engagements and particular campaigns, the terrible casualties of the war have made it appear more attritional than was the case. Once the Germans, in 1914, lost the ability to mount a victorious campaign of manoeuvre on the Western Front, and a front line was stabilized, this did not mean that their opponents simply wore them down. Instead, the Germans were eventually outfought and defeated – in 1918, both in offensive and in defensive warfare. Moreover, individual campaigns had strategic point even if implementation did not meet planned outcomes. Thus, in 1915, the British, French and Italians planned attacks in order to reduce German pressure on Russia and thus avoid the risk that Russia collapse. In 1916, the Germans intended to hit the French hard at Verdun, before focusing on Britain, which was seen as the major foe. In turn, in 1916, the British took over most of the burden of the Somme offensive in order to help the French who were suffering heavily at Verdun. It is important to emphasize such points in order to underline the extent to which there was strategic purpose and coherence as well as reasons for attacks, instead of the general popular view of pointlessness and poor command. So also with the war at sea.[4]

The heavy casualties on land owed much to the war being waged by well-armed industrial powers that were willing and able to deploy much of their young male populations. In the last, the powers benefited from pre-war patterns of military activity, notably conscription, but also from the nature of labour organization, the hierarchical character of society and the impact of nationalist values. Before the outbreak of the war, the Socialist International had pursued pacifism and had rejected wars seen as bourgeois and capitalist. In 1913, the French Socialists had unsuccessfully opposed the extension of military service from two to three years. In the event, instead of opposing war, the French Socialists and the German Social Democrats had demonstrated their respective patriotisms in 1914. Trade unions had co-operated with governments and there was little avoidance of conscription.

Despite the repeated failure of military operations on the Western Front to secure their objectives in 1914–17 (and up to mid-1918), and the heavy costs of the conflict, both sides showed the adaptability and endurance of modern industrial societies. They did so in a way that enabled them to continue a large-scale, long-term war. In addition, had the campaigns been waged in a different manner, been, for example, more manoeuvrist and less static, there is no reason to assume that casualties would have been lower. Instead, troops would have been more exposed to both offensive and defensive fire. Indeed, trench systems served to stabilize the line and to protect troops. The latter was particularly necessary given the very heavy casualties that the combatants took in 1914.

However, once these trench systems had been constructed, it proved very difficult to regain mobility, and certainly operational mobility, although the combatants repeatedly sought to mount decisive attacks that would enable them to do so. In large part, the inability to break through was due not to the inherent strength of trench systems, but, instead, to the force–space ratio on the Western Front. Moreover, trench systems became more sophisticated as the original, improvised defences were replaced by defences in depth. These were less vulnerable to attack, not least because positions were increasingly located on reverse slopes, while more barbed wire was used. As a result, trench systems became less vulnerable to a single attack and to field artillery. Instead, systemic attacks supported by masses of artillery became necessary. These attacks, however, were far more costly in manpower, *matériel* and time.[5] The same was true on the Isonzo front, where the Italians, as allies, from 1915, of Britain and France, launched eleven offensives in 1915–17, taking very heavy losses to push the Austrians back only six miles.

In contrast, where the force–space ratio was lower, it was harder to ensure concentration and mass. At the same time, it proved possible, in these circumstances, to achieve breakthroughs, to make major gains and to obtain decisive results. This was particularly the case on the Eastern Front, which was far more extensive than its Western counterpart. On the Eastern Front, Germany and Austria fought Russia, with Germany proving particularly successful. For example, in the German breakthrough at Gorlice–Tarnów in Poland in 1915, artillery and gas proved more effective than on the Western Front that year. However, prior to the Russian collapse in 1917, the Germans did not make conquests comparable to those they were to make in just one campaign in 1941. Confronted by repeated Russian victories over the Austrians, notably in 1914 and in the Brusilov offensive in 1916, the Germans took over command of the Austrian military, which was poorly led.

Russia was finally knocked out of the war in 1917, as a consequence of the combination of defeat by the Germans and serious internal problems in sustaining the war. The size of the Russian army, and the fact that the fighting was on Russian soil, greatly exacerbated the tremendous strain of the conflict. Whereas the Germans did not advance on Moscow, as Napoleon had done in 1812, these internal problems in a lengthy conflict were far more serious than the situation in 1812. These issues interacted to create a crisis in support for Tsar Nicholas II. He was overthrown and replaced in February 1917 by a republican government under Kerensky, which sought to continue the war as part of the alliance system. However, the Germans maintained their military pressure, the Russians were unsuccessful, and Kerensky was overthrown by the Bolsheviks (the victorious Communist faction) in a coup in late 1917.

The German success on the Eastern Front put the Allies' limited achievements on the Western Front that year in perspective. The new Russian leadership under Lenin negotiated the Peace of Brest-Litovsk with Germany the following year, accepting major territorial losses. This indicated the changes war could bring, as well as the extent to which Germany appeared successful in the war until well into 1918. By that summer, Germany was in control of far more territory than at any earlier stage during the war. Moreover, as far as Europe was concerned, the alliance against Germany was now far weaker than in 1914–17.

Like other treaties during conflicts, for example that of Prague in 1635 and Lunéville in 1801, the terms of Brest-Litovsk hardly demonstrated the indecisiveness of conflict in this period. Indeed, Russia, in 1918, had to accept territorial losses greater than those inflicted on it in any previous war. Moreover, other powers were also hit hard in the war. After defeating Austrian attacks in 1914, Serbia was conquered by attacking Bulgarian, German and Austrian forces in 1915, as (largely) was Romania by the same powers in 1916: anticipating Allied victory and territorial gains through co-operation, Romania had entered the war earlier that year only to be swiftly defeated by attacking forces that combined spend and manoeuvre, unbalancing the Romanians who failed to respond to the dynamism of the attack.[6]

In addition, Italy was nearly knocked out of the war by the Austro–German Carporetto offensive of 1917, and might well have fallen, but for the dispatch of Allied reinforcements to help establish a new line. This offensive saw far more Italian territory captured than had been the case with all the Italians attacks on the Isonzo front. Indeed, campaigning as a whole appeared more effective in 1917 than in 1915 or 1916. The Austro–German offensive, however, failed to benefit from Austrian naval support, which was an aspect of the broader weakness in army–naval co-operation during the war.

On the Western Front, in contrast, British, French and German generals had to confront the problems of the strength of the defensive. The available manpower made it possible to hold the front line with strength and to provide reserves, the classic need for all linear defence systems. For the offensive, generals, whether the Germans at Verdun in 1916, or the Allies later in the year on the Somme, faced the difficulty of devising an effective operational system and tactical method that would not only achieve break-through, but also then be able to sustain and develop it. This was far from easy, not least because of the problems for troops of advancing across terrain badly damaged by shellfire, as well as the difficulties of providing reserves in the correct place, of maintaining the availability of sufficient high-explosive shells for the all-crucial artillery and of providing adequate information to commanders about developments. Deficiencies in communications led directly into command problems.

At sea, in the absence of a decisive fleet engagement, the British and Germans each relied on the long-term solution of blockade; the British by surface vessels and the Germans by submarines. The adoption of convoys in 1917 helped lessen the serious challenge of the latter.

The length of the war arose, in part, from the time taken to develop tactics able to restore mobility to the Western Front, and, in part, from the time necessary to ensure the provision of sufficient munitions. The balance of resources was also important: the Germans ran out of reserves of troops in 1918, in part due to their heavy losses during the Spring Offensive of that year, and in part because they did not move sufficient troops back from the Eastern Front. This was due to a determination to pursue additional territorial gains in the collapsing Russian empire, again a clear political goal.

In contrast, the Allies had a fresh source of troops as a result of American entry into the war in 1917. American troops were deployed in large numbers on the Western Front. They played an important role in 1918, notably in the successful Allied offensive in the last stage of the year, and would have done even more so had the war continued into 1919. American warships were also important to the naval balance and in the struggle against German submarines. Furthermore, unlike in the Second World War, the Allies did not have Japan as an enemy. Instead, a member of the victorious alliance, Japan successfully attacked German colonies in the Western Pacific and China, and dispatched warships to the Indian Ocean and Mediterranean to help against German submarines.

As a major instance of improved wartime performance, and notably in an action–reaction process in which new challenges were confronted and overcome, the effectiveness of armies in attack on the Western Front rose during the war, and particularly so in 1918. The same was also true of air power. First, the Germans developed stormtrooper techniques, using them with considerable success in their spring 1918 offensive on the Western Front, as they had earlier done at Riga against the Russians (1916) and at Caporetto against the Italians (1917). These techniques relied on carefully planned surprise assaults employing infiltration, and focusing on opponents' strong points in order to destroy their cohesion. Élite attacking units were equipped with weapons such as flamethrowers that provided firepower as well as mobility.

As a consequence of these techniques, the Germans achieved break-throughs, but poor generalship ensured that these were not adequately exploited in 1918. The Germans mounted a series of sequential attacks, rather than an attempt to focus on one part of the Allied front and achieve and develop a sustained breakthrough there. Furthermore, there were no realizable political goals to accompany the offensive. Instead, the Germans misleadingly assumed they could use shock to force an Allied collapse. They planned to drive the British forces out of France and, thus, to lead France to surrender. To this end, the Germans attacked both the British and the French, the latter in an attempt to draw French reserves away from being able to support the British. However, the latter goal failed which provided a key underpinning for the British. In addition, the Germans failed to focus on the rail junctions that were crucial to British logistics: they focused their forces on Allied units, rather than on Allied vulnerabilities.

The offensive also led to heavy German losses and to a new extended and vulnerable front line that left their tired forces vulnerable to attack. More generally, and prefiguring the situation with the German army during the Second World War, the German offensive technique in 1916–18 relied on élite units, rather than on raising the quality of their army as a whole.

Secondly, thanks in large part to the use of aerial reconnaissance, the British focused on improving artillery firepower and accuracy, and, more importantly, on artillery–infantry coordination. As a result, they were able to dominate the three-dimensional battlefield and to apply firepower more effectively than in earlier attacks. Their 1918 campaign was a great success in this respect. Seeking to raise the effectiveness of the army as a whole, British improvements and adaptability outweighed those of the Germans, and this brought great benefits in the more fluid closing stage of the war. Artillery readily outranged machine guns.[7]

Artillery played a greater role in the Allied success than tanks, although the Allies, unlike the Germans who built few, appreciated the potential of the latter. Like other new weapons, tanks commanded attention. Indeed, they had a capability that other weaponry lacked, for example for flattening barbed wire, as well as a major visual impact. However, as was only to be expected of a weapon that had not had a long process of peacetime development and preparation, there were major problems with its mechanical reliability. Moreover, tanks proved vulnerable to broken terrain, artillery and mines. Some of the statements subsequently made on behalf of the wartime impact of the tank, as of aircraft, reflected the bold, and also often competing, claims about weapons systems made by their protagonists in the 1920s and 1930s, rather than an informed critical assessment of operations in the First World War.

The Allied offensive of 1918, an offensive to which France and the United States made major contributions alongside British and British imperial forces, was not only effective and sustained, but also important to the development of modern warfare. In place of generalized firepower, there was systematic coordination, reflecting precise control of both infantry and massive artillery support, plus improved communications. Combined arms techniques were mastered by both the British and the French. This emphasis was also seen in Allied plans for the offensive projected in 1919. For example, there was interest both in the large-scale use of tanks and in using radio contact between aircraft and ground forces to enhance co-operation. Plans for a major use of tanks in 1919, however, exaggerated their mechanical capabilities and assumed an operational capability that the specifications and tactical effectiveness of tanks did not merit. There was a parallel with optimistic projections about air power, notably concerning the potential of bombing.

In 1918, the main German forces, no longer adeptly commanded, were defeated on the Western Front, and collapsed, whereas, in 1945, they were to be defeated, far more conclusively, by the Soviets. The anti-war ethos of the 1960s, an ethos that focused its historical consciousness on the First World War, ensured that this achievement was underrated. It was the leading achievement of the British and French armies in the twentieth century. Moreover, the Second World War came to play the role of a good war and to dominate attention. As a result, the value of Allied victory in the First World War was underplayed.

Wartime military casualties were very heavy, including 1.7 million deaths in Germany and 1.4 million in France. There were also heavy civilian losses. The First World War, furthermore, had profound political and social consequences in both the short-and the long-term. The intractability and strains of the war had led to an escalating violence that hit hard at the social fabric while radicalizing war aims. The latter, in turn, drew on a strident nationalism that helped make compromise impossible and led to greater pressure to make all-out efforts. Brutality towards conquered areas, such as by the Germans in Belgium and France, the Austrians in Serbia and the Austrians and Russians in Galicia (southern Poland), was part of a wider intense social dislocation that included forced recruitment, deportations and 'ethnic cleansing'. More generally, the disruption of war hit medical care and the provision of food.[8] Across Europe, established norms rapidly collapsed, both with regard to the conduct of war within Europe and in terms of responses to existing conventions. This situation looked towards German war-making in the Second World War, although then the authoritarianism of the Germans in 1914–18 was joined by a more radical racial ideology.

The First World War led, in 1917–18, to the fall of the Austrian, German, Russian and Turkish empires, and thus created long-term instability across much of Eurasia as successor regimes sought to cope with the consequences and to shape change to their benefit. Meanwhile, during the war, there were mobilizations of resources on a tremendous scale, with inevitably serious economic and financial consequences. For example, over five million troops were sent from Britain to fight in France and Belgium. In order to meet the demands for resources, government authority rapidly expanded. The consequences were transformative. War economics and economic warfare distorted domestic and international economics, and destroyed the liberal pre-war system of free trade. In France, for instance, a state of siege was imposed on 2 August 1914, greatly increasing the power of the military and permitting requisitioning and censorship.

Both voluntarily and by compulsion, participation in the state rose. For example, in Britain, not only was conscription introduced in 1916, but also the number of Britons holding government securities rose to over sixteen million. Participation in the war effort was actively pursued through propaganda campaigns. Confronted by the popular wish to see a just war, and convinced that war was a test of national quality and spirit, states devoted much attention to them, using techniques very different to those of a century earlier. In 1917, having decided 'that it was desirable that a separate Department of State should be set up to deal with the general question of propaganda', the British government established a Department of Information. The conflict between nations, and not simply their militaries, predicted by some writers before the war, had become a reality.[9]

The military, political, social and economic burdens extended to neutrals. For example, in order to protect their country, the Dutch prepared for war. The army became 450,000-strong, the power of the military over industry increased and, by 1918, 75 per cent of the country had been placed under a state of siege.[10] Neutrals such as Denmark, Norway and Sweden had their merchant shipping greatly affected by the Allied blockade of Germany and by German submarine attacks on shipping.

Governments were not only strengthened. Instead, they, as well as established practices, were put under serious pressure. The costs of the war caused very high levels of inflation (prices rising by 340 per cent in France during the war) and of government debt that greatly challenged the position of the middle classes, as well as the public finances. Currencies were devalued while taxes rose. For example, income tax was introduced in France. In addition, there was a major loss of confidence in established ideologies, political orders, social hierarchy, Providence and the future of humankind. Anti-war feeling developed as just one of the far-reaching consequences, and it was more strongly marked in the 1920s than in the decade before the First World War.

Furthermore, social mores were affected by a wartime decline of deference and also by the rapidly shifting role of women in the militarized wartime societies. With men called to fight, the economic sphere extended for women and notably in industry. In addition, large numbers of women and children replaced rural male workers, especially in France. Furthermore, many women accompanied the military as nurses. This reflected the extent to which the social contours of conflict changed. Large numbers of women had accompanied armies in the early modern period. As 'camp-followers', they provided a domestic environment for many of the soldiers. While some women were prostitutes, others were wives and partners. Cooking and nursing were part of the life. These roles had diminished in the nineteenth

century, not least as the bureaucratization of war meant that more activities were regulated and were provided by soldiers, of whom then there
was relatively scant shortage. Manoeuvres away from home bases and an
emphasis on speed in campaign contributed to the situation. Regulation
was even more the case in the twentieth century, but many women were
absorbed into support functions. However, roles were carefully segregated.
Women served as nurses, but food preparation on campaign was by men.
The situation was less differentiated, indeed in part segregated, for the
irregular forces of non-state actors, but they were a minority of the forces
deployed in Europe. Many women were also left as widows by the war,
including 600,000 in France.

The First World War led into a series of struggles, notably, but not only,
in Eastern Europe. These in part reflected the search for new frontiers
by new states, as well as the treatment of competing ethnic groups and
political ideologies. Thus, in Upper Silesia, Germans fought Poles, while a
Communist takeover in Hungary was ended by a Romanian invasion.

The widest ranging of the struggles was the civil war in Russia between
the Bolsheviks (the victorious Communist faction) and their opponents
in 1918–20. This war was complicated by international intervention
against the Bolsheviks, particularly by the British and the French, but
including not only Eastern Europeans, such as the Romanians, but also the
Americans, Canadians and Japanese. The composition of the coalition was
very different to the anti-Russian coalitions in 1812 and 1854–6, and this
difference reflected the major change in the world system that had already
occurred prior to the First World War. In part, the size of Russia was the
key issue, as it was a Pacific as well as a European power. The Russian
Civil War was won by the Bolsheviks. They benefited greatly from the
ruthlessness with which they suppressed opposition and directed resources,
from the serious divisions among their opponents and from the unpopu-
larity of the 'White' or anti-Bolshevik cause with the peasantry, which saw
scant reason to welcome counter-revolution. The Bolsheviks held Moscow
and St Petersburg and, with them, the central position and the industrial
centres and communication nodes. Moreover, the White generals consistently failed to coordinate their attacks on the Bolsheviks, providing the
latter with important opportunities for sequential campaigning, and thus
for using their forces more effectively to achieve a winning local superiority.

The Russian Civil War also entailed efforts by the Bolshevik government
to regain control by force of regions where non-Russian ethnic groups
had sought to win independence. Russian control was reimposed in the
Caucasus, Central Asia and Ukraine; but not in the Baltic states (Estonia,
Latvia, Lithuania), Finland or Poland. The Russo–Polish War, in which
the invading Russians were heavily defeated in the Battle of Warsaw of
1920, demonstrated the characteristics of the warfare of the period. It
was highly fluid, and this type of warfare was to be as common as the
fronts and fixed sides that tend, as a result of the First World War, to

dominate modern conceptions of early twentieth-century warfare. Rapidly advancing Russian forces did not win the popular support anticipated. Moreover, their brutality helped encourage a strong nationalist response. Like those invading East Prussia in 1914, the Russian forces were poorly co-ordinated. The Poles benefited from French equipment and advice. The well-executed Polish counter-offensive against the Russians both defeated their over-extended forces and drove them back out of Poland. British naval intervention helped thwart the Bolshevik efforts to gain Estonia and Latvia.

Poland was one of a number of states that created new militaries from 1918. Others were Czechoslovakia, Finland, Estonia, Latvia and Lithuania, while Hungary and Austria became two separate states. Indeed, the rise in the number of European armies (and to a far lesser extent navies) is an important feature of the military history of the period, albeit one overlooked due to the habitual focus on Western Europe and on the issue of new technology.

Civil warfare on a very different scale to that in Russia was seen in Ireland in 1921–2. As an aspect of the nationalism and challenge to empires that accompanied, and even more followed, the First World War, there had been an unsuccessful nationalist rebellion in Dublin in 1916, the Easter Rising. Fighting resumed after the war, but in a different form. The Irish Republican Army (IRA) organized its active service units into flying columns which staged raids and ambushes in order to undermine the stability of British rule. Assassinations and sabotage were also employed. The IRA was short of arms (many of which were gained by raids on the British) and was outnumbered by the army and the police, but it was able to take the initiative and to benefit from the limited options available to those trying to restore control. There were significant improvements in the methods used to fight the IRA, but political support was lacking.

Unwilling to persist, the British government abandoned control over most of the island. As so often with counter-insurgency struggles, there were claims that, had it persisted, victory could have been obtained. However, whatever the truth of this, the government was faced by a range of difficult imperial commitments. The IRA thus benefited from such issues as the Russian Civil War and from new British commitments in the Middle East. Once the British had withdrawn from the bulk of Ireland, the IRA split, with a faction rejecting the peace settlement. This led to a fresh struggle, but, in this, the forces of the new Irish state successfully overcame opposition. In part, this success was a matter of more brutal conduct than that of the British, notably the execution of prisoners. In addition, the 'anti-Treaty' rebels lacked a psychological drive comparable to that they had experienced against the British.

A very different civil war, in scale, severity and international context, was that in Spain in 1936–9. This struggle began with an unsuccessful military rebellion by right-wing Nationalists under General Franco, supported by a large section of the population, against the left-wing Republican government, which was also supported by a large section. As with other civil wars, the Spanish one revealed and created tensions within the military, while also leading to the establishment of paramilitary forces that played a major role. Thus, on the Republican side, those of the military, who remained loyal, were challenged by the role of socialist, anarchist, regional and other militia volunteers. The military rebellion, the arming of workers and the major place for militias, all encouraged this situation. There were different political strategies at stake, strategies that reflected tensions seen with the Russian Revolution. In Spain, the Communists (who were on the Republican side), on the pattern already followed in Russia, supported the organization of the militias into a regular army with the relevant established practices and ethos. This stress on clear discipline, necessary training, hierarchical rank and defined organization cut across alternative means of providing force and control. The established practices were very much part of the European tradition, one that, as a consequence, tended to contain and restrict such alternatives as organization on radical-ideological grounds. In both, the French and the Russian revolutions, there was a relatively rapid reversion to established patterns of organization. At the same time, this standardization, in Spain as on earlier occasions, under-lined the symmetrical character of European warfare.

In doing so, and ensuring that the Republicans and the Nationalists fought a similar war, the emphasis was put on two alternative forms of difference between the two sides. One, in common with many conflicts, was command experience and skills. Here, the Nationalists benefited from the extent to which commanders and officers had fought in Morocco in the 1920s against local opponents, whereas their counterparts lacked such experience. Secondly, again a common element, came the international context, which very much involved ideological rivalry. The Soviet Union provided assistance to the Republicans, notably with aircraft, but less so than the more direct intervention the Nationalists received from Germany and Italy. Each sent large numbers of personnel as well as equipment.[11] The international context, military as well as diplomatic and political, was significant in the major struggles throughout the period covered by this book. This was an aspect of the multi-polar character of the European system.

The resource and organizational dimension was also significant in Spain, as the Republicans, despite having the state apparatus, could not feed their population, raise revenue and control inflation. This specifically affected military logistics, with the army short of food. In contrast to the Russian Civil War, the side that held the central position lost, while that which benefited from most external support and military experience won. This contrast underlines the need for caution in the analysis of reasons for victory.

To contemporaries, terror bombing was a notable feature of the Spanish Civil War, particularly with the German bombing of the city of Guernica, but also with Italian or German bombing of other targets including the cities of Barcelona and Cartagena. This perception encouraged a more general tendency in the 1920s and 1930s in which advocates for air power, looking to a future conflict between great powers, claimed that it had dramatically changed the nature of war, while such a belief affected the response to the terror bombing seen during the Spanish Civil War. Bombers were presented as a strategic arm, able to attack enemy industry, and to sway an opponent's domestic opinion by bombing its cities and wrecking morale. Thus, the impasse of the trenches was to be overcome in a short, sharp and modern conflict. These arguments were pushed hard by those, especially in Britain, who supported a separate service organization for air power: the Royal Air Force, created in 1918, acted as a lobby for air power. In other countries, especially France, the emphasis, instead, was on air power as a support for the army: on tactical rather than strategic means and goals.

Such debates were pushed to the fore from the mid-1930s. The catalyst was the rise of Adolf Hitler to power in Germany, in 1933, and his proclaimed determination, from 1935, to ensure a wholesale overthrow of the peace settlement at the close of the First World War. This ambition led to fears of a coming major war. Germany had far more resources than Italy, where the right-wing dictator, Benito Mussolini, had not yet brought conflict to Europe.

The Germans made much of their commitment to mechanization and created their first three panzer (armoured) divisions in 1935. These were designed to give effect to the doctrine of armoured warfare that was developed in Germany, in particular by Heinz Guderian. Initially drawing heavily on Britain's use of tanks in the First World War, and on subsequent British thought, the Germans developed their own distinctive ideas in the 1930s. They planned to use tanks en masse in order to achieve a deep breakthrough, rather than employing them, as the French did, as a form of mobile artillery in support of infantry. The panzer divisions were to seize the initiative, to move swiftly and to be made more effective by being combined arms units incorporating artillery and mechanized infantry. Indeed, tanks were to be the cutting-edge of the successful German blitz-krieg (lightning strike) operations in 1939–41, although good battlefield leadership and the ability to raise the tempo of campaigning was key, as was effective training.

In practice, however, the German army did not match the claims made for it by propagandists, and was less of a war 'machine' than they suggested. The mechanization of its infantry was limited, its logistics was overly dependent on horse transport and the German economy was not geared up for a long war. Moreover, much German doctrine in the 1920s and 1930s related to infantry rather than tanks. This point underlines the problem of reading back from subsequent concerns and perception in order to establish significance and an apparently clear pattern of development.

The Second World War began with the large-scale Japanese invasion of China in 1937, and first involved European powers in conflict when Japanese and Soviet forces clashed in 1938 and, even more, 1939. The war in Europe began later. The successful German occupation of Austria in 1938 and Czechoslovakia in 1939, and that of Albania by Italy also in the spring of 1939, were military actions, but did not amount to war. Instead, it started that autumn with the German invasion of Poland, a step that led Britain and France into war with Germany, while the Soviet Union subsequently joined the Germans in conquering Poland. There were a series of swift German successes: against Poland in 1939, Denmark, Norway, the Netherlands, Belgium and France in 1940, and Yugoslavia and Greece in early 1941. These successes led Hitler to a conviction of his own inevitable success and destiny; a pattern earlier seen with Napoleon.

However, German war-making, as had earlier been the case with those of Napoleon, Moltke the Elder and the Bolsheviks during the Russian Civil War, was actively helped by poor strategic and operational choices by its opponents, to an extent that later commentators, many fascinated by the German victories, tend to underplay. The Polish and French failure to retain sufficient reserves ensured that the Germans were able to maintain the initiative they had gained by first launching the attack. The extended perimeter of opposing forces in Poland in 1939, France and the Low Countries in 1940 and Yugoslavia in 1941 also gave the attacking Germans major advantages. So did their ability to win and use air superiority, to retain the tempo of armoured advances, which disoriented their opponents and sapped their will to fight, and to operate in terrain their opponents considered impassable or very difficult. They did this to decisive effect in the Ardennes in 1940, and in the Balkans the following year.

However, alongside success, these campaigns demonstrated some of the deficiencies of the German military and war machine. These included a lack of adequate mechanization. In France in 1940, Britain and France together fielded more and better tanks than the Germans, and the British army in particular was highly mechanized, which was a reflection of the nature of Britain's advanced economy and relatively mechanized society. In turn, the Germans lacked the doctrine, planning, training and equipment for an invasion of Britain, as well as the heavy bombers and long-range fighters for an effective campaign of air attack designed to gain air superiority and to inflict enough damage to force Britain to peace. Indeed, the German air assault in 1940–1 failed, not least due to an able British defence that made good use of radar. However, London suffered serious devastation.[12]

As a reminder, that goals and tasks were also significant, the German strategic weakness of having no adequate way to move from victory to a mutually acceptable and thus viable peace settlement, in short from output to outcome, was also highly significant. The Germans in effect sought to create an imperial system. Hitler's approach to allies was entirely instrumental, while those conquered were even more harshly treated. Aside from economic exploitation, and racial discrimination and violence, there was a brutality designed to crush, and notably so in Poland and Serbia. This policy worked against what might otherwise have been an attempt to create a viable anti-Soviet and anti-Communist alliance, one, moreover, that drew on the widely diffused nature of anti-Semitism.

Yet, by the start of June 1941, it was by no means clear that Germany was bound to fail. Allied to Italy, the Soviet Union, Hungary, Romania, Slovakia, Bulgaria and Finland, and with Spain, Portugal, Switzerland, Ireland and Sweden neutral, and all bar Britain conquered, Hitler appeared in a highly dominant position. Outside Europe, Japan was Germany's ally, while the United States was neutral, both in a situation very different to that in the spring of 1918.

When Hitler attacked the Soviet Union in June 1941, in Operation Barbarossa, the deficiencies already seen with German operations were to be compounded by the vastness of the territory that had to be conquered, as well as by the availability of massive Soviet reserves. Lulled by over-confidence in the value of a swift offensive, by their swift success over France in 1940 and by their tactical and operational skills and ability, the Germans had not planned or prepared adequately for the conflict, and, in particular, lacked the necessary logistical support. They were convinced that the Soviet military had been gravely weakened by the comprehensive and brutal purges launched in 1937 and had been overly impressed by the serious difficulties the Soviet army had encountered at the hands of outnumbered Finland in the 'Winter War' of 1939–40.

In practice, helped by the heavy use of artillery and by a focus on the main axis of operations, the Soviets had finally succeeded against Finland in 1940, rather like the Austrians, Prussians and Russians advancing against Napoleon in 1814. Moreover, the absence of any German political strategy short of total success was all-too-apparent in the case of the Soviet Union, as it had earlier been in Eastern Europe. Hitler believed in the primacy of will and the inherent racial and cultural superiority of German soldiers. The end pursued was a total victory that individual successes were not in fact going to obtain.

The Red Army suffered heavy defeats at the outset of Barbarossa and, in these and initial counter-attacks, lost large quantities of men, tanks and aircraft. Major Soviet armies were outmanoeuvred and forced into surrender, in Belarus and Ukraine. However, Soviet doctrine, with its emphasis on defence in depth and its stress on artillery, proved effective once the initial shock and surprise of the German attack had been absorbed. The German advance fell seriously behind schedule, while Soviet resistance was not ended. Soviet resilience in often relentless fighting, and the Soviet ability to learn from early defeats, meant that the war rapidly became attritional. That was a type of conflict for which the Germans were not prepared, and in which they could not prevail against the Soviet forces.[13] German casualties were higher than anticipated, as was the loss of armour.

More generally, the war indicated that employing tanks, as the Germans did, to try to revolutionize conflict, was of limited value in the face of 'counter-tank' practices, such as the use of anti-tank weapons and the employment of tanks in mobile defence. Combined with the lack of petrol, spare parts and ammunition, and with the debilitating and damaging conse- quences of the weather, including summer dust, autumn mud and winter freezing, these problems ensured that the German tank divisions could not act as the intended operational centre of gravity. Largely intoxicated by the scale of advance, the high command, however, ignored these flaws and so, even more, did Hitler.

The need to advance on a broad front slowed the impetus of the German attack, as did serious logistical problems. In addition, the Soviets proved better at operating in the difficult winter conditions of Russia. Furthermore, once their advances had been held in late 1941, and again in late 1942, the Germans suffered from the absence of sufficient manpower, artillery and supplies. Moreover, the front line was far more extended than had been the case when the offensive was launched. The Germans lacked strong opera- tional reserves to cope with the major Soviet counter-attacks that were launched in December 1941 and November 1942.

This was a failure not only of Germany but also of its alliance system. Allies, including Italy and Romania, sent large numbers of troops, and volunteers were also raised, for example in France and Spain. The role of allied forces was subsequently underplayed or misrepresented in their military history. For example, in the Finnish version of history, Finland's participation in 1941–4 in Germany's war against the Soviet Union is presented as the 'Continuation War', a separate effort that took forward the Finnish–Soviet Winter War of 1939–40, and was not joined to Germany's efforts. While this account captured Finland's wartime independence, it is also misleading. More generally, there was a significant continuity for many states, for example Romania, between opposition to the Soviet Union during the Russian Civil War and during the Second World War.

In their war with the Soviet Union, the Germans were badly hampered by Hitler's maladroit interventions and by a more systemic overconfidence, an unwillingness to work out realistic plans and to implement them and a failure to appreciate that earlier successes in Western Europe did not provide a template for war against the Soviet Union. Embracing their harsh racial beliefs, the Germans both underestimated the Soviets and brutalized them. The Soviet ability to mount a successful counter-attack in December 1941, at the Battle of Moscow, indicated the continued resilience of their centralized and authoritarian governmental system, and its ability to mobilize resources, albeit at the cost of considerable hunger and much brutality. Japan's decision to focus on war with Britain and the United States ensured a non-aggression pact with the Soviet Union that enabled the Soviets to transfer troops from Siberia to the Moscow front.[14]

Stabilizing, let alone advancing, the front proved an enormous strain on German resources, although the Soviet counter-attack was finally held in early 1942. Moreover, launched later against a Soviet army that was more effective and better prepared than in June 1941, the 1942 German offensive – Operation 'Blue' – was jeopardized by an ill-conceived and poorly executed plan. Aside from contradictory original goals, Hitler's developing conviction that the city of Stalingrad, on the River Volga, had to be captured, foolishly substituted a political goal for the necessary operational flexibility. Despite a massive commitment of resources, the attacking Germans were fought to a standstill in the rubble of a much shelled and bombed city. When, in an adroit, surprise operation, the Soviets counter-attacked, winning rapid success, notably against weak Romanian units in flanking positions, Hitler again failed to respond with the necessary flexibility and forbade a retreat from Stalingrad by the Sixth Army before it was encircled. It was then fought and starved into surrender.

The Germans, nevertheless, proved formidable foes on the defensive and succeeded in stabilizing the front. In part, this was thanks to Field Marshal Manstein's embracing of mobile warfare and skilful employment of counter-attacks in early 1943, but the difficulties of sustaining the Soviet offensive also played a role. However, the Germans were outnumbered and outfought thereafter, and their attempt to regain the initiative with the Kursk offensive that summer totally failed. In that offensive, the scale and goal were far more limited than Operation 'Blue', but the attempt to drive in a large and well-defended Soviet salient was beaten. It is instructive that the respective casualties of the two sides are still contested, as is the narrative and analysis of the campaign.[15]

Failure at Kursk resulted in a crisis in confidence within Germany, one to which the overthrow of Hitler's ally Mussolini, the Fascist dictator of Italy, and the heavy British bombing of Hamburg contributed greatly. In turn, the war helped lead the Germans to keep going, as the alternative of defeat, notably to the Soviets, appeared terrifying. Hitler was able to manipulate a toxic cocktail of fanaticism and terror.

As the war progressed, the Soviet army proved increasingly successful in attack, and adept at developing co-operation between armour, artillery and infantry, and at making the latter two mobile. Highly effective attacks were launched, notably in March and April 1944, when the Germans were driven back across the Rivers Bug, Dniester and Pruth and into the Balkans, and, in June-September that year, when, in Operation Bagration, Belarus was overrun and much of the German Army Group Centre, the major German force on the Eastern Front, destroyed by about 1.7 million Soviet troops.

Ultimately, by April 1945, in less than two-and-a-half years' fighting, the Red Army drove the Germans from the Volga to the Elbe. This was a distance greater than that achieved by any force in Europe for over a century, and one that showed that a war on fronts, across an enormous range and against bitter resistance, did not preclude one of the frequent movement of those fronts. This was not simply an advance on one axis, but one across much of Eastern Europe. Soviet operational art towards the end of the war stressed firepower, but also employed mobile tank warfare: attrition and manoeuvre were combined in a coordinated sequence of attacks. Once broken through, mobility and this sequence allowed the Soviets to prevent their opponents from falling back in order to establish a new front. In doing so, the Soviets benefited from the progressive deterioration of the German army, not least as its fighting quality was hit by heavy casualties. Moreover, the bulk of the German air force was employed on home defence against the devastating Anglo–American air assault on Germany.

Although the Red Army absorbed the bulk of the German forces, the latter also fought the Western Allies, principally Britain and (from December 1941) the USA. Unlike with Russia in 1917, the Germans, after their conquest of France in 1940, were unable to benefit from knocking out a major opponent militarily. Sequential conflict, of the type attempted by Napoleon in 1805–12, proved impossible. Just as Britain had posed a strategic dilemma for Napoleon, so Britain, unconquered, served as a base for air attack on German-dominated Europe, for diversionary operations in the Mediterranean and, eventually, for the full-scale invasion of Western Europe.

The Mediterranean campaign, which began when Italy and Britain went to war in June 1940, initially focused on North Africa (1940–3) and Greece (1941). From late 1942, when the Americans invaded French North Africa, the Mediterranean provided the British and Americans with crucial experience in amphibious operations. In 1943, after the Germans and Italians were defeated in Tunisia, the Allies invaded first Sicily and then mainland Italy, and the latter led to the overthrow of Mussolini. In response, German forces were committed to what became a new front in Italy. On the other hand, the Allied defeat of Italian and German forces in the Mediterranean involved a lengthy conflict and the commitment of considerable Allied resources in a secondary theatre.

Britain's ability to act as a base was dependent on the ability to win the Battle of the Atlantic. This involved keeping Atlantic sealines open against German attacks, principally from submarines, but also from surface raiders and from aircraft. The submarine assault was far more serious than that during the First World War because the German conquest of Norway and France in 1940 provided bases lacking in the earlier conflict. Moreover, Britain faced more of a naval struggle because it was also at war with Italy and Japan, from June 1940 and December 1941 respectively.

Conversely, the lack of air–sea co-operation weakened the German assault, as did the extent to which investment long focused on surface warships rather than submarines. The latter made major inroads into the British merchant marine, but America's entry into the war in December 1941 greatly increased the resources available for fighting the submarines as well as the size of the merchant marine. The Allies also benefited from developments in anti-submarine techniques, developments that more than kept pace with the challenge mounted. Aircraft were used to considerable effect and in 1943 Portugal made available its bases on the Azores, which closed the 'air gap' in the Atlantic. Further north, the deployment of aircraft to Iceland from 1940 was important: a Danish dependency, it was occupied by the British once Denmark was conquered by the Germans. Intelligence information was also significant, with the breaking of German codes helping locate submarines.

In contrast to the Germans, the United States mounted, against Japan, the most successful submarine campaign in history. Contingencies played a major role, not least Japan's lack of a focus on opposition to submarine attacks. Nevertheless, the contrast is instructive. The Allied success against German submarine attack reflected fighting quality, in the shape of acquiring and disseminating relevant skills, as well as beating Germany in an asymmetrical struggle of resources. As a result, it was possible not only to supply embattled Britain with food and raw materials, but also to build up forces there capable of invading Continental Europe as well as of sustaining a large-scale offensive.

On 6 June 1944, D-Day, in the largest amphibious operation in European history, Anglo–American forces successfully landed in Normandy in northern France. Superior Allied resources played a key role in this success, notably in air control and in overwhelming naval support, but so also did fighting quality. The Germans failed to stop the invasion at the water line, to mount successful counterattacks or to prevent the Allies from exploiting their landings.[16] Indeed, despite the difficulties of breaking out from the beachheads and later from Normandy, notably in the face of anti-tank guns, the Germans were outfought over the following three months.

The Allied breakout from Normandy was followed by a deep exploitation, much of it by American mechanized forces, which drove the Germans out of France and Belgium. The British advance, which was also impressive, involved a heavier use of artillery. However, their mobility reduced to positional warfare, the Allies were held near the German frontier.[17]

That December, the Allies were put under pressure by a German counter-attack, Operation Autumn Mist, in the Battle of the Bulge. The decision to attack the Americans reflected the political factors that dominated the prioritization that was central to strategy. Hitler moved the Fifth and Sixth Panzer armies, core units facing the Soviets, in order to attack the Americans, hoping that a surprise offensive would lead to their defeat and the collapse of their will. Although in part mounted by poorly trained and equipped scratch forces, the attack achieved some success, not least because the Germans, in contrast to when attacking in the Ardennes in 1940, deliberately waited for cloud cover that would thwart Allied aircraft. As a lesser repeat of the German spring offensive in 1918, the offensive was held and left the Germans with a more extensive defensive line and with fewer troops to defend it. The German resistance to the Soviet advance on Berlin, launched on 12–13 January 1945, was also much weakened.[18] In early 1945, the Anglo–American armies resumed the advance, fought their way to, and across, the Rhine and joined the Red Army, which had captured Berlin, in forcing unconditional surrender on the Germans.

The Germans had also been battered since 1943, and even more in late 1944 and early 1945, by an Anglo–American air offensive of hitherto unprecedented fury. This brought great destruction to the German economy, affecting the production of weaponry, while also leading to the diversion of German air strength to home defence. Despite the limited precision by high-flying aircraft dropping free-fall bombs, strategic bombing was crucial to the disruption of German communications and logistics, largely because it was eventually on such a massive scale, and because they could not be attacked by any other means. Attacks on communications seriously affected the rest of the German economy, limiting the transfer of resources and the process of integration that is so significant for manufacturing. The reliance of European industry on rail was far greater than today and that increased its vulnerability to attack, because rail systems lack the flexibility of their road counterparts, being less dense and therefore less able to switch routes. The relationships between economics, transport systems and logistics have always been significant in military history. The Allied emphasis switched from attempting precision attack, which proved difficult to execute given the technology of the period, onto area bombing, with its attendant goals of disrupting the war economy and destroying urban life in order to hit morale and the work force.

The effectiveness as well as the morality of bombing has been the subject of considerable debate. Moral issues were raised by George Bell, Bishop of Chichester, and by others; and have been pressed much more vigorously since. The most frequently cited instance is that of Dresden, a reference to the heavy casualties caused by the Anglo–American bombing of the city of Dresden on 13–14 February 1945. However, the general consensus at the time was that the bombing campaign was a deserved return for earlier German air attacks (as well as current rocket attacks by V–1s and V–2s), and also was likely to disrupt the German war effort and hit morale. As far as the latter was concerned, the hopes of interwar air power enthusiasts were not fully realized. During the war, most military leaders did not argue that bombing alone could win. Instead, it was generally accepted that bombing should be part of an integrated strategy. Nevertheless, it was claimed that area bombing would cause heavy casualties, which would affect civilian morale. This was certainly true of Italy in 1943. The extent to which civilian morale in Germany was broken is controversial, but it is possible that the impact of bombing on civilians has been underestimated by the habitual conclusion that the bombing did not end the war. There was more to German resilience than Hitler's determination, and the inability to stop the bombing encouraged a sense that defeat was likely, indeed was already occurring. Propaganda about the inability of Allied bombing to damage targets within Germany was discredited. Whether these benefits justified heavy civilian casualties, and also a high level of losses among Allied aircrews, is a question that has modern resonance given current sensitivity about civilian casualties, but, by 1944, total war was being pushed as precisely that, and was anyway being waged by Germany.

It is possible to debate alternative use of the resources devoted to air attack. However, there were serious practical and institutional restrictions to any reallocation of resources, as well as economic difficulties confronting the retooling of manufacturing. As a result, the feedback process of judging policy could not be expected to work even had information flows been more accurate and speedy, as is rarely the case in war.

In his New Year's address in 1945, Hitler assured his audience that 'like a Phoenix out of the ashes, the German Will has risen anew from the rubble of our cities ... and thousands of People's Assault battalions have been established'. However, German defeat in 1945 was total. Hitler committed suicide as Soviet forces fought their way into Berlin. The city had fallen before – to the Russians in 1760 and the French in 1806, but there had not been a struggle on this scale or with these consequences. Only once Germany was conquered, did the Soviet Union join in the war against Japan that had begun for Britain and the United States in December 1941. That war was brought to a close with the Americans dropping two atomic bombs on the cities of Hiroshima and Nagasaki in August 1945. Although not employed in Europe, the use of this terrifying new weapon constituted a major act in European military history and one with rapid consequences. In 1947, the British mapped the 'estimated effect of a shallow underwater burst atomic bomb on Portsmouth Harbour and ships present'. This map reflected the lessons learned by British observers at Operation Crossroads in 1946–7, when two atomic bomb tests (air and underwater detonations) and subsequent surveys of their effects were conducted by the United States at Bikini Atoll in the Pacific. The onset of the Cold War meant that the threat of Soviet nuclear attack became a major issue for British defence planning.

As with the First World War, the Second led to a large-scale mobilization of national resources, a massive extension of the powers of government and an attempt to regiment and direct society. Propaganda played a key role, not only with news but also with the arts, for example film and music. In Britain, historical war films, such as that of Shakespeare's play *Henry V* (1944), were seen as a way to stiffen public morale. The same was true for other combatants, as with the German film *Kolberg* (1945), which depicted a key turning point in 1762. In 1945, Goebbels gave Hitler a biography of Frederick the Great (r. 1740–86) in order to encourage the idea that fighting on resolutely would be rewarded with a sudden change in circumstances. In the Soviet Union, 'Socialist Realism' was emphasized as part of the control of the arts, but there was also a deliberate use of historical trophes of nationalism, notably in film.

At the same time, it is all-too-easy to present such a state-dominated account. The point of this propaganda rested on the very nature of the public–private partnership that has been a key theme of this book. For all combatants, there were major concerns about morale and resilience, and these encouraged attempts to gather intelligence, as well as to ensure that the 'Home Front' was kept supplied with food and opinion. This was certainly true of democracies and reflected a broader process of democratization there. In 1937, John Buchan, the Governor-General of Canada, who had played an important role in the successful British First World War propaganda effort, declared, in a speech to the Canadian Institute of International Affairs:

The day has gone when foreign policy can be the preserve of a group of officials at the Foreign Office, or a small social class, or a narrow clique of statesmen from whom the rest of the nation obediently takes its cue. The foreign policy of a democracy must be the cumulative views of individual citizens, and if these views are to be sound they must in turn be the consequence of a widely diffused knowledge.

Yet, totalitarian societies, including Germany and the Soviet Union, also had to be concerned about public opinion, and had to get their mechanisms of authority and power to work to that effect, which was a difficult task. The Gestapo responded with great concern to the public mood after the British firebombing of Hamburg in 1943.

Such firebombing was an aspect of the more general hardship created by this war. The attack on civilians was most brutally seen with the German genocidal mass murder of about six million European Jews in the Holocaust. The German slaughter of other civilians was also heavy, for example 120,000 Poles killed in Warsaw in 1944, in large part in suppressing the Warsaw Rising and in the related slaughter of civilians. The killing of civilians through bombing and other military acts did not compare in intention or action with German mass murder, but, nevertheless, was devastating. So also was the more general disruption through hunger, flight, violence, loss of homes and family separation. The German invasion of the Soviet Union proved particularly destructive. Left without food or shelter, Soviet prisoners of war died in very large numbers. Moreover, the German attacks had a major effect elsewhere. For example, about eight million French, Belgian and Dutch civilians fled in May–June 1940, when the Germans invaded. German aircraft machine-gunned refugee columns. This was the most dramatic of a wave of disruptions that included Allied bombings in 1942–4 which led to fresh civilian casualties and flight, although there was no such machine-gunning of fleeing civilians.[19] A similar trajectory was seen elsewhere.

The German surrender in 1945 might appear the obvious place to end a chapter on war in Europe in the first-half of the twentieth century, however, one of the valuable consequences of arbitrary chronological classifications, in this case that on the half-century, is that it leads to the inclusion of a number of conflicts in the second half of the 1940s. These were all on a very different level of scale to the Second World War, but also focus attention on a contrasting type of conflict. The role of counter-insurgency warfare was to the fore in the Greek Civil War, where, in part by deploying critical mass, the anti-Communist side prevailed,[20] and, more obscurely, in the Soviet suppression of anti-Communist forces in Eastern Europe, for example Poland, the Baltic Republics, Albania and Ukraine. In the case of the Greek Civil War, British and, later, American aid also played a role in the defeat of the Communists, as did eventual divisions in the Communist bloc.

As an instance of another conflict that has attracted insufficient attention, the successful opposition to Communist insurgents in Spain was a continuation of the Spanish Civil War (1936–9). A large number of Communists had taken shelter in France where many fought in the Resistance to German occupation. The Germans also slaughtered large numbers of Spanish refugees. In 1945, the fall of Hitler and Mussolini led to a widespread assumption that Franco would also be overthrown and, based in France, a Communist insurrection began in northern Spain. However, it failed. In part, this was because of the brutality of the governmental repression and in part to the extent to which part of northern Spain was very much an anti-Communist area. In addition, the insurgents' need for food led them to raid villages and thus to lose the prospect of local support. With food a key weapon, the government took pains to keep the amount of food in the region limited.

There was a degree of continuity between conflicts in the late 1940s with counter-insurgency warfare in the Second World War, most clearly with resistance to German occupation for example in Greece, Yugoslavia and Poland. However, the emphasis between types of conflict was very different between the two halves of the decade. This was because, despite particular tension over Berlin in 1948–9, the confrontation of conventional forces in the Cold War between the Communist and anti-Communist blocs did not lead to large-scale conflict. This point underlines the issues of judgement involved in deciding what to include in any study and how best to analyze wars. The situation in Europe in the late 1940s also prefigures the complexities of the Cold War, in particular its combination, on a global scale, of conventional confrontation with large-scale counter-insurgency warfare.

In the Berlin Crisis, the Soviets blockaded West Berlin, which was occupied by American, British and French forces, whereas East Berlin and East Germany comprised the Soviet occupation zone. West Berlin was an enclave within East Germany. This blockade was met by an Anglo–American airlift, an impressive display of air power, including during a bitter winter: 278,228 flights, the majority American, supplied 2.3 million tons of supplies, enabling West Berlin to survive the crisis. Air deliveries became greater in scale than pre-airlift rail deliveries. The Soviets harassed the aircraft, for example firing flak nearby, but did not try to shoot them down and there was no fighting. The American airlift was organized from the massive Rhein-Main Air Base, just south of Frankfurt. This, America's leading air transport terminal in Europe, was of key significance for the American presence in West Germany. As a result, the roads focusing on Frankfurt were rapidly repaired and improved. This was an instance of the important local impact and infrastructure of the Cold War.

The Berlin Crisis helped lead to the formation in 1949 of NATO, the North Atlantic Treaty Organization, an anti-Communist military bloc that included much of Western Europe. Whereas in 1945–8, culminating with Czechoslovakia in 1948, Communist parties with Soviet support had taken over all of Eastern Europe, bar Greece and (neutral) Finland, there was a determination to prevent any further westward movement. Moreover, American aircraft capable of dropping atomic bombs, alongside bomb components, were deployed in Britain from 1950. The Cold War was now to the fore.

CHAPTER SEVEN

The Erosion of the
Nation-Army, 1950–2000

This half-century was at once a unit, one easily spanned by the experience of many individuals, and yet also a study in stark contrasts. In 1950, Europe was harshly divided into two bitterly opposed camps, and large-scale war between them appeared a ready prospect, one likely to lead to, or be linked with, a Third World War. That the First had been followed by a Second appeared to create a sequence. Moreover, the swift deterioration in international relations from 1945 between the major powers, a deterioration not matched after 1918, seemed to make this more probable.

In 2000, on the other hand, the idea of a major war within Europe appeared extremely unlikely. The settlement of the Kosovo crisis of 1999, with only limited hostilities, and without the intervention of Serbia's patron, a now weakened Russia, appeared to highlight the more general situation. Unlike in 1914, the Balkan crisis had not led to a wider war. Moreover, by 1999, much of the young male civilian population had had little or no experience of military service, and certainly of wartime service.

The transformation was highly significant, as was the process of change; but the contours of this transformation can be presented in very different ways. An emphasis of a task-based, politically driven account would see not only the military but also society as responsive to the needs and implications of these tasks. While that approach has merit, it is also necessary to give due weight to the autonomy of the social sphere and to link it to cultural as well as political developments.

In contrast, it is possible to offer an interesting perspective, one that is chronologically and politically broader than the idea of a 1960s-based reaction against military themes. That idea is indeed valid, as well as important, but it does not provide a full account, and, in particular, one that encompasses an understanding of the relevant political dynamics. Instead, it is possible to see a reaction throughout the period, one continuing from the Second World War, instead of just starting in the 1960s. This was a reaction to the earlier period of total war. This reaction was in the shape of an attempt to strengthen civilian control over the military; or, to vary the perspective, an attempt to build on the earlier process of the total mobilization of society in order to ensure such control. Stalin and Hitler built up their militaries, but also sought to impose control on them. Hitler, indeed, had far more control over his generals than Wilhelm II had done. In Britain, moreover, the military was more under effective governmental control in the Second World War than it had been in the First.

Both Western democratic systems and their Communist counterparts were suspicious of the military. Each maintained heavy investment in the armed forces in order to pursue the Cold War that lasted from 1946 to 1989. However, the emphasis was on a comprehensively armed confrontation between the Communist and capitalist blocs that, alongside the proximity to war, remained under civilian control. At the same time, the willingness on both sides to plan and prepare to use nuclear weaponry as part of an active defence[1] scarcely matched popular wishes. This point opens up the possibility of seeing government and the military as nodal areas and political abstractions within a more complex political system that involved overlap and co-operation as much as difference and disagreement. In part, military history then becomes the playing out of this situation, a playing out that changed, as well as reflected, norms.

At the level of international organization, the pattern within individual armies was matched by the civilian control of the competing military blocs: NATO for the West, established in 1949, and the rival Warsaw Pact for the Communist states founded in 1955. These alliances reflected the role of non-European powers (if the Soviet Union is seen as at least partly non-European), or at least of one non-European power (the USA) in European military affairs. The alliances also indicated the significance of control over Central Europe to the major world powers. This represented a continuation from the age of European dominance in the nineteenth century, and one that contrasted very much with the situation in the late fifteenth when the Mediterranean had been more important.

NATO led to a large-scale American military commitment to Western Europe. Aside from army and naval units, a network of air bases to support American aircraft was a crucial component and much NATO infrastructure expenditure was spent on developing them. The role of air bases in the Azores helped explain why, although not a democracy, Portugal was a founding member of NATO. The 1951 defence agreement with Iceland, a NATO member, ensured that the United States could use the base at Keflarik, which it, in turn, paid to develop. In 1953, the United States and Spain signed an agreement giving the Americans rights to establish air bases, although Spain, a Fascist dictatorship, was not invited to join NATO. These and British air bases were crucial both to the resupply of American forces in NATO, and in providing strategic depth in the event of a Soviet advance into Western Europe overrunning much territory, as was feared would occur.

Within Europe, the nation-under-arms was seen not only as an expression of citizenship and national identity; but also, in part, as a means to ensure civilian control which helps explain a tension with some military leaders. Thus, in Italy and West Germany, on the pattern of the earlier arguments of the French Third Republic (1870–1940), conscription was presented not only as militarily necessary (in this case in the Cold War), but also as a way to contain the consequences that might flow from a professional military and, more specifically, an authoritarian and anti-democratic officer corps. Karl Marx's warning about 'Bonarpartism' on the part of military leaders had a counterpart in anxieties in the West. However, these anxieties are underplayed because military efforts in France and Italy to act against government, notably in France over the Algerian question, did not lead to their overthrow. This again serves as a reminder that what did not happen is very important in military history. In 1961, in the face of the threat that a generals' putsch in Algiers, France's foremost colony, would spread to France, the French government deployed tanks to protect the National Assembly. Control was maintained.

Concern in other areas was encouraged by the role of the military in the authoritarian right-wing dictatorships in Portugal and Spain, and also because the Greek military successfully mounted a coup in 1967. In turn, the trajectories of these regimes reflected the role of force, but also its complex interplay with politics. In Portugal, an authoritarian government was overthrown by a coup in 1974 by the Armed Forces Movement, a largely left-wing movement opposed to continued warfare in defence of Portugal's colonial position in Africa. Attempts by the Communists to take this government in an increasingly radical direction, however, failed as the Communists lacked sufficient support within the army. This led to the failure of an attempted coup in 1975. Instead, in 1976, the army handed over power to civilian politicians and thereafter remained essentially outside politics, which, itself, was an important aspect of the political situation.

In Greece, the right-wing military junta sought in 1974 to strengthen its wavering domestic popularity by backing the long-standing demand for *enosis*, union with Cyprus. The latter was an independent state with a Greek-speaking Christian majority, but where the Turkish Muslim minority was protected by the Turkish Cypriot role in the governing 'partnership' arrangement. This issue brought nationalism and military politics into concern. In 1974, with Greek backing, this Cypriot government was overthrown and replaced by another that was designed to implement *enosis*, a Greek variant on Hitler's *Anschluss* with Austria in 1938. Moreover, the 'ethnic cleansing' of Turks was begun by the Greeks, as an attempt to create a fundamental change. However, a rapid military response by Turkey – an invasion of much of the island that was accepted by the USA – led to the humiliation of the far weaker Greek junta. Its authority gone, the junta handed over power in Greece to democratic politicians. Thereafter, on the Portuguese pattern, the military remained outside politics. Cyprus stayed divided and about 165,000 Greek Cypriots were driven from the Turkish zone. Established by force, this verdict continues to dictate life in Cyprus. In part, this matched the compulsory population transfers between Greece and Turkey in 1923. In that respect, nationalism, religion and ethnicity have proved longer barriers than the politics that divided Germany during the Cold War, when West Germany was the state created out of the American, British and French occupation zones and East Germany that from the Soviet zone.

In Spain, the authoritarian Franco regime had continued in power after victory in the Civil War of 1936–9, using considerable brutality in the immediate postwar years in order to impose control and overcome guerrilla opposition. In 1975, Franco died and the transition to democracy, accompanied by the return of monarchy, was relatively orderly. Despite concerns, there was no military coup, and democracy was established, with the first elections since 1936 held in 1977. However, paranoid anxieties on the far right, as well as a response, drawing on a genuine hatred of democracy and on nostalgia for old ways, to the destruction of the old, Francoist order, led to an attempted coup on 23 February 1981. As an instance of 'might-have-beens', this was a significant moment in European military history. Colonel Tejero of the Civil Guard took over the *Cortes* (parliament), while General Milans del Bosch, the head of the Valencia military region, called a state of emergency and pressed King Juan Carlos to establish a military government. This was very much a make-or-break moment for democratic Spain. Juan Carlos acted promptly and clearly, using television, an instructive counter to the immediate reach of the military, to broadcast his affirmation of the constitution and democratic rule. His stance ensured that most of the army did not support the coup, which then collapsed. The political dynamic of the occasion required a degree of affirmation which the military did not receive.

This failure helped to break the logjam of the Spanish past. The divided army was now weaker, and the military budget was reduced. The army became increasingly professionalized. Membership of NATO from 1982 meant that officers' horizons shifted hugely, so that combatting 'the enemy within' no longer became its primary purpose. This change was a key aspect of a more long-term departure in Spain from the alignments and issues of the past. The attempted coup and the transformation of the military indicated the central significance of military developments for broader patterns of social and political history, and notably for episodes in the latter.

The militaries of Eastern Europe remained under the control of its Communist governments. The latter did not find it necessary to purge their leadership comprehensively, as Stalin had done in the Soviet Union in 1937. Instead, these militaries were used to suppress political tendencies that were judged unwelcome. Reformist Communist movements were forcibly overthrown in Hungary in 1956 and in Czechoslovakia in 1968. These were the largest operational use of military forces in Europe in the second half of the century. In each case, there was a major deployment of Soviet forces.

The determined use of armour, backed up by air attack helicopters, crushed popular opposition in Hungary in 1956. Petrol bombs proved an inadequate response from the outnumbered resistance. NATO forces did not intervene, in large part because of the danger of setting off a full-scale war that would have involved the use of hydrogen bombs, the even more potent development from atomic bombs. In hydrogen bombs, a nuclear detonator heated hydrogen isotopes sufficiently to fuse them into helium atoms, releasing an enormous amount of destructive energy. In 1955, President Eisenhower of America had referred to the danger, as a result of a thermonuclear conflict, of the end of human life in the Northern Hemisphere. In addition, there was no NATO border with Hungary, while British and French forces were committed to conflict with Egypt in the Suez Crisis. The key response in 1956 was the American one, which demonstrated the role of political decisions made outside Europe. Once control was reimposed, the implicit role of the Soviet military remained important to the security of the new system.

In turn, in 1968, about 250,000 Soviet troops, supported by Bulgarian, Hungarian, Polish and East German contingents, invaded Czechoslovakia. The invasion benefited from the airlift of troops into Prague. Heavily outnumbered, fearful of the consequences for the people and without any prospect of Western support, the Czech government did not offer armed resistance, and the invasion was far less violent than that of 1956. Non-violent protest, such as demonstrating in front of tanks, did not preserve Czech independence. The invasion, however, was not accompanied by the summary executions seen in Hungary in 1956.

Meanwhile, the Warsaw Pact more generally acted to consolidate the Communist bloc and to underline Soviet dominance of it. Soviet weaponry, commanders, doctrine and training were crucial for the militaries of other Warsaw Pact states. For example, between 1946 and 1990, Bulgaria received almost $16.7 billion worth of military and defence industrial assistance from the Soviet Union.[2] However, Romania demonstrated increasing independence, notably by refusing to take part in the invasion of Czechoslovakia in 1968.

The integration of Warsaw Pact economies was most pronounced in the manufacture of weaponry and the resulting military–industrial complex acted to create a more general integration. Co-operation within the Warsaw Pact was crucial to the economic integration within the Soviet bloc. International co-operation was essentially a military project, and one involving dominance but also continual negotiation. As so often, lesser powers helped direct, or at least affect, the attitudes and actions of stronger allies. The Soviet Union tolerated openings towards the West, notably by Hungary, and occasionally exploited them to its benefit. However, the Soviets also sometimes called a halt to these openings. Although signs of hegemonic co-operation based on mutual interests began around 1960, the Soviet imperial outlook remained predominant all the way until the end of the Soviet bloc in 1989. The Soviets compelled the Eastern bloc states to participate in three massive armaments programmes in 1951, 1961 and 1976, providing them with credit for the purchase of arms if necessary. Parts and components that Hungarian companies needed to assemble and manufacture constituted an increasingly large proportion of Hungary's imports of military equipment. Thus, the military dynamics of debt emerged alongside the fiscal and economic character of a heavily militarized alliance system.[3]

There were signs of greater economic autonomy in the Warsaw Pact from the 1970s. Both East–West détente in the mid-1970s and the avail-ability, thereafter, of large-scale Western, especially West German, loans, notably to East Germany, Poland, Hungary and Romania, encouraged this process. However, the Soviet-dominated military system and its related economic and social dimensions, which included conscription, acted to create a significant measure of coherence.

In a very different context to Czechoslovakia in 1968, Britain deployed troops from 1969 in order to thwart separatism in Northern Ireland. This deployment was successful, with troops, in Operation Motorman, in 1972 moving into 'no-go areas' of Londonderry and Belfast, hitherto controlled by the Provisional IRA, a violent radical Marxist separatist group based in the Catholic community. This operation led the IRA to follow the course of terrorism, rather than that of waging guerrilla warfare, and terrorism proved far more difficult to overcome. The British made extensive use of helicopters to supply fortified posts, as roads were vulnerable to mines, and employed intelligence-gathering in order to strike at terrorists and to thwart their operations; but there was a limit to what could be achieved. At the same time, the terrorists were unable to drive the army out of Northern Ireland. The situation was complicated when Protestant 'loyalist' movements developed that, in turn, were committed to sectarian violence. As the Provisional IRA struck at the Unionist Protestant community, as well as the British military, while the 'loyalists' attacked Catholics, the situation drifted from crisis towards chaos. The attritional character of terrorism and counter-terrorist operations was apparent, but the British army contained the situation sufficiently to allow negotiations that produced a peace settlement in 1998. Terrorism had clearly failed by then. The lack of foreign-armed intervention was a significant factor, although the terrorists benefited from the supply of arms and money from Libya and from American sympathizers.

Although it remained the dominant model during the Cold War, the nation-under-arms, or the nation-army, became less prominent as an attractive thesis to important strands of opinion. The anti-authoritarianism of the 1960s helped weaken the appeal of this thesis in Western Europe, as did the example of the American abandonment of conscription. In Eastern Europe, the fall of the Communist system in 1989–91 brought to the fore an already widely held disenchantment with conscription and the brutality it frequently entailed, notably with violent, often murderous, bullying.

The declining popularity of conscription provided political and social space for a contrary emphasis on the professionalism of long-service regular forces. This emphasis also reflected technological change in the shape of the more complex weaponry that the military now had to operate. Many conscripts lacked the aptitude for training to operate these systems. The heavy costs of equipping, housing, feeding and training large numbers of conscripts were also a factor. There were distinctive military aspects, but the move against conscription was also an aspect of a more general abandonment of low-skill occupations as labour forces became more differentiated and with a far greater emphasis on skill and training. In contrast, numbers and physical strength became less significant. There was also the perceived need to engage in long-range and long-term expeditionary warfare, a warfare for which conscripts appeared inappropriate. The extended build-up of United Nations coalition forces, including British and French units, before the Gulf War attack on Iraq was launched in 1991, demonstrated both these characteristics. Thus, the requirements from forces in expeditionary warfare were very different to the crucial home-defence component of the Cold War military, and particularly the NATO states and the neutral powers.

The increased emphasis on advanced military technology stemming from expeditionary warfare further enhanced the American position in weapons procurement. This element had been to the fore during the Cold War and notably with air power. Under the Mutual Defence Assistance Program, the USA provided aircraft on generous terms to allies such as Denmark and the Netherlands, and this helped bind NATO around American weapons and systems. So also did the concept of interoperability. At the same time, a European arms industry survived. This industry was particularly important for the production of the basic weaponry necessary for the large conscript armies, and notably for handheld firearms. There was also European production of advanced weaponry. Britain, France and Sweden manufactured cutting-edge fighters, and Britain, Germany and Sweden state-of-the-art tanks. The profitability of this production owed much to foreign sales and, in particular, the ability to benefit from the increased wealth of oil economies. Thus, Britain sold Tornados to Saudi Arabia as part of a major package that helped bring prosperity to the arms industry, notably BAE Systems.

However, the potential of profit was affected by competition from non-European producers, and to a far greater extent than prior to the Second World War. In particular, the desirability of attracting American diplomatic support repeatedly led to orders being placed with American companies. So also did the degree to which the Americans were at the technological cutting-edge, as was seen with the role of America's electronics industry in the weaponry and systems that were discussed in the 1990s in terms of a 'revolution in military affairs'.

Attempts to create a viable rival European defence industry met repeated problems, both political and industrial. Procurement and production were overly affected by political considerations, notably locating investment to meet particular national, regional and political needs. This led to a pattern of sub-optimal production. The European Commission has now followed NATO in trying to shape European defence markets, but this has not proved successful. Conversely, the situation might have been more dire but for these efforts. The EU (European Union) had certainly had some success in passing, although not always enforcing, regulations, for example for the competitive retendering of parts of a prime contractors' supply chain. This was intended to improve the efficiency of the defence industrial supply chains as well as to harmonize the European defence market. However, protectionism was a major constraint as was a concern to maintain the integrity of supply chains in the event of other governments disapproving of policy, as with the 2003 Gulf War. The British were worried about a reliance on Belgium for ammunition.

The dependence of the military on the private sector was repeatedly demonstrated in procurement, most obviously in electronics. The computer capacity offered by the military was regularly surpassed by what was available to individual purchasers through private-sector technology companies. At the same time, the independence of the private sector was demonstrated with the pressures on government created by industrial consolidation as well as the related emergence of global giants and the need for privatization in order to attract liquidity. Thus, developments at the national level are very much located within international pressures.

The last stages of the Cold War had seen no willingness to employ the large forces available, alongside a paradoxical determination to keep them ready for conflict. International relations appeared to stabilize in the mid-1970s as aspects of a process of détente. American–Soviet strategic arms limitation talks led to agreements in 1974 and 1976, while the Helsinki treaty of 1975 recognized the position and interests of the Eastern bloc. West Germany's *Ostpolitik* normalized its relations with Communist countries and led to the recognition of the East German border with Poland, thus abandoning ideas of German revanchism. The engagement with the Communist bloc provided by loans and trade further diminished tension, and notably for West Germany.

However, Cold War tension revived in the early 1980s, and for a variety of reasons. The Soviet invasion of Afghanistan at the close of 1979, which was a key issue for the United States and Britain, was less contentious in Western Europe than the deployment of new missiles by the Soviet Union and the United States. In West Germany, there was widespread popular opposition to the deployment of American cruise and Pershing II missiles in order to provide enhanced short and intermediate-range defences against Soviet attack. This deployment was a response to that of the mobile SS–20 by the Soviet Union, but this, in turn, increased Soviet anxieties about being attacked. In 1983, fearing an attack by NATO that was not in fact planned, the Soviet leadership considered launching a pre-emptive invasion of Western Europe. The Soviets developed bacteriological weapons for use in such an attack, although much of their military lacked any cutting-edge capability.

In the 1980s, the Western forces sought to prepare themselves for a successful non-nuclear war, even while they also readied for its nuclear counterpart. In particular, the doctrine of AirLand Battle proposed a synchronization of air and land forces in order to provide an effective mobile counter to any Soviet attack and to the Soviet concept of Deep Battle. Western forces sought to enhance their mobility and to move away from doctrine, deployment and training focused on a static defence of Western Europe.

In the event, there was no international conflict in the early 1980s and, from 1985, the new Soviet leader, Mikhail Gorbachev, sought to reduce international tensions. In 1987, he and the American President Ronald Reagan settled the issue of intermediate-range nuclear missiles, a key cause of rising tension. The Intermediate-range Nuclear Forces Treaty prohibited ground-launched ballistic and cruise missiles with ranges of between 500 and 5,500 kilometres.

Moreover, issues within the Soviet bloc were handled very differently to Hungary in 1956 and Czechoslovakia in 1968. In 1980–1, it was decided in Moscow not to send Soviet forces to Poland to prevent a probable democratic takeover by the Solidarity movement, a popular mass movement based initially on the rejection by workers of Communism, supposedly a workers' movement. Instead, the Polish army was used for the task in December 1981, and it was handled in a less violent fashion than 1968, let alone 1956. Martial law was declared, a military council was appointed to govern Poland, thousands were detained without trail and scores were killed; but, crucially, there was no Soviet invasion and no organized Polish resistance. The Soviet Defence Minister, Dmitriy Ustinov, supported Soviet military intervention. Solidarity's actions, including strikes, challenged the geopolitical logic of the Warsaw bloc, notably the rail links between the Soviet Union and its forces in East Germany. However, in the increasingly comatose last period of the era of the leadership of the Party by Leonid Brezhnev (1964–82), Ustinov's Politburo colleagues were reluctant to send in the army, and the Soviet Union was warned not to by President Reagan. In addition, Poland was probably too big to invade easily. There was also anxiety that the Poles would fight, unlike the Czechs in 1968, and concern about the effect that an invasion of Poland would have on Soviet troops, especially on the morale of men from neighbouring western Ukraine and Belarus.

It was always dangerous to see an event as a clear choice, let alone a pattern. Instead, there is the need to locate each episode in its context. Nevertheless, 1980–1 suggests a major shift against the use of force amongst the Soviet leadership, and certainly as compared to its use in Czechoslovakia in 1968. This change appears even more the case in light of the unwillingness of the divided Communist leadership to use large-scale force to prevent the overthrow of Communist regimes in Eastern Europe in 1989.

This was the case in 1989 in all countries bar Romania. In December there, a full-scale anti-Communist revolt in Timişoara, a city with a large ethnic Hungarian population, led the government to send in tanks, which fired on the demonstrators, as well as to deploy factory workers armed with clubs. However, in the face of a crowd of over 100,000 people, the army there changed sides. On 21 December, in the capital, Bucharest, a popular demonstration in the face of an address by the dictator, Nicolae Ceauşescu, was crushed by the gunfire and armoured cars of the Securitate, the Romanian Secret Police, who also used tanks to smash through hastily erected barricades and to crush demonstrators. Over 1,000 were killed. However, the following day, renewed demonstrations led Ceauşescu to flee. The army eventually acted in support of the public agitation, providing force sufficient to overawe the Securitate and to overthrow the regime. Ceauşescu was detained, tried and killed by the army. In East Germany, the police used water cannon and batons, while the protestors responded with Molotov cocktails and stones, but no one was killed.

In the Soviet Union, in 1990–1, force was employed to try to maintain the cohesion of the federal state. There was small-scale action against nation-alists in Georgia (1989), Azerbaijan (1990), Lithuania (1991) and Latvia (1991), and this action led to some killing, for example nineteen protestors in Georgia. These steps, however, were small-scale and did not intimidate the nationalists. In Russia, in August 1991, there was an attempted coup in Moscow, designed to overthrow the reform movement and to restore Communist control. The coup, which was responsible for the death of three people, failed to gain traction in the face of large-scale, hostile public demonstrations in Moscow. Its failure led to the rapid overthrow of the Soviet Union, which no longer appeared to have any political logic.

The first post-Communist government of Russia was led by Boris Yeltsin, President from 1991 to 1999. He had led the opposition to the attempted coup in 1991. A far greater effort than that seen to preserve the Soviet Union was made to resist Islamic independence movements in the part of the northern Caucasus that remained under Russian rule. The Russians responded by invading the rebellious region of Chechnya in December 1994. They captured the capital, Grozny, in 1995, after a lengthy siege in which they employed devastating firepower. The heavy damage produced by artillery and airstrikes in a built-up area indicated a lack of serious concern about civilian casualties as well as limited preparedness for anything other than operations of this type. Thereafter, success in crushing resistance proved elusive and, in 1996, the Russians withdrew under a peace agreement. The 1994–6 campaigns revealed the deficiencies of the badly led, ill-equipped, undertrained, poorly motivated and below-strength Russian forces. Under Yeltsin, there was a marked lack of expenditure on the Russian military, which was not protected from the economic meltdown of the period. Equipment was not maintained while there was very little training and operational effectiveness decreased. However, a renewed Russian attack in 1999–2000 led to the fall of Grozny.

There was a similar lack of expenditure in other Eastern European states, as adverse economic and fiscal circumstances caused successive crises, while the military was neglected and its morale collapsed, hitting recruitment. Training was neglected, as was procurement while corruption, bullying, alcoholism and drug-abuse became more common. In Bulgaria, the defence budget was cut from $550 million in 1990 to $230 million in 1994.[4]

Meanwhile, a major and sustained effort was made to maintain the cohesion of Yugoslavia, a federal republic under Communist control since the Second World War: Serb control, not Communism, was the issue. In 1992, having failed to coerce distant Slovenia into remaining in Yugoslavia, the Serbs tried to prevent neighbouring Croatia from gaining independence, and this war spilled over into Bosnia. Western settlements were eventually imposed, in Bosnia in 1995 and in Kosovo in 1999, at the expense of the expansionism and ethnic aggression of a Serbian regime that had unsuccessfully looked for Russian sponsorship. The brutal slaughter of civilians by the Serbs, and, to a lesser extent, by their opponents, reflected the extent to which ethnic groups were seen as the units of political strength, and thus as targets. The civil war in Bosnia led to attempts at international peacemaking including, in 1993, the creation of a UN no-fly zone. However, the Bosnian Serbs, the major cause of destabilizing aggression, violated the no-fly zone. Moreover, in 1995, the Bosnian Serbs murdered about 7,000 unarmed Muslim males in the town of Srebrenica. Air strikes, heavily restricted by political considerations, failed to stop the fall of Srebenica nor, indeed, to affect Serb conduct.

Subsequently, the Bosnian Serbs accepted a settlement in part due to NATO air attack and diplomatic pressure, but American-supported ground military action by the Croats and Bosnian Muslims was possibly more or as significant. They acted as de facto ground forces to NATO's campaign while conversely NATO supplied air power to indigenous ground forces. NATO action was heavily dependent on the United States, although with other NATO powers involved, including Britain, the Netherlands and Turkey. Italian air bases on the other side of the Adriatic were crucial. NATO forces were well-prepared and, apart from France, moved smoothly into a combined campaign. Coalition activities encouraged a greater degree of interoperability as well as the standardization of operating procedures. However, there were serious problems in agreeing targeting criteria. A lack of political support for wide-ranging bombing meant that NATO ran out of agreed targets to hit, although this was not known by the Serbs. Air attacks were intended to destroy Bosnian Serb military offensive capability and began with the destruction of their air defence system. The bombing then switched to what was intended as a calibrated means to bring the Bosnian

Serbs to the negotiating table. In hitting the communications of the Bosnian Serb army, the air attack lessened its mobility and command and control capability and denied it air support. The Croatian army's 1995 Operation Thunder, in which it destroyed the Serb insurgency in Croatia was along similar lines: NATO took out Serb air defences and the Croats overran Serb ground defences.

Faced subsequently by separatist pressure in the autonomous region of Kosovo from its majority Albanian population, the Serbs used the same brutal tactics as in Bosnia. The NATO response, an air campaign in 1999, took far longer to achieve its goals than had been anticipated, publically and privately, and caused far less damage to the Serb military than was claimed. Serbian resolve was underestimated. In part, the Serbs made effective use of camouflage, while the restrictions on targeting again greatly affected NATO air attacks. The weather had a severe impact on NATO air operations, a large number of which were, as a result, cancelled or affected. Laser-guided weapons require largely cloud-free skies in order to lock-on, and thus work. Weather remained a highly important factor in air operations, one overlooked in much of the technological triumphalism offered by commentators. Supposedly all-weather aircraft proved, in practice, to have more limited capability.

Moreover, although the Serbian high- and medium-altitude anti-aircraft systems proved ineffective, the shoulder-fired missiles of Serbia's M–NPAD (Man-Portable Air Defence Systems) affected NATO's willingness to mount low-altitude flights, and thus to be effective in ground attack. Instead, the Serb withdrawal from Kosovo, in 1999, appears to have owed much more to a conviction that a NATO land attack was imminent, as well as to the withdrawal of Russian support. At the same time, the bombing of Serbia hit the economic interests of the political élite, encouraging pressure for a political settlement. Aside from frequent attacks on war industries and logistics, there was a focus on oil refining and storage, and electricity generation and transformation, as well as on bridges. The cityscape of Belgrade continues to show the significant damage caused by bombs and cruise missiles, notably with the destruction of government buildings. Fear of future losses as the weather improved in summer may have been a factor in affecting Serbian attitudes in 1999. The United States provided the foremost contribution in 1999, and France the second. Other NATO powers that took part included Britain, Denmark and the Netherlands. Italian air bases were crucial while Britain and France each deployed a carrier.

The air offensive had not immediately prevented the large-scale expulsion of Kosovars from their home. Indeed, the brutal Serbian 'ethnic cleansing' campaign, Operation Horseshoe, increased as the air attack was mounted, with the Serbs freed from restraint and raising the size of their force in Kosovo. The crisis suggested that air power, as so often, would be most effective as part of a joint strategy, instead of as a strategic tool alone. Rather than thinking in terms of binary divides, ground and air threats were not totally separate as the possibility of a ground invasion encouraged a concentration of defending forces that made them more vulnerable to air attack. However, the Kosovo crisis underlined the difficulties of assessing military effectiveness and impact, and, thus, capability.

The Kosovo crisis, the last major stage of the Yugoslav breakup, demonstrated the ultimate reliance of European developments in the twentieth century on the use or non-use of force. This was true of the international system, of changes within states and of social transformations. The varied end of the Cold War encapsulated this reliance, as did the earlier course, and end, of totalitarian rule in Greece, Portugal and Spain. The role of NATO in the defence of Western Europe was also part of the equation: it provided the security for the economic growth, social transformation and political development that followed 1949, as well as the military context for the end of the Cold War and for the subsequent international transformation of Europe in the 1990s. This security owed much to the American nuclear umbrella, which was anchored by NATO, as well as to the presence of substantial American land, sea and air forces in Western Europe.

To leave force out of the account of post-1945 European history, or to treat it as marginal, is seriously mistaken. It is, for example, curious to read accounts of Europe in the 1960s that mention the social changes of the period and, more particularly, the pronounced current of radicalism towards its close, but that underplay the role of force, whether the coup in Greece, the intervention in Czechoslovakia or the large-scale confrontation between East and West, one that included a serious crisis in 1961 as the Soviet Union sought to exploit Western vulnerability over Berlin by erecting the Berlin Wall.

Moreover, this confrontation played a major role in the strategic situation elsewhere. A key reason why President Lyndon Johnson of the United States sought to fight a limited war in Vietnam was that he was concerned that an escalation in hostilities there would lead to a riposte in the shape of a Soviet attack on Western Europe. A similar strategic equation had been a play during the Korean War in 1950–3. Moreover, this equation affected the naval dimension. The focus of American naval power in the 1960s in support of the commitment to Vietnam meant that the American navy in the Mediterranean was greatly challenged by the build-up of Soviet naval forces there. This captures the limitation of trying to separate out European military history, as the build-up was designed to affect the power politics of the Middle East, which became particularly acute from 1967, but also was important to the security of Europe's 'southern flank'. An awareness of Western Europe's vulnerability in the face of massive Soviet conventional superiority posed major problems for NATO and for the United States.

The presence of nuclear weaponry east and west of the Iron Curtain ensured, moreover, that, for the first time, the capacity to destroy life in Europe was part of its military history. At the peak in 1986, the Soviet Union had 40,159 operational nuclear arms, the USA 23,317, France 355,

Britain 350, China 224, Israel 44 and South Africa 1. Full-scale nuclear war would have been a true apocalypse, one that was different to the apocalyptic fears of the fifteenth and sixteenth centuries, but similarly traumatic. This presence helped encourage the pressure for civilian control of the military and, even more, of international relations.

At the same time, it is unclear that nuclear armaments determined the course of the military history of the period. It is possible to argue that the threat posed by their use acted as a deterrent to action, and thus ensured that there was no move to war, unlike in 1914 and 1939–41. This avoidance of conflict then becomes an important aspect of the military history of the period; indeed can be presented as making large-scale war obsolescent. Moreover, given the consequences of the use of atomic weaponry, this avoidance was crucial to the history of the species. The threat from nuclear arms certainly helped elide the contrast between vulnerable armed forces and a less vulnerable society, a contrast that had already been greatly lessened by bombing in the Second World War. In addition, this threat contributed to the politicization of war in terms of hostile public responses. Public pressure from the late 1950s for nuclear disarmament was an aspect of the hostility to military identities and themes that was an important aspect of the counterculture and of anti-Americanism. These gathered pace from the late 1960s, in part encouraged by the hostile response to the Vietnam War. In a new form, this response encapsulated Europe's interaction with wider developments and military trends.

An alternative analysis is offered if it is argued that the avoidance of war during the Cold War reflected a range of factors, and not simply, or even necessarily primarily, the nuclear deterrent. Indeed, displacing the latter from a central causal role represents a questioning not only of the key role of technology, but also of the particular state-controlled arms industry that produced these specialized weapons. A host of issues are involved in this avoidance of war, including the possible viability of a non-nuclear conflict between the major blocs. Such a war was part of the range of possibilities. At any rate, the collapse of the Communist bloc and Soviet Union without the use of such weapons, or, indeed, war, suggested that they were not necessarily a central element in modern history.

The 1990s, therefore, left the legacy of the second half of the century still more complex. For example, alongside the conflicts in Bosnia, Croatia, Kosovo and Serbia in that decade, the second half of the twentieth century saw weaponry of unprecedented lethality deployed in Europe and to target in. In particular, the hydrogen bombs developed in the 1950s were far more destructive than their atomic predecessors. Moreover, the deployment of missiles with nuclear warheads ensured a range, speed and certainty of delivery totally lacking in the case of bombers. Changes in technological capability were to continue, not least in an action–reaction cycle. For example, stealth technology enabled aircraft to circumvent radar detection. Such aircraft were in use in combat in Europe from the 1990s. So also with cruise missiles. However, the military interventions in former Yugoslavia in the 1990s were atypical in that the conflicts of the half-century in Europe generally did not permit a testing of the latest technology. That, however, meant that it was, and remains, very difficult to determine how far new technology should be seen as a cutting-edge dynamic in military development or, instead, whether the emphasis, rather, should be on technology as a means to an end, and, moreover, as a means that did not alter fundamental issues focused on the relationships between war and political, social and economic contexts.

While military themes played a declining role in the culture of Western Europe in the second half of the twentieth century, and, notably in its closing decades, they were revived in Eastern Europe after the end of the Cold War as the states of the period struggled in the 1990s to offer a new nationalism. In post-Communist Russia, the Second World War served as the focal point for Russian patriotism and martial sentiment. Indeed, in 2014–15, the government was repeatedly to invoke the memory of the 'Great Patriotic War' in order to justify the Russian annexation of Crimea and to defend the actions of pro-Russian separatists in east Ukraine. Victory Day, celebrated on 9 May, became Russia's most important non-religious holiday in the post-Communist era. At the same time, in Eastern Europe, there was a tendency to define an acceptable nationalist military past in terms of opposition to Russia. Thus, in the Baltic Republics, those who had fought Russia were, to a degree, rehabilitated whether or not they had aligned with Nazi Germany. In Poland and Hungary, it became possible to emphasize past conflict with Russia. Moreover, this was related to political preferences. The fall of the Warsaw Pact led to a period of neglect of the military and the military–industrial complex. Swiftly, however, the subsequent drive by many states to join the EU and NATO led to an attempt to revive both. The military was reconfigured away from Warsaw Pact tasks and away from conscription. Instead, there was an attempt to create a more professional volunteer military and to reorganize the military–industrial complex accordingly.[5]

There was no comparable contemporary challenge in Western Europe, but, instead, a desire to overcome the past by, as it were, downplaying much of it. This was certainly the case with a general rejection of past bellicosity and martial values, and a widespread reluctance to mark battles other than in terms of sorrow over the casualties.

CHAPTER EIGHT

Modern Society, 2000 to the Present: The Abandonment of War?

The trends of the late twentieth century initially appeared to gather pace in the early twenty-first, and without any significant qualification of them. In particular, the disinclination of most Europeans to engage in conflict was seen with further moves against conscription. Indeed, in 2012, Germany abandoned it. Linked to this process came a significant fall in the willingness to spend on the military and to match promises about defence expenditure, a fall that very much reflected popular assumptions. In 2008–10, sixteen of the European NATO states still cut their military expenditure. Whereas, in 1990, the European members of NATO accounted for 34 per cent of its military spending, by 2011 the percentage had fallen to 21 per cent. Looked at differently, much of this was because of a massive increase in American expenditure (by 77 per cent in real terms from 1999 to 2010), and, in 2011, the European NATO states spent just under $270 billion, a formidable sum. However, the agreed NATO guideline was for 2 per cent of GDP (Gross Domestic Product) to be spent on defence, whereas, in 2011, only the USA, Britain, France, Greece and Albania met this target. That year, the Libya campaign indicated serious weaknesses in NATO military capability, but, in 2014, the declared average expenditure on defence of Europe's NATO members was 1.6 per cent of GDP and the real percentage probably closer to 1.3. Thanks, indeed, to rising Asian expenditure, Asia came to supplant European military expenditure. Total European defence spending in real terms fell by an average of 2.5 per cent annually in 2010–13, with Britain, France and Germany being the sole NATO European powers in the top ten of global spenders in 2013. Expenditure fell on both equipment and on costs arising from military numbers, which, on the whole, also fell. The end of conscription helped ensure a cut in the latter.

Germany, Europe's most successful economy and the dominant state in the EU, was particularly remiss in military expenditure, and there were also questions about the combat-readiness of German forces. There were certainly serious limitations with the German military. In 2014, it emerged that, short of resources and poorly prepared, the German military would be totally unable to meet its NATO commitments, a point publicly admitted by the Defence Minister. A German parliamentary report in 2014 revealed that, at most, seven of the navy's forty-three helicopters were in a shape to fly and only one of its four submarines was operational. The frigates ordered in 2007 and designed to enter service by 2017 are impressive, not least with their hybrid population system, but the four are intended to replace eight Cold War-era predecessors and lack some of their submarine-hunting and anti-aircraft capabilities. As an instance of the public–private partnerships involved in weapons procurement, the warships were built by a consortium led by the shipbuilding arm of Thyssen Krupp.

In Britain, there was controversy in 2015 over whether the 2 per cent benchmark would be met, and criticism of the government, notably from defence professionals, for its failure to confirm the guideline, which it eventually did. However, there was far less popular support for ring-fencing defence expenditure than for spending far more on health, and defence issues played only a very minor role in the 2015 general election campaign.

Moreover, in the 2000s, as another instance of a more widespread disenchantment with defence strength and expenditure, there was a move to reduce, if not get rid of, nuclear weapons. The establishment, in 2008, of Group Zero, a pressure group to this end, was followed, in 2010, by New START, an arms agreement between President Obama of the USA and Dmitry Medvedev of Russia, who had endorsed the aims of Global Zero. The two powers agreed to cap their deployment of strategic warheads at 1,550 each. Obama, moreover, did not deploy missile defences to Poland and the Czech Republic as the George W. Bush administration had planned to do and as Russia very much opposed. This was a key step that left NATO much weaker when Russia increased its pressure on the West in 2014–15, not least with rhetoric about the possibility of nuclear attack.

There was also pressure on Britain and France in the late 2000s to contribute to the process of nuclear disarmament; pressure that neither government was keen to yield to. However, in Britain, and notably in Scotland, there was much opposition to upgrading the nuclear deterrent. In Scotland, which came close to voting for independence in 2014, there was much support for nuclear disarmament and, specifically, for closing the nuclear submarine base at Faslane, a key NATO base.

War in the 2000s was largely seen by Europeans as a matter of policing against those unwilling to accept pacific norms that were endorsed (or should be endorsed) by all states and most people. During that decade, there were paramilitary operations in Europe, notably in Spain against Basque separatists, but there were no conflicts of any significance in Europe west of the revived Russian assault on Chechnya and, later, a swift Russian attack on Georgia in support of Russian-backed separatists in Abkhazia. There was no recurrence of the conflict in former Yugoslavia.

Meanwhile, European military interventions outside Europe were repeatedly presented in terms of moral interventionism, rather than selfish state interest. This tendency was notably the case with the discussions surrounding NATO's commitment to Afghanistan, its first non-European mission. Thus, a moral politics acted as a powerful parameter. This, apparently, pointed the way to future developments in which Europe acted as a culture without bellicosity, deploying only to support international norms. This approach appeared particularly appropriate given the coalition nature of many European governments, the extent to which left-of-centre political parties favoured such an approach and the nature of public opinion. A postwar politics appeared as a part of a postmodern world, alongside a post-industrial economy and a post-class society. Meanwhile, as part of the post-Cold War 'peace dividend', and in response to an emphasis on rapid deployment and to commitments in the Islamic world, most American forces in Europe were withdrawn to the United States. The American military presence in Europe fell from over 400,000 personnel at the height of the Cold War to 64,000 in 2015, including only 27,000 soldiers. As a key element, heavy equipment was stockpiled in Western Europe, with the equipment to be used for units that were to be airlifted in from the United States in the event of crisis.

Growing disenchantment with the commitments to Afghanistan and Iraq in the late 2000s, in turn, affected broad tranches of European public opinion, as well as governments troubled by their intractable character, and militaries concerned about casualties and the effects on morale, and on preparedness for other tasks. As a result, some European powers pulled forces out of Afghanistan or Iraq, or hedged their use with restrictive guidelines. In Afghanistan, Germany did not send its forces to the more troubled south and preferred to focus on policing rather than military functions. The net effect of moral politics, dominant norms, popular disenchantment and governmental caution was to lessen political and public support, let alone enthusiasm, for expeditionary warfare, however much sanctioned by international bodies, whether NATO or the United Nations (UN). By extension, this shift in attitudes affected views on military service as a whole. This was especially so in Germany, but less so in France and Britain.

This degree of disenchantment, in turn, affected the military and led to repeated complaints, by troops, and on their behalf, about what was seen as a breach of the 'military covenant', namely the agreement between society and the military under which the latter put themselves in harm's way in return for a degree of care and support from society. These complaints were particularly strongly expressed in Britain. There, the earlier end of conscription during the Cold War itself, as well as the degree to which it had never been as well-established as had been the case in the Continent, had encouraged the development of the concept of the 'military covenant' as an alternative to the notions of shared arrangements presented by the idea of the citizenry under arms by means of conscription.

These alternatives entailed differing versions of an aspect of what has hitherto in this book been termed the public–private partnership. The tension involved in this relationship by the 2010s helps underline the extent to which it is not necessarily sensible to write in terms of a developmental, still more teleological, approach. This caveat is further encouraged because of the extent to which there was in the 2000s and 2010s an enhanced use, including by governments, of private security agencies and a related privatization of military functions. This situation, however, did not amount to a return to the mercenaries of the sixteenth century. Although there was much talk of privatization, and some practice, notably in Britain, neither the discussion nor privatization extended to core capacities in terms of fighting units.

Instead, it was largely at the already-developed margins of co-operation with the private sector that the use of non-military assets gathered pace. This was particularly so for such tasks as air transport and refuelling. Transport and logistics had been areas in which there had been co-operation in the past, and, in one respect, there was a move back from the highpoint of centralized control in the early twentieth century and during the Cold War. This control had reflected the long-standing interest in regulation and bureaucratization seen with the growth of government aspirations and functions in the nineteenth century followed by the mobilization of resources and energies during the period of war and defence from 1914 to 1989. However, the impact of neo-liberalism, accentuated by successive fiscal crises, by the desire for a 'peace dividend' and by the pressures of expenditure on social welfare, was such as to encourage a marked move away from centralized state control and provision in the 1990s, 2000s and 2010s.

In part, this move encouraged tensions with the military which saw itself as commodified and as subject to the austerity facing other branches of state service, and without any understandings of special functions and risks. In part, the emphasis on a 'military covenant' was a response to this situation. It also reflected an attempt to argue for the military as a unit, not least in response to the danger that otherwise there would be a fragmentation, including tensions within the military, as had been the case in some countries on occasion during the twentieth century. As a separate issue, the relationship between neo-liberalism and left-wing anti-militarism was scarcely close, but there were shared consequences in challenging military assumptions and governmental and political assumptions about the military.

In one respect, the challenge from Russia in the 2000s and, even more, 2010s was incorporated into the standard European analysis of conflict by presenting the Putin government as rejecting norms, not least as it pursued, or at least playacted, traditional trophes of aggressive nationalism. As such, Russia was taken to demonstrate the undesirability of such an approach and of the related bellicosity. The attack on Georgia in 2008 was a brutal display of power politics in support of separatism within Georgia: external force successfully supported internal force.

At the same time, the challenge from Russia provoked moves to return to a more militarized environment. Thus, in 2015, Lithuania restored conscription because of growing Russian aggression in Ukraine. There was a continuation of established social norms in that this conscription was for men only. Lithuania followed up by announcing an increase in the defence budget. Estonia already had conscription. In March 2015, the German Cabinet adopted a draft budget for 2016 that would raise the Defence Ministry's budget from €33 billion in 2015 to €34.2 billion and also committed to spend €35 billion by 2019.

The Russian seizure of Crimea from Ukraine in 2014, and the support of violent separatism in eastern Ukraine in 2014–15, led to talk of a renewed Cold War, as well as many references back to the origins of the First World War in 1914.[1] The mistaken argument that the First World War had stemmed from the inability to operate international relations, as opposed, as was in fact the case, to the bellicosity and deliberate steps of particular states, notably Austria and Germany, made the modern situation of distrust and confusion appear far more disturbing.

Concern in 2014–15 about the possibility of war was encouraged by bold Russian talk about large-scale rearmament, including 800 new aircraft, 1,400 new helicopters and 6 carrier groups by 2020. A third of Russia's rising military budget is devoted to strengthening nuclear forces. Several new intercontinental ballistic missiles are planned, including the multi-warhead Sarmat. By early 2015, three of the projected Borei-class submarines had already entered service. This deployment was designed to allow Russia to keep ballistic-missile submarines on permanent patrol for the first time since the end of the Cold War. These weapons were not simply deterrents, but, instead, were increasingly incorporated into Russian war-fighting doctrines. Also in 2015, Russia tested the R–500, a new cruise missile capable of carrying a nuclear payload and suspected of having a range prohibited by the American–Soviet Intermediate-range Nuclear Forces Treaty of 1987. This led to American consideration of deploying intermediate-range nuclear missiles in Europe.

By 2015, Russia had an estimated 4,300 nuclear warheads, compared to 4,764 in the USA and 250 in China. The other European powers with nuclear warheads are France and Britain with 300 and 225 respectively. In the 2010s, France modernized its nuclear forces, updating its submarines, aircraft, missiles and warheads. This process includes the introduction of forty new Rafaele aircraft able to carry cruise missiles. Britain prepared for an updating of its nuclear capability, which is submarine-borne. Meanwhile, in 2014–15, Russia deployed advanced missile systems to Crimea and resumed the Cold War tactic of frequent flights by long-range aircraft designed to test NATO defences. Air attacks on Denmark and Sweden, a key deterrent to them expressing support for the Baltic Republics, were practised, while there was also a probing of British air space. Over the Arctic, there was concern that Russia might seek to exploit climate change to the detriment of other powers, notably Norway and Denmark, the latter the protector power of Greenland. In 2015, in the Victory Day celebrations in Moscow, air defence missile launchers, intercontinental ballistic missile carriers and tanks, including the new T–14 were displayed. The T–14 was presented as superior to Western rivals such as the American Abrams and British Challenger, although, during the rehearsal, the T–14 on display stalled for fifteen minutes.

In 2015, the centres of tension were Ukraine and Estonia. The Russians staged large-scale snap exercises near the border of Estonia, while their aircraft routinely probed its airspace. In 2015, Russia threatened the United States with the use of nuclear arms and other forms of conflict if NATO challenged its position in Crimea, armed Ukraine or provided support to the Baltic Republics against Russian pressure, notably backing for dissident ethnic Russians who are numerous there.[2] Yet, despite such action being threatened, Russian tanks have not advanced on Kiev as they certainly could have done.

This activity led to much criticism, notably by the United States, but also within Britain, of NATO's failure to demonstrate resolve and maintain expenditure. This was ironic as Obama's decision not to deploy missile defences to Poland and the Czech Republic had been an aspect of the problem. As a result of the 1997 'Founding Act', under which NATO promised Russia that no combat units would be permanently deployed on the territory of any new member of the alliance, no NATO forces were permanently based east of Germany, despite article V of the NATO treaty which committed NATO powers to defend each other with 'armed force' and the admission of the Baltic Republics to NATO in 2004. The NATO 'very high readiness task force', announced in 2015, was only 5,000-strong, and divisions within NATO were readily apparent, notably over whether Ukraine should be rearmed and its forces trained. Whereas Britain and the USA supported this idea, France and, in particular, Germany were opposed, seeing it as provocative to Russia and a threat to peace.

Indeed, strains in NATO were readily apparent, as they had earlier been when intervening in Libya in 2011. That intervention had seen Britain and France prominent, and Germany conspicuously not so. Italy had not only taken a role but also provided key air bases. Other NATO powers had taken part, but had found it difficult to influence decision-making. As a consequence, Norway withdrew from the mission. As a reminder of the relative weakness of Europe's NATO powers, the initial air assault on Libyan air defences had greatly depended on American participation.

In 2015, under Operation Atlantic Resolve, the United States rotated military units into Europe for exercises with allies, such as Platinum Eagle 15 with the Romanian army. Moreover, the United States and NATO developed plans to pre-position military vehicles, including heavy tanks, in

Eastern Europe, possibly in Estonia, Latvia, Lithuania, Poland, Romania and Bulgaria. Russia saw the latter as a violation of promises made after the fall of the Soviet Union not to expand the alliance eastwards, promises Western leaders insisted were never made. On 24 June 2015, employing the intimidation increasingly common in Russian policy, Yevgeny Lukyanov, the Deputy Secretary of the Russian Security Council, said that Poland and Romania 'had better think about something different' instead of hosting American 'missile defence elements aimed at our strategic nuclear forces ... They automatically become our targets.'[3]

There were concerns in 2014–15 about whether NATO forces possessed the sophistication and training necessary to counter the 'hybrid' means the Soviets had demonstrated in Crimea: Russian control had been gained, not by sending in an invasion army, but by indirect means, notably rapidly exploiting the potential interaction of force and politics and using well-armed and well-trained special operations forces and local supporters in an effective, but deniable, fashion.[4] This was not the conflict of conventional dominance, and it underlined the need for armies to possess a counter-insurgency capability directed against the efforts of other major states that did not inherently need to use the means of insurgency but that might follow this course. The possibility that Russia might intervene in Estonia or other states to 'protect' ethnic Russians from alleged discrimination was part of the political equation of fear that led to concerns about possible conflict. The Baltic Republics lack tanks and air forces or navies of any scale. There was talk, in place of the site of Cold War anxiety about a Soviet advance, of a new 'Fulda Gap' between Russia and its Kaliningrad enclave of the Baltic, with the Soviets thus advancing to cut off the Baltic Republics from reinforcement by land. With its ability to use 'volunteers', many clearly soldiers with their insignia removed, and also to threaten nuclear attack, Russia had a spectrum of choices NATO lacked. These were aspects of a hybrid warfare doctrine and capability presented in 2013 by General Valery Gerasimov, Chief of the Russian General Staff, as central to a new strategy. Cyber-warfare was an important aspect of this range, for the doctrine announced the employment of 'military means of a concealed character, including carrying out actions of informational conflict and the actions of special operations forces'.

The Western response focused initially on finance, with a determination to exacerbate financial pressures in Russia that owed much to the fall in the price of oil. However, the war and the related economic disruption led also to problems for Ukraine, which, in 2015, threatened a partial debt default. In place of earlier interventions in Afghanistan and Libya, NATO, meanwhile, was having to revert to its core mission of planning self-defence against Russia. In particular, by 2015, Latvia appeared vulnerable. Whichever of the Baltic Republics was under pressure from Russia, there was the risk of the latter seeking to intervene in force. If NATO then responded, a response that would entail tackling Russian air defences in the region, Russia might well see this as an escalation enabling them to threaten to use, or indeed use, intermediate nuclear missiles.

At the same time, the military challenge posed by Russia was very different to that mounted by the Soviet Union. Russia not only lacked the large-scale forces the Soviet Union had had in the 1980s, but also the necessary military, governmental and economic support systems. Moreover, the alliance network provided by the Warsaw Pact, its troops, infrastructure and defence in depth, had gone. Although Russia had significant allies in Asia, particularly China, and was thus in a much better strategic position than had been the case in the later stage of the Cold War, there was no equivalent ally in Europe. There were NATO countries that sought good relations with Russia, especially Bulgaria and, from 2015, Greece, but not to the point of alliance, although the projected Turkish Stream gas pipeline involved the movement of Russian natural gas west via Turkey and Greece. During the 2003 Gulf War, in contrast, Romania guaranteed American access to airfields and allowed America to set up military bases. In 2015, a large number of Poles joined unofficial militias intended to act in the event of conflict with Russia. Similarly, Estonia has a 30,000-strong 'Defence League' that is armed by the government, has infantry training once a month and, in the event of an invasion, would be mobilized under the command of professional soldiers.

In addition, European states bordering Russia, those that had been part of the Soviet Union, were, with the exception of Belarus, hostile, and generally very much so. That, indeed, explained the significance of the Ukraine crisis: the pro-Russian government there had been overthrown in early 2014 as a result of large-scale popular demonstrations, a process endorsed by Ukraine's western neighbours in Eastern Europe, notably Poland, as well as by Western Europe. The possibility of Ukraine joining NATO was raised. Ukraine was seen in Russia as an integral part of the identity of the latter.[5] For Russia, in 2014–15 to focus on Ukraine, and also be considered a threat to the Baltic Republics, notably Estonia and Latvia, was for Russia to represent a very different challenge to the rest of Europe compared to that which the Soviet Union had posed.

This contrast led to questions about the applicability of calls for rearmament elsewhere in Europe. Different challenges to this equation of Russian threat and military response arose from concerns about other security issues, notably in the Islamic world. Indeed, these issues raised the question whether Russia should, or could, be seen as an aberrant member of an anti-Islamic bloc, as in its willingness to arm Iran; a member, however, that could be brought onside. Alternatively, it was unclear whether the emphasis should be on the challenge posed by Russian policy, both to Europe and to the world system. Views were expressed by politicians and other commentators and contrasting accounts of the past and varying perspectives on the future were deployed accordingly.

A less confident position for Europe was suggested in 2015, when President Xi of China attended the celebrations of Victory Day in Moscow.

Chinese troops took part in the parade for the first time, while Russia and China staged joint naval exercises in the eastern Mediterranean. President Putin sought to align the Eurasian Economic Union, a league of Russia, Belarus and Central Europe, with China and notably with China's plan to link China to European markets via Central Asia in the Silk Road Economic Belt.

The absence of war hitherto in this period, other than the Russian intervention against Georgia in 2008 and the insurrection in Ukraine in 2014–15, ensures that conflict cannot be related to transformations in the European international system such as the major and sustained fiscal and political crisis in the Eurozone in the early 2010s. This crisis was not responsible for Russian expansionism, indeed adventurism, for it was already clear that most Western European powers were unlikely to act against Russia, while the key element was American policy. The principal concern is that military action initiated by Russia will lead to such a transformation in the international system. The rhetoric of Russian policy, at once nationalist, revisionist and embittered, contributed to the sense of crisis, indeed fear.

Security issues related to the Islamic world led to suggestions that Europe's southern border was as much under threat as its eastern one,[6] but with the threat being different. Rather than the challenge coming from the actions of an expansionist state, Russia, there was the combination of serious instability in North Africa, especially Libya, and a millenarian ideology in the shape of an Islamic fundamentalism that left no role for other cultures. The particular anxiety in 2015 was that terrorists might use the cover of large-scale refugee flows from North Africa, notably into Italy, in order to move into Europe and begin hostile operations there. This fear was compounded by the rapid growth of large and unintegrated immigrant communities and by acts of terrorist violence, particularly, in 2015, in France and Denmark. The zone of anxiety included Spain as a frontier country, but with large immigrant communities in countries further north, such as Britain where there was terrorist violence in 2005, a feeling of concern, if not crisis, was widespread. In 2015, the EU proposed military action against people traffickers from North Africa, a measure rejected by Libya and considered unwelcome by the UN.

In some respects, this threat underlined the repeatedly non-linear character of military history and also the uncertainty about how best to respond to challenges. The primacy of political, social and ideological contexts over military means emerged clearly in considering how best to respond to the challenge of terrorism, a challenge that became more vivid with suicide bombings. This issue of response was very much seen in the extension of judicial supervision over military action. In Europe, human rights laws, specifically the European Convention on Human Rights (ECHR), were applied to limit the activities of the military not least by taking precedence over the more permissive Geneva Conventions and their international humanitarian law. The Geneva Conventions accept that in war lethal force can be a matter for first resort against the enemy, whereas the ECHR allows lethal force to be used only in exceptional circumstances. The latter puts commanders in a very difficult position. Shooting people in war can, therefore, make states liable for the breach of their human rights. Moreover, governments could be liable for negligence claims brought by injured servicemen. In 2014, the British Supreme Court ruled that the European Convention applied to soldiers in foreign war zones.

Equally, the challenge of terrorism and the relevant contexts were not a constant. In particular, externally directed terrorism, as part of a wider conflict with Islamic fundamentalism, offered a very different threat to its domestic counterpart. The contrast with the far left-wing and right-wing terrorists of the 1970s and 1980s in Europe was readily apparent.

The role of politics was abruptly demonstrated from another direction in 2015, when Jean-Claude Juncker, the President of the European Commission, proposed the formation of a EU army, a view strongly opposed by Britain. The call also underlined the significance of the military to ideas of political legitimacy and purpose, for the issue captured the question of the extent to which the EU could operate as a proper state and give force to a foreign policy, and its ambition for further centralization. Moreover, suspicion of the USA played a major role in the call, as the proposal for such an army inherently was a move to create a European equivalent of NATO. For both these reasons, the plan enjoyed support in Germany; but not in Britain where the American alliance was seen as far more significant, valuable and desirable.

A different theme in the defence debate in the early twenty-first century was provided by the argument that expenditure on social welfare and on other domestic agendas was more significant as a form and guarantor of security and stability than military expenditure. This argument represents another iteration of the long-standing tendency to see the strength of societies as a key element in the rivalry of states, with differing forms of measurement being a crucial indicator of social and political trends. As a consequence of this tendency, the linkage between military requirements and state developments remains far more complex than a focus on the size of armed forces might imply. However, expenditure on social welfare and health is consistently far greater than that on defence.

A separate but related strand, again emphasizing the domestic dimension, was provided by the use of the military as the arm of the state in situations judged crises. In the 2000s, in Britain, for example troops were deployed to replace striking firefighters and to help deal with 'mad cow' disease, while the prospect in 2000, due to industrial action in the shape of a blockade of the oil refineries, of a long-term breakdown in petrol deliveries encouraged a reliance on the military as the ultimate substitute for the police. In 2012, the army successfully provided security for the Olympic Games in London. In France, Italy and Belgium in the 2010s, troops were deployed in cities such as Marseille, Naples and Brussels where, aside from justified anxieties about terrorism, large-scale criminality excited public concern and governmental attention. In each case, the army was seen as a crucial adjunct to the police. Moreover, terrorist attacks in Paris in early 2015 ensured that the largest single deployment of French troops that year was in French cities. For example, troops were placed on guard outside the synagogue in Lyon. Conversely, urban rioting in London in 2012 did not lead to a reliance on the army: instead, police forces were tapped to move men.

This aspect of military history does not tend to attract attention, but it underlines the extent to which the significance of the military in part rests on it being a body of trained men (and, increasingly, women) accustomed to taking orders and available to fulfil governmental instructions. That the practical conditionality of this availability is less than in the sixteenth century reflects the extent to which political history, notably state development, has affected the military. The use of the military, as of the police, is greatly affected by legal constraints. However, there is no need today to consider the equivalent of the mercenary or aristocratic commanders of the sixteenth century with their independent positions and views. The nearest equivalent is that of warlords in areas where state authority has collapsed, for example the Russian separatist part of Ukraine in 2014–15, and in the Balkans in the 1990s. That very linkage today between these individuals and the absence of state control indicates the contrast with the early modern period. What had been central then was regarded as a political pathology by the 2010s, and one that was shared by unstable parts of Africa and Asia.

CHAPTER NINE

Conclusions

The continuing validity of Charles Tilly's adage is unclear, not least because it underplays the ideological dimensions of strategic culture. To take the state-building and politics of the 2010s, the role of war in encouraging the building of a new European state and, alternatively, of challenging, indeed weakening, it is unclear. So also is the possible impact of a Russian challenge. That may well lead in the areas most threatened to a rallying to the state as the expression of the nation, but the threat may also lead to divisions within the state. The extent to which NATO will be reinvigorated is unclear, as, notably, is the likely trajectory of popular views. In considering Tilly's adage, particular uncertainty arises from globalization and whether the response would be hostile and, therefore, whether globalization made, and would make, war more or less likely. In addition, global networks create new patterns and sites of vulnerability, including, for Europeans, outside Europe.

The relationships between states, militaries and social structures, practices and attitudes in the present circumstances, are unclear, varied and in flux. In part, that helps establish the significance of the topic, but also the precariousness of schematic accounts. The capacity of different political systems for engendering consent and syncreticism is also unclear, but, repeatedly, that capacity has been important in grounding and confirming success in conflict. This helps to make military history an aspect of total history, and other branches of history an aspect of military studies, which is the correct conclusion.

The centrality of war to European history is a narrative and analysis that would have surprised few up to the late twentieth century. However, a decline of war as a subject for study and, indeed, a dominant force in the account of the past and the explanation of the present, became readily apparent from then. This was particularly the case in Europe, and notably in Western Europe. It had many manifestations. War was treated, in the words of the leading French historian Fernand Braudel, as an 'epiphenomenon', one that was essentially a surface event that did not change the great structures and currents of history;[1] a profoundly mistaken assessment of the relationship between structures and events.[2] More prosaically, but also indicative, I can recall being told by the historian Jan Glete that the

Journal of Military History, the leader in the field, was not available in Swedish libraries.

More generally, historical works tended to underplay military history, to ignore the detail and to prefer a simplistic handling of military issues and, notably, the one that emphasized the role of political and social factors. It was as if military history was demilitarized. This was very apparent in 'War and Society' courses, or those on 'The Memory of War', the latter a key element of the 'cultural' approach to the topic. Each, indeed, is a very important topic, but it is frequently presented as if it is *the* subject and *the* means of approaching military history. This is not the case.

This decline of war as a subject, both in its own right and as a contribution to broader issues in history, was encouraged by the anti-war mood of the 1960s, the *détente* of the 1970s and the end of the Cold War and conscription. Complacency also became a major element. These developments affected not only the public, but also the academic profession, much of which lacked any real understanding of the nature of war. The experience of conflict, common in the 1970s among the middle-aged as they looked back to their youth and childhood, was no longer the case for most European men by the 2000s and 2010s. Moreover, the experience of military service became less common and insistent.

Instead, other issues were to the fore in domestic politics and public concerns, while war appeared a discretionary matter of out-of-area expeditions. The extent to which much of Europe did not take part in the two Gulf Wars with Iraq, especially the 2003 conflict, was also significant. Britain and Poland were the allies of the United States in that conflict, while France and Germany conspicuously opposed the 2003 war, and Italy and Spain were among those who sent no troops. Germany's move from being in the front line of the Cold War to a much more restrained role, as far as preparation for, and participation in, conflict were concerned, was highly significant.

When forces were deployed, both within Europe, notably in the Balkans in the 1990s, and outside, there were tight rules of engagement and careful restrictions on targeting. In particular, there was great caution in any activity likely to lead to civilian casualties. There was also much reluctance to take steps that might lead to the loss of military personnel. Casualty restriction became a goal and means of conflict. Aside from creating very difficult tactical, operational and, even, strategic parameters, this, in turn, established new norms and expectations that posed considerable difficulties.

The situation would have been different had negotiations for Turkey to join the European Union succeeded as they have not hitherto been. Turkey was (and is) a state, not only with conscription, but also with a strong military ethos, and one that was engaged against insurgents, as well as having, in Syria, Iraq and Iran, highly troublesome neighbours. The military commitment was different to that represented by other states that had retained conscription as an aspect of patriotism, notably Switzerland, for the ethos of the latter was far from bellicose. Thus, the definition of Europe is highly significant when considering how best to present European military history, both the geographical definition and its cultural counterpart. This point is not new, but remains highly pertinent. Moreover, it will be so in the future. Indeed, the presence, potential and issue of the EU add a potent political dimension.[3] So also do the role of Russia and the position of neighbours not in the EU or NATO.

If the present poses challenges to the understanding of the significance of past conflict, so also do changes in the very nature of history over the last half-century. The emphasis on social history and on social science forms of analysis did not automatically mean a lack of interest in war. Indeed, each could prove a highly productive way to consider the wider experience of conflict, notably in terms of 'War and Society', as well as to approach the nature of military institutions as societies. However, as an aspect of the changing nature of the subject, there was a decline in the engagement of most academics with military history, and notably insofar as conflict itself was concerned. Partly as a consequence, the interactions of societies, states and international systems with war and the military were increasingly handled by experts in societies, states and international systems, and many lacked sufficient knowledge of war and the military. As a result, there was a tendency, in many works, to treat both war and the military in a fairly simplistic fashion or with reference to social science theory.[4] In particular, there was, in this literature, a lack of engagement with the specifics of campaigning and battle.

This tendency was compounded because much of the work on war and the military was produced by non-academics writing for a popular market. They tended to focus on tactical and operational accounts of battles and campaigns. As a result, there was relatively little attention from this direction to work on societies, state and international systems, as well as to theoretical perspectives on tactical and operational issues. Consequently, the subject was, at once, relatively short on conceptual discussion, notably insofar as tactical and operational issues were concerned, and often characterized by misguided discussion as far as the broader contextual questions were at issue.

The argument in this book is that there is no central analytical core in military history, nor any clear linear pattern in developments. Instead, a number of factors interacted and did so without any hierarchy of causation or set pattern of interaction. At times, the international system provided the basic dynamic driving change, but there was also a high degree of autonomy in technological and organizational changes. Moreover, the motives for war were far more complex than those suggested simply by the exigencies and opportunities of the international system. Domestic political pressures were also of key significance, and notably as mediated in the context of political cultures and social systems that welcomed conflict or were, at least, attuned to it.

As an aspect of this point, the notion of the military as a category separate to society is frequently misleading or limiting. The domestic drive can be seen in particular in the pressure for war in the political culture and society of Europe for most of the period. This pressure reflected both the drive for *gloire*, reputation and status that was so important for aristocratic society and the need to win each in order to keep the monarch powerful, a situation that extended to the governments of republics. The most significant element was that war, the prospect of it, its conduct and the consequences, throughout proved important.

Ideological factors linked international and domestic elements, helping overcome cultural, social, collective and individual inhibitions against violence and encouraging the formulation of goals in terms of conflict, and, notably, of sustaining conflict in the face of opposition. This linked the 'Wars of Religion' of the sixteenth and seventeenth centuries to the French Revolutionary Wars, the Russian and Spanish Civil Wars, the Second World War and the Cold War. They were not the sole conflicts in which there was a clearly ideological dimension. At the same time, what may today not appear ideological, or so clearly ideological, also had that dimension, notably the wars of dynasticism in 1450–1789 and those of nationalism in 1800–1918. Moreover, as the First World War showed, these conflicts could be as determined and bloody as the wars of ideology.

Further challenging the idea of a central analytical core comes the need to judge each period on its own terms and not to view the character of military history and, notably the practice of operations, through the prism of one particular period's practice and culture. The frequent tendency to adopt a perspective on the centuries from 1450 to 1850 based on developments from 1850 to 1980 is a particular flaw. This tendency leads not only to a misunderstanding of the earlier period, but also of its later counterpart. The tendency to do so is linked not only to a misreading of military history, but also to an emphasis on the 'war and society' approach. That approach leads to a stress on the experience of 'total war', rather than to an ability to contextualize it in terms of a far more varied experience of conflict.

Moreover, whether geopolitics, ideology or warfare are considered, the period 1850 to 1980 can no longer be readily understood as modernity, in light of the developments that have occurred subsequently. The key element is cultural, in particular the rejection, in individualistic and hedonistic societies, of notions of the need and obligation to serve, and, indeed, of the desirability of war and military service. As a consequence, military tasking in recent years has also differed from the earlier situation, both in terms of international relations and with reference to domestic politics. A shifting present very much ensures that the modern, modernity and modernization all alter. Given the implication that modernization equates with development, and that the latter deserves approbation, this point is important in considering narratives of change.

The values of the present age were captured in a cartoon by Peter Brooks in the *Times* on 3 October 2014. This depicted a British jet carrying nine missiles, each with a price tag from £30,000 to £790,000 with the pilot saying, 'If we don't hit schools and hospitals in Iraq, we certainly will back home'. This was a reference, not only to the extent to which defence and social welfare are competing forms of expenditure, but also to critical attitudes towards the use of force itself.

The critique of conventional accounts offered here leads also to another form of critique, namely the different question of whether Europe is the best level of geographical analysis or whether the emphasis, instead, should be on particular parts of Europe. The issue, moreover, can be seen not as a fixed option, but as entailing a placing or categorization that varied with time. Thus, what Atlantic Europe meant in 1800, 1900 and 1950 was very different in each case, but also very different to the situation in 1600, fundamentally contrasting as that was to the situation in 1450. This very possibility for changing categorization encourages analysis, for it moves away from any rigid designation of regions, and also questions the process of giving them descriptive clarity and causative power.

In some respects, there is the danger that regional stereotyping, whether for alleged exceptionalism or for caricature, replaces that at the national level. This is very much a theme of Chapter 2, in which the consequences of failing to understand Mediterranean perspectives and the consequences of this failure for the analysis of Spain are discussed.

At the same time, the use of a regional perspective may be more valuable than is suggested in the previous paragraph. Certainly, there is a matrix composed of Northern, Eastern, Southern and Western Europe. Furthermore, these descriptions at various times were employed to imply inherent, indeed exceptional, characteristics, as well as to suggest distinctions and descriptions for analytical purposes. There can, however, be a particular teleology at play, and it may be misleading, as is raised in the discussion of the Balkans and, more generally, of Eastern Europe. Each, it is generally implied, was, as it were, foredoomed to backwardness, an assessment that acquired particular force from the eighteenth century. So also, as discussed in Chapter 2, with the consideration of Spain and, more generally, of the Mediterranean.

At the same time, alongside conceptual and methodological problems with a regional perspective on European military history, there is a foundation for this approach. It is valid to note the role of oceanic links and maritime commitments, and the manner in which these were far more valuable for states in Western, Southern and Northern Europe, than for Eastern European counterparts. The Black Sea lacked an oceanic reach. Indeed, in geopolitical terms, and without suggesting any cultural essentialism, Eastern Europe is closer to Eurasia as a concept and reality than Western Europe. In part, this is a reflection of the role of Russia, the rise of which has been a feature throughout the period, albeit with particular periods of crisis, notably the early 1610s, 1708–9, 1812, 1918–19 and 1941–2. Thus, Muscovy, pressing on and incorporating the cities of Novgorod and Pskov in 1478 and 1510 respectively, is, as it were, part of a pattern linked to alleged Russian plans in 2015 to spark rebellion and, in concert with Russian special forces, declare an independent 'Bessarabian People's Republic', based in the city of Odessa.[5] Moreover, the struggle between the maritime powers, both in Europe and overseas, ensured that the Western European powers ended up as the dominant ones in the maritime and oceanic spheres. The Baltic and Mediterranean polities, in contrast, were essentially regional. The Jenkinson speech to Parliament mentioned in Chapter 1 can be reconsidered in this light.

Within Europe, furthermore, there was, to a degree, the replication of wider contrasts that have been noted on the broader Eurasian scale. These ranged from military choices, notably the degree of reliance on cavalry as opposed to infantry, to social contexts, in particular the character of landed society.[6] The subsequent working through of these, and other, geographical contrasts has not always attracted sufficient attention, and certainly not on the level seen with synoptic accounts of Eurasian history as a whole. Nevertheless, historical geography very clearly demon-strates contrasts in the case of industrial activity, urbanization and other socio-economic indicators and also in the possibilities that differential development led to. For example, the struggle with the Turks (Ottomans) in the nineteenth century was very different in character to that in the early modern period when the pressure of Turkish expansion ensured great efforts and significant innovation on the part of opponents, notably Russia but also Austria.[7]

On top of these Eurasian differences, there are the contrasts between regional, or sub-continental, power systems. Related to the politics of this issue, the frequency of conflict between the different powers of the Continent varied greatly in intensity. This variation established networks of conflict, networks that did not always match state divisions or, depending on the method of depiction, suggested patterns of particular linkage. These networks, in turn, varied with power and ambition, and altered chronologi-cally. Thus, Sweden fought German powers in the seventeenth century and the early eighteenth, as it did not in the nineteenth (after 1813) or twentieth.

Major conflicts could lead to an overlap between regional struggles, most obviously with the Napoleonic Wars, the two world wars and the Cold War, in part because these conflicts became umbrella wars encompassing a range of powers and disputes. Less comprehensively, major powers could become involved in regional struggles, for example in Italy from the fifteenth to the late nineteenth century, and in the Balkans. This process became more significant when competing major powers played a role, as with the Italian Wars in 1494–1559 or the Low Countries from the 1560s to the 1740s. In the former, France, Spain and Austria played major parts and, in the latter, France, Spain, Austria and Britain.

The pattern of regional conflict could have consequences not only for tasking and strategy, but also for force structures. A classic instance of variations in the latter case, one valid to militaries even with very similar weapons and tactics, was that between states inherently on the defensive, and therefore more prone to adopt fortifications, and those for whom an emphasis on the offensive encouraged a stress on siege artillery, and a lesser need for fortifications.

The regional dimension of European military history repays attention. This dimension highlights the question of the value of adopting the European level, as well as the validity of the idea of a distinctive European way of war or, conversely, distinctive set of parameters; and, if so, the issue of what European, and indeed Europe, mean as far as military history is concerned. The argument here is for a limited exceptionalism, one that is clearer for the period up to the early nineteenth century, after which exceptionalism is tempered, from a different direction, by the extent, nature and role of other Western states, first, in the New World and, then, in the former Dominions of the British empire, such as Australia and Canada.

To turn to the period up to the early nineteenth, the multi-polarity of Europe, far from being unique, was seen elsewhere, notably in the eighteenth century in India, where the decline of the Mughal empire was followed by competition between the Mughals, Marathas, Afghans and regional rulers notably of Bengal, Hyderabad and Mysore. Nevertheless, this multi-polarity was not as grounded elsewhere in state structures, political loyalties and international assumptions about appropriate behaviour, as it was in Europe. For example, the struggle involving China, Japan and Korea in the 1590s can be seen in terms of multi-polarity, but that was certainly not how China saw the situation. Instead, there was a sense of Japan as challenging a divinely ordained Chinese imperial system. These contrasts were an important aspect of the ideological situation.

Multi-polarity in Europe led not so much to an exceptionally high rate of conflict, but to an understanding of this conflict as inevitable, with related assumptions about the need for, and possibility of, state development to produce the necessary resources. Moreover, these conflicts were linked to the growth of national consciousness, whether described, subsequently, in terms of nationalism or of proto-nationalism, and whether expressed or not in imperial structures. Irrespective of how far the term nationalism is adopted, the pattern of national identification through conflict seen for example in the case of England, France and Scotland in the fourteenth and fifteenth centuries had, in part, been restricted in the sixteenth and seventeenth centuries by the pressures of ideological rivalry and the consequences of dynasticism which, depending on circumstances, could challenge or support ideas and practices of nationhood and national politics. At the same time, the ideological rivalries and power politics of the Reformation led to a marked increase in the rhetoric of nationalism, not least as international authority in the case of the Papacy was rejected and as individual states became the units of confessional activity. This increase was particularly notable in Scandinavia, England and Scotland. The collapse of the dynastic link between Poland and Sweden in the 1590s was, in part, a product of opposition in Lutheran Sweden to a Catholic ruler. Yet, religion was not the sole factor. Despite a common Catholicism, Portugal rejected the dynastic link with Spain in 1640.

National identification through conflict became more prominent from the late eighteenth century and, even more, in the nineteenth, albeit with similar ideological and dynastic restrictions to the earlier age of religious conflict from the 1520s to 1640s. The intensity and outcome of this interplay was not matched elsewhere in the world. Rivalry between what may be described as proto-nationalism and, later, nationalism and, on the other hand, these competing identities and drives helped explain much of the conflict of the period and, therefore, why states invested their hope, efforts and resources so heavily in war. Invested, however, makes the individual and collective decisions to do so sound reasonable and based on calculations of profit and loss. This was not in fact the case. The context and process of decision-making, instead, should be approached in terms of emotions and beliefs as well as calculations. These emotions and beliefs combined to ensure bellicosity. This, however, did not mean that war occurred all the time. Instead, there were particular occasions when decisions were taken to engage in war. These occasions reflected bellicosity in more specific terms.

Since 1945, the situation appears different, but that conclusion is less obvious if the context is that of Russia and Eastern Europe. The public display in Moscow in 2015 of new weaponry, such as the RS–24 Yars intercontinental ballistic missile, reflected a fascination with weaponry and pride of display not seen in most of Western Europe. Whether this amounted to deterrence or threat or both is a matter for discussion, as is whether such a stance was a rational matter of graduated power politics, or a vicarious commitment to glory and the appeal of force. At any event, the notion that past values are no longer pertinent appears far less relevant than had seemed to be the case in the 1990s. In 2014, Russia's aggression in Ukraine amounted, with Crimea, to the first annexation of sovereign territory in Europe since the Second World War.

Rivalries between nationalism and alternative identities also contributed to the extent to which states were only one category of player in the wars and warfulness of the period. Ideological resistance, the defence of particular interests and opposition to the particular acts and demands of regular forces encouraged a violent response to states and broke down the monopolization of war by the military. Examples included confessional activism during the Wars of Religion from the 1520s to the 1640s, stemming from the Protestant Reformation, and the comparable ideological engagement, first, of the French Revolutionary and Napoleonic period, and, subsequently, of the twentieth century. Thus, the bitter resistance to

French forces in southern Italy in 1798 and 1806, and in Spain in 1808–14, prefigured that to German and Soviet armies in the twentieth century. This was not simply a matter of popular violence in response to conquest by ideologically hostile foreign forces. There was also the same pattern within states, as with the Carlist wars in nineteenth-century Spain and the Civil War there of 1936–9.

Moreover, the extent of civil warfare in Spain in the 1640s and 1700s underlined the manner in which it was not only in periods and terms of clear ideological struggles such as the 1800s and 1930s that the state faced ideologically motivated resistance and, as a result, did not wield control. There were also instances in which this point was true in the international category, such as the Genoese rising against Austrian occupation in 1746 and the subsequent successful resistance of the city to Austrian attempts to recapture it. Thus, popular participation cut across the general impact of state-building on the military, as well as the nexus identified by Charles Tilly. The weaknesses of the modern state may make this point even more relevant in the future.

Therefore, the thesis of the relationship between war and state transformation suffers not only from the misleading tendency to present war as a single-purpose activity with a clear trajectory, but also from the failure to place due weight on the many significant cultural and sociological factors involved in military organization, activity, capacity and effectiveness. These factors could cut across what might appear, in a schematic approach, to be the best form of organization in terms of bureaucratic efficiency or the accumulation of coercion and capital. This approach offers a crude and ahistorical utilitarianism in the shape of modern-style bureaucratic processes, one that underplays the inherent complexity of war.

NOTES

Preface

1   C. J. Esdaile, 'The British Army in the Napoleonic Wars: Approaches Old and New', *English Historical Review*, 130 (2015): 123–37.

2   W. C. Horsley (trans), *The Chronicles of an Old Campaigner* (London, 1904), pp. 184–5.

3   See, for example, C. S. Gray, *Strategy and Defence Planning. Meeting the Challenge of Uncertainty* (Oxford, 2014).

4   K. Helleiner, 'The Vital Revolution Reconsidered', *Canadian Journal of Economics and Political Science*, 23 (1957): 1.

5   G. Satterfield, *Princes, Posts and Partisans. The Army of Louis XIV and Partisan Warfare in the Netherlands, 1673–1678* (Leiden, 2003).

6   For a different focus, see D. Armitage, *Civil War: A History in Ideas* (New York, 2016).

7   Stone to Black, email, 29 April 2015.

8   Anon., *The Chimera: Or the French Way of Paying National Debts, Laid Open* (London, 1719), cited in J. Macdonald, *A Free Nation Deep in Debt: The Financial Roots of Democracy* (Princeton, NJ, 2003), p. 205.

9   E. Gibbon, *The History of the Decline and Fall of the Roman Empire*, edited by J. B. Bury (7 vols, London, 1897–1901), IV, 167; H. J. Mackinder, 'The Geographical Pivot of History', *Geographical Journal*, 23 (1904): 421–44.

Introduction

1   C. Tilly, *Coercion, Capital, and European States, AD 990–1990* (Oxford, 1990) and 'States, State Transformation, and War', in J. H. Bentley (ed.), *The Oxford Handbook of World History* (Oxford, 2011), pp. 190–1; S. P. Reyna, 'The Force of Two Logics: Predatory and Capital Accumulation in the Making of the Great Leviathan, 1415–1763', in Reyna and R. E. Downs (eds), *Deadly Developments: Capitalism, States and War* (Amsterdam, 1999), pp. 23–68. For Tilly's other relevant arguments as 'too simple', J. A. Goldstone, 'Political Trajectories Compared', in J. H. Bentley, S. Subrahmanyam and M. E. Wiesner-Hanks (eds), *The Cambridge World*

History. VI. The Construction of a Global World, 1400–1800 CE. Part I: Foundations (Cambridge, 2015), p. 453.

2   C. J. Rogers (ed.), *The Military Revolution Debate: Readings on the Military Transformation of Early Modern Europe* (Boulder, CO, 1995).

3   C. Freeman, 'How to Defeat a Caliphate', *Spectator*, 30 May 2015, pp. 14–15.

4   D. Parrott, *The Business of War: Military Enterprise and Military Revolution in Early Modern Europe* (Cambridge, 2012).

5   N. Younger, *War and Politics in the Elizabethan Counties* (Manchester, 2012).

6   I. Sherer, '"All of Us, in One Voice, Demand What's Owed Us": Mutiny in the Spanish Infantry during the Italian Wars, 1525–1538', *Journal of Military History*, 78 (2014): 893–926.

7   M. M. Rabà, 'All servizio dell' Impero. Grandi signorie feudali e difesa della supremazia asburgica in Italia settentrionale. Il caso Emiliano, 1547–1559', *Rivista di Studi Militari*, 2 (2013): 75–118.

8   I. Wallerstein, *The Modern World System II: Mercantilism and the Consolidation of the European World-Economy, 1600–1750* (New York, 1980).

9   C. Treblicock, '"Spin-Off" in British Economic History: Armaments and Industry, 1760–1914', *Economic History Review*, 22 (1969): 480.

10 R. Middleton, 'Naval Administration in the Age of Pitt and Anson, 1755–1763', in J. Black and P. Woodfine (eds), *The British Navy and the Use of Naval Power in the Eighteenth Century* (Leicester, 1988), pp. 109–12; J. MacDonald, *Feeding Nelson's Navy: The True Story of Food at Sea in the Georgian Era* (London, 2004); C. Wilkinson, *The British Navy and the State in the Eighteenth Century* (Woodbridge, 2004); G. E. Bannerman, *Merchants and the Military in Eighteenth-Century Britain: British Army Contracts and Domestic Supply, 1737–1763* (London, 2008); D. Syrett, *Shipping and Military Power in the Seven Years War: The Sails of Victory* (Exeter, 2008); R. J. W. Knight and M. Wilcox, *Sustaining the Fleet, 1793–1815: War, the British Navy and the Contractor State* (Woodbridge, 2010); R. Morriss, *The Foundations of British Maritime Ascendancy: Resources, Logistics and the State 1755–1815* (Cambridge, 2011); J. Davey, *The Transformation of British Naval Strategy: Seapower and Supply in Northern Europe, 1808–1812* (Woodbridge, 2012); C. Buchet, *The British Navy, Economy and Society in the Seven Years War* (Woodbridge, 2013).

11 D. Brunsman, *The Evil Necessity: British Naval Impressment in the Eighteenth-Century Atlantic World* (Charlottesville, VI, 2013).

12 G. J. Bryant, *The Emergence of British Power in India 1600–1784: A Grand Strategic Interpretation* (Woodbridge, 2011).

13 R. J. W. Knight, *Britain against Napoleon: The Organisation of Victory, 1783–1815* (London, 2013).

14 C. Antunes, 'Introduction', in Antunes and J. Gommans (eds), *Exploring the Dutch Empire. Agents, Networks and Institutions, 1600–2000* (London, 2015), p. xiv.

15 Michael Fallon, Secretary of State for Defence, 'Why We are not Feeble', *Sunday Telegraph*, 21 June 2015, p. 18.

16 Richard to Jeremy Browne, 14 Aug. 1759, BL. RP. 3284.

17 W. Cobbett (ed.), *The Parliamentary History of England from the Earliest Period to the Year 1803* (36 vols, London, 1806–20), 19, col. 948.

18 See, for example, D. Copeland, *Economic Interdependence and War* (Princeton, NJ, 2014), and C. S. Gray, *Strategy and Defence Planning. Meeting the Challenge of Uncertainty* (Oxford, 2014).

19 P. K. O'Brien, 'A Global Perspective for the Comprehension of Fiscal State Formation from the Rise of Venice to the Opium War', in R. Harding and S. S. Ferri (eds), *The Contractor State and its Implications, 1659–1815* (Gran Canaria, 2012), pp. 233–4.

20 T. J. Dandelet, *The Renaissance of Empire in Early Modern Europe* (Cambridge, 2014).

21 P. P. O'Brien, *How the War was Won. Air-Sea Power and Allied Victory in World War II* (Cambridge, 2015).

22 G. Chet, 'Teaching in the Shadow of the Military Revolution', *Journal of Military History*, 78 (2014): 1073–4.

23 N. Housley, *Crusading and the Ottoman Threat, 1453–1505* (Oxford, 2012).

24 B. S. Hall, 'The Corning of Gunpowder and the Development of Firearms in the Renaissance', in B. J. Buchanan (ed.), *Gunpowder* (Bath, 1996), pp. 93–4.

25 C. J. Rogers, 'The Medieval Legacy', in G. Mortimer (ed.), *Early Modern Military History, 1450–1815* (Basingstoke, 2004), pp. 6–24, esp. 20–3.

The Fracturing of the European System, 1450–1600

1 J. Black, *War in the World. A Comparative History 1450–1600* (Basingstoke, 2011).

2 G. Parker, *The Military Revolution: Military Innovation and the Rise of the West, 1500–1800* (Cambridge, 1988; 2nd edn, Cambridge, 1996); C. J. Rogers (ed.), *The Military Revolution Debate: Readings on the Military Transformation of Early Modern Europe* (Boulder, CO, 1995).

3 D. A. Bell, 'Global Conceptual Legacies', in D. Andress (ed.), *The Oxford Handbook of the French Revolution* (Oxford, 2015), pp. 642–58.

4 W. H. McNeill, *The Age of Gunpowder Empires, 1450–1800* (Washington, 1989).

5 D. Peers (ed.), *Warfare and Empires: Contact and Conflict between European and Non-European Military and Maritime Forces and Cultures* (Aldershot, 1997), p. xvii.

6 Robertson, *Charles V* (3 vols, London, 1769), I, 134–5.

7   A. N. Kurat, 'The Turkish Expedition to Astrakhan in 1569 and the Problem of the Don-Volga Canal', *Slavonic and East European Review*, 40 (1961): 7–23.

8   G. Casale, *The Ottoman Age of Exploration* (Oxford, 2010).

9   E. Tenace, 'Messianic Imperialism or Traditional Dynasticism? The Grand Strategy of Philip II and the Spanish Failure in the Wars of the 1590s', in T. Andrade and W. Roger (eds), *The Limits of Empire: European Imperial Formations in Early Modern World History* (Farnham, 2012), pp. 280–307, commenting on G. Parker, *The Grand Strategy of Philip II* (New Haven, CT, 1998), p. 273.

10 R. Murphey, 'Süleyman I and the Conquest of Hungary: Ottoman Manifest Destiny or a Delayed Reaction to Charles V's Universalist Vision', *Journal of Early Modern History*, 5 (2001): 197–221.

11 Charles abdicated the Imperial title on 3 August 1556 in favour of his brother who was free to decide when it should take effect. This formally took effect on 14 March 1558 when Ferdinand agreed this with the Electors.

12 J. Tracy, *Emperor Charles V, Impresario of War: Campaign Strategy, International Finance, and Domestic Politics* (Cambridge, 2002); H. Kleinschmidt, *Charles V: The World Emperor* (Stroud, 2004); L. Silver, 'Shining Armor: Maximilian I as Holy Roman Emperor', *Museum Studies: Art Institute of Chicago*, 12 (1985): 8–29.

13 C. Nall, *Reading and War in Fifteenth-Century England: From Lydgate to Malory* (Woodbridge, 2012).

14 D. Goodman, *Spanish Naval Power, 1589–1665. Reconstruction and Defeat* (Cambridge, 1996).

15 C. Phillips, *Six Galleons for the King of Spain: Imperial Defense in the Early Seventeenth Century* (Baltimore, MD, 1986).

16 G. I. Halfond (ed.), *The Medieval Way of War. Studies in Medieval Military History in Honor of Bernard S. Bachrach* (Farnham, 2015), pp. 185–204.

17 G. Parker, 'The "Military Revolution, 1560–1660" – A Myth?', in C. J. Rogers (ed.), *The Military Revolution Debate: Readings on the Military Transformation of Early Modern Europe* (Boulder, CO), p. 39; M.'t Hart, *The Dutch Wars of Independence: Warfare and Commerce in the Netherlands, 1570–1680* (Abingdon, 2014), p. 64.

18 F. Braudel, *The Mediterranean and the Mediterranean World in the Age of Philip II* (London, 1966).

19 J. F. Guilmartin, *Gunpowder and Galleys: Changing Technology and Mediterranean Warfare at Sea in the Sixteenth Century* (Cambridge, 1974); M. Philippides and W. K. Hanak, *The Siege and the Fall of Constantinople in 1453* (Farnham, 2012).

20 C. Imber, 'The Reconstruction of the Ottoman Fleet after the Battle of Lepanto', in *Studies in Ottoman History and Law* (Istanbul, 1996), pp. 85–101.

21 Y. Park, *Admiral Yi Sun-shin and His Turtleboat Armada: A Comprehensive Account of the Resistance of Korea to the 11th Century Japanese Invasion*

(Seoul, 1973); S. Turnbull, *Samurai Invasion: Japan's Korean War, 1592–1598* (London, 2002).

22 W. E. Lee (ed.), *Empires and Indigenes. Intercultural Alliance, Imperial Expansion and Warfare in the Early Modern World* (New York, 2011).

23 M. C. Fissel, *English Warfare, 1511–1642* (London, 2001), p. 282.

24 M. A. Bakhit, *The Ottoman Province of Damascus in the Sixteenth Century* (Beirut, 1980), pp. 94, 98, 225; A. C. S. Peacock (ed.), *The Frontiers of the Ottoman World* (Oxford, 2009).

25 For a more generally instructive scepticism, G. Ágoston, 'Firearms and Military Adaptation: The Ottomans and the European Military Revolution, 1450–1800', *Journal of World History*, 25 (2014): 85–124. Among his other important works, '"The Most Powerful Empire": Ottoman Flexibility and Military Might', in G. Zimmar and D. Hicks (eds), *Empires and Superpowers: Their Rise and Fall* (Washington, 2005), pp. 121–71, 'Disjointed Historiography and Islamic Military Technology: The European Military Revolution Debate and the Ottomans', in M. K. Durukal (ed.), *Essays in Honour of Ekmeleddin Ihsanoğlu* (Istanbul, 2006), pp. 567–82, 'Knowledge, Technology and Warfare in Europe and the Ottoman Empire in the Early Modern Period', in S. Kenan (ed.), *The Ottomans and Europe: Travel, Encounter and Interaction* (Istanbul, 2010), pp. 471–80, 'War-Winning Weapons? On the Decisiveness of Ottoman Firearms from the Siege of Constantinople (1453) to Mohacs (1526)', *Journal of Turkish Studies*, 39 (2013): 129–43. See also C. Issawi, 'The Ottoman–Habsburg Balance of Forces', in H. Inalcik and C. Kafadar (eds), *Süleyman and His Time* (Istanbul, 1993), pp. 145–51.

26 G. J. Bryant, 'Asymmetric Warfare: The British Experience in Eighteenth-Century India', *Journal of Military History*, 68 (2004): 431–69.

27 T. Andrade, *Lost Colony: The Untold Story of Europe's First War with China* (Princeton, NJ, 2011).

28 P. C. Allen, *Philip III and the Pax Hispanica, 1598–1621: The Failure of Grand Strategy* (New Haven, CT, 2000).

29 E. Tenace, 'A Strategy of Reaction: The Armadas of 1596 and 1597 and the Spanish Struggle for European Hegemony', *English Historical Review*, 118 (2003): 855–82. See also G. Parker, *The World Is Not Enough: The Imperial Vision of Philip II of Spain* (Waco, TX, 2001) and *Success Is Never Final: Empire, War, and Faith in Early Modern Europe* (New York, 2002).

30 J. Black, *War in the World. A Comparative History 1450–1600* (Basingstoke, 2011) and *Beyond the Military Revolution. War in the Seventeenth-Century World* (Basingstoke, 2011). For an emphasis on political factors as also shaping military practice, see P. H. Wilson, 'Meaningless Conflict? The Character of the Thirty Years' War', in F. C. Schneid (ed.), *The Projection and Limitations of Imperial Powers, 1618–1850* (Leiden, 2012), p. 32.

31 G. Parker, *The Military Revolution: Military Innovation and the Rise of the West, 1500–1800* (Cambridge, 1988; 2nd edn, Cambridge, 1996).

32 K. Chase, *Firearms: A Global History to 1700* (Cambridge, 2003); A. Stanziani, *Bâtisseurs d'empires. Russie, Chine et Inde à la croisée des*

mondes, xvᵉ–xixᵉ siècle (Paris, 2012) and *After Oriental Despotism. Eurasian Growth in a Global Perspective* (London, 2014).

33 G. Parker, *Global Crisis: War, Climate Change and Catastrophe in the Seventeenth Century* (New Haven, CT, 2013).

34 K. DeVries, *Medieval Military Technology* (Peterborough, Ontario, 1992), pp. 143–68, 'The Impact of Gunpowder Weaponry on Siege Warfare in the Hundred Years War', in I. A. Corfis and M. Wolfe (eds), *The Medieval City under Siege* (Woodbridge, 1995), pp. 227–44, and 'The Use of Gunpowder Weaponry by and against Joan of Arc during the Hundred Years War', *War and Society*, 14 (1996): 1–15. For continuities, A. Ayton and J. Price (eds), *The Medieval Military Revolution: State, Society and Military Change in Medieval and Early Modern Europe* (London, 1998); C. J. Rogers, 'The Medieval Legacy', in G. Mortimer (ed.), *Early Modern Military History, 1450–1815* (Basingstoke, 2004), pp. 6–24, and F. Tallett and D. J. B. Trim (eds), *European Warfare, 1350–1750* (Cambridge, 2010).

35 S. Morillo, 'Guns and Government: A Comparative Study of Europe and Japan', *Journal of World History*, 6 (1995): 75–106. For comparison, see also T. Andrade, H. H. Kang and K. Cooper, 'A Korean Military Revolution?: Parallel Military Innovations in East Asia and Europe', *Journal of World History*, 25 (2014): 51–84.

36 E. B. Monshi, *History of Shah Abbas the Great* (Boulder, CO, 1978); M. Haneda, 'The Evolution of the Safavid Royal Guard', *Iranian Studies*, 21 (1989): 57–86.

37 R. S. Love, '"All the King's Horsemen": The Equestrian Army of Henri IV, 1585–1598', *Sixteenth-Century Journal*, 22 (1991): 511–33.

38 G. Parker, 'The Limits to Revolutions in Military Affairs: Maurice of Nassau, the Battle of Nieuwpoort (1600), and the Legacy', *Journal of Military History*, 71 (2007): 366–9.

39 H. J. Mackinder, 'The Geographical Pivot of History', *Geographical Journal*, 23 (1904): 421.

40 Ibid., pp. 432–3.

41 D. Parrott, *The Business of War. Military Enterprise and Military Revolution in Early Modern Europe* (Cambridge, 2012).

42 S. Kyriakidis, *Warfare in Late Byzantium, 1204–1453* (Leiden, 2011), p. 223.

43 M. Greene, *Catholic Pirates and Greek Merchants: A Maritime History of the Early Modern Mediterranean* (Princeton, NJ, 2011); P. N. Miller, *Peiresc's Mediterranean World* (Cambridge, MA, 2015), pp. 293–8.

44 J. Black, *Kings, Nobles and Commoners. States and Societies in Early Modern Europe* (London, 2004).

45 J. B. Wood, *The King's Army: Warfare, Soldiers and Society during the Wars of Religion in France, 1562–1576* (Cambridge, 1996).

46 K. DeVries, 'Gunpowder Weaponry and the Rise of the Early Modern State', *War in History*, 5 (1998): 127–45.

47 W. Cook, 'The Cannon Conquest of Násrid Spain and the End of the Reconquista', *Journal of Military History*, 57 (1993): 43–70.

48 C. Tilly (ed.), *The Formation of National States in Western Europe* (Princeton, NJ, 1975); Tilly, *Coercion, Capital, and European States, AD 990–1990* (Oxford, 1990); B. Downing, *The Military Revolution and Political Change: Origins of Democracy and Autocracy in Early Modern Europe* (Princeton, NJ, 1990). For a Chinese equivalent, Xu Erbin, *Military Revolutions in a Transitive Society: Military Reformations and Social Change in 14th–17th Century Europe* (Harbin, 2008).

49 R. M. Eaton and P. B. Wagoner, 'Warfare on the Deccan Plateau, 1450–1600: A Military Revolution in Early Modern India?', *Journal of World History*, 25 (2014): 50.

50 B. Teschke, 'Revisiting the "War-Makes-States" Thesis: War, Taxation and Social Property Relations in Early Modern Europe', in O. Asbach and P. Schröder (eds), *War, the State and International Law in Seventeenth-Century Europe* (Farnham, 2010), p. 58.

51 D. Parrott, *Richelieu's Army: War, Government and Society in France, 1624–1642* (Cambridge, 2002); G. Rowlands, *The Dynastic State and the Army under Louis XIV: Royal Service and Private Interest, 1661–1701* (Cambridge, 2002).

52 D. Grummitt, 'The Defence of Calais and the Development of Gunpowder Weaponry in England in the Late Fifteenth Century', *War in History*, 7 (2000): 253–72.

53 G. Hanlon, *The Twilight of a Military Tradition: Italian Aristocrats and European Conflicts, 1560–1800* (London, 1996); W. Maltby, *Alba* (Berkeley, CA, 1983).

54 N. Murphy, 'Henry VIII's First Invasion of France: The Gascon Expedition of 1512', *English Historical Review*, 130 (2015): 43.

55 L. Martines, *Furies. War in Europe 1450–1700* (London, 2013).

56 G. Alfani, *Calamities and the Economy in Renaissance Italy: The Grand Tour of the Horsemen of the Apocalypse* (Basingstoke, 2013).

The Creation of Lasting Standing Forces, 1600–1700

1 D. Parrott, 'Strategy and Tactics in the Thirty Years' War: The "Military Revolution"', in Rogers (ed.), *Military Revolution Debate*, p. 232.

2 G. Foard, *Naseby: The Decisive Campaign* (Barnsley, 1995).

3 G. Robinson, *Horses, People and Parliament in the English Civil War: Extracting Resources and Constructing Allegiance* (Farnham, 2012).

4 G. Mortimer, 'War by Contract, Credit and Contribution: The Thirty Years War', in Mortimer (ed.), *Early Modern Military History, 1450–1815* (Basingstoke, 2004), pp. 115–16.

5 G. Phillips, *The Anglo-Scots Wars 1513–1550* (Woodbridge, 1999), p. 257;

J. Raymond, *Henry VIII's Military Revolution: The Armies of Sixteenth-Century Britain and Europe* (Woodbridge, 2007).

6   D. Lupton, *A Warre-Like Treatise of the Pike, or, Some Experimental Resolves, for lessening the number, and disabling the use of the pike in warre* (London, 1642), pp. 99–100.

7   J. A. Lynn, *Giant of the Grand Siècle: The French Army, 1610–1715* (Cambridge, 1997), p. 4–76.

8   Douglass, *Schola Martis, or the Arte of War ... as Practised in Flanders*, BL. Add. 27892 fols 213–17.

9   D. Chandler, *The Art of Warfare in the Age of Marlborough* (Staplehurst, 1976), p. 111; D. Blakemore, *Destructive and Formidable: British Infantry Firepower 1642–1765* (London, 2014).

10 Anon., *The New Exercise of Flintlocks and Bayonets; appointed by the Duke of Marlborough* (London, 1708), p. 6.

11 Caesar, *The Commentaries of C. Julius Caesar* (London, 1677).

12 Sir James Turner, *Pallas Armata, Military Essayes of the Ancient Grecian, Roman, and Modern Art of War* (London, 1683), pp. 169, 178–86.

13 B. Simms, *Europe. The Struggle for Supremacy. From 1453 to the Present* (London, 2013).

14 D. Showalter, 'Europe's Way of War, 1815–64', in J. Black (ed.), *European Warfare 1815–2000* (Basingstoke, 2002), p. 27. For another critique of Whiggery and progressivism, D. Parrott, review published in *War in History*, 4 (1997): 479.

15 H. Duccini, *Faire voir, faire croire: L'Opinion publique sous Louis XIII* (Paris, 2003).

16 NA. SP. 84/202 fols 73, 126, 84/207 fol. 124.

17 The painting now hangs in the Musée des Beaux-Arts de Lyon.

18 NA. SP. 78/124 fol. 289.

19 P. Sonnino, *Louis XIV and the Origins of the Dutch War* (Cambridge, 1988).

20 C. Taylor, *Chivalry and the Ideals of Knighthood in France* (Cambridge, 2013).

21 P. H. Wilson, *German Armies. War and German Politics 1648–1806* (London, 1998).

22 G. Parker, *Global Crisis: War, Climate Change and Catastrophe in the Seventeenth Century* (New Haven, CT, 2013).

23 NA. SP. 80/15 fol. 122, 80/16 fol. 6.

24 Report by Roger Meredith from The Hague, 14 Jan. 1676, NA. SP. 84/200 fol. 1.

25 NA. SP. 84/202 fol. 128.

26 J. Ehrman, *The Navy in the War of William III: Its State and Direction, 1689–1697* (Cambridge, 1953).

27 N. A. M. Rodger, *The Command of the Ocean: A Naval History of Britain, 1649–1815* (London, 2004), p. 579.

28　J. A. Lynn, 'The Evolution of Army Style in the Modern West, 800-2000', *International History Review*, 18 (1996): 507–45.

29　J. Glete, *War and the State in Early Modern Europe: Spain, the Dutch Republic, and Sweden as Fiscal-Military States, 1500–1660* (London, 2002).

30　J. Shovlin, 'War and Peace. Trade, International Competition, and Political Economy', in P. J. Stern and C. Wennerlind (eds), *Mercantilism Reimagined. Political Economy in Early Modern Britain and Its Empire* (Oxford, 2014), p. 315.

31　F. Wakeman, *The Great Enterprise: The Manchu Reconstruction of Imperial Order in Seventeenth-Century China* (Berkeley, CA, 1985).

The Aristocratic Order and the Pressures on it, 1700–1800

1　C. Storrs, 'Philip V and the Revival of Spain, 1713–48', in T. J. Dadson and J. H. Elliott (eds), *Britain, Spain and the Treaty of Utrecht, 1713–2013* (London, 2014), p. 84.

2　G. Ágoston, 'Firearms and Military Adaptation: The Ottomans and the European Military Revolution, 1450–1800', *Journal of World History*, 25 (2014): 123.

3　Cabinet Minute, 29 Sept. 1756, BL. Add. 51376 fols 85–6.

4　Robert Keith, British envoy in Vienna, to Newcastle, 17 Jan. 1753, NA. SP. 80/191; Frederick II to Lord Marshal, Prussian envoy in France, 20 Jan. 1753, *Polit. Corr.*, IX, 315; Vergennes, French envoy in Mannheim, to Saint-Contest, French Foreign Minister, 5 Feb. 1753, AE. CP. Palatinat 78 fol. 104.

5　For example, Report from Spain, 23 July 1738, Lucca, Archivio di Stato, Anziani al Tempo della Libertà, 634 fol. 59.

6　For the argument that dynasticism functioned as a moderating norm by limiting claims, containing stakes and requiring the regulation of shifts in sovereignty, J. Shovlin, 'War and Peace. Trade, International Competition, and Political Economy', in P. J. Stern and C. Wennerlind (eds), *Mercantilism Reimagined. Political Economy in Early Modern Britain and Its Empire* (Oxford, 2014), p. 315.

7　J. Ostwald, *Vauban under Siege: Engineering Efficiency and Martial Vigor in the War of the Spanish Succession* (Leiden, 2007).

8　See illustrations in A. Husslein-Arco (ed.), *Prince Eugene's Winter Palace* (Vienna, 2013), esp. pp. 41, 59, 77–84.

9　J. Ostwald, 'The "Decisive" Battle of Ramillies, 1706: Prerequisites for Decisiveness in Early Modern Warfare', *Journal of Military History*, 64 (2000): 664.

10　J. B. Hattendorf et al. (eds), *Marlborough: Soldier and Diplomat* (Rotterdam, 2012).

11 Bedford, Bedfordshire Record Office, Lucas Papers 30/9/17/3. I would like to thank Lady Lucas for permission to use these papers.

12 W-G. Monahan, *Let God Arise: The War and Rebellion of the Camisards* (Oxford, 2014).

13 AE. CP. Espagne 419 fol. 67.

14 Keith to Robert, 4th Earl of Holdernesse, Secretary of State for the Northern Department, NA. SP. 80/197 fols 104–24.

15 Townshend to John, 3rd Earl of Bute, 17 Sept. 1761, Mount Stuart, Bute papers, 7/23.

16 Anon., *A Letter to the People of England, Upon the Militia* (London, 1757), p. 10.

17 Memoranda of James Harris MP, Jan. 1779, London, History of Parliament transcripts.

18 Auckland to Morton Eden, 10, 31 Aug. 1792, BL. Add. 24444 fols 55, 169, 179.

19 Sheridan, 4 Ap. 1797, W. Cobbett (ed.), *Parliamentary History of England*, vol. 33 (London, 1818), cols 226–7.

The Rise of the Bureaucratic State and of Mass Society, 1800–1900

1 C. Bassford, *Clausewitz in English: The Reception of Clausewitz in Britain and America 1815–1945* (New York, 1994).

2 C. Telp, 'The Prussian Army in the Jena Campaign', in A. Forrest and P. H. Wilson (eds), *The Bee and the Eagle: Napoleonic France and the End of the Holy Roman Empire, 1806* (Basingstoke, 2009), pp. 155–71.

3 J. A. Lynn, 'Toward an Army of Honor: The Moral Evolution of the French Army, 1789–1815', *French Historical Studies*, 16 (1989): 171–2.

4 T. C. W. Blanning, *The French Revolution in Germany: Occupation and Resistance in the Rhineland, 1792–1802* (Oxford, 1983); D. Laven, *Venice and Venetia under the Habsburgs, 1815–1835* (Oxford, 2002).

5 C. J. Esdaile, *Outpost of Empire: The Napoleonic Occupation of Andalucia, 1810–1812* (Norman, OK, 2012).

6 B. Colson, *Napoleon on War* (Oxford, 2015), p. 124.

7 H. J. Davies, *Wellington's Wars: The Making of a Military Genius* (New Haven, CT, 2012).

8 Stanhope to Duke of York, 19 June 1815, BL. Add. 34703 fol. 22.

9 A. Forrest, *Waterloo* (Oxford, 2015), p. 52.

10 D. Lieven, *Russia Against Napoleon* (London, 2010).

11 Hill to Rev. Jacob Ley, 7 July 1815, Hill papers, private owner.

12 C. Esdaile, *Women in the Peninsular War* (Norman, OK, 2014).

13 London, National Army Museum, 1975-09-62–1.

14 J. M. House, *Controlling Paris: Armed Forces and Counter-Revolution, 1789–1848* (New York, 2014).

15 R. Holroyd, 'The Bourbon Army, 1815–1830', *Historical Journal*, 14 (1971): p. 551.

16 BL. Add. 54483 fol. 22.

17 F. C. Schneid, *The French-Piedmontese Campaign of 1859* (Rome, 2014).

18 K. Epstein, *Torpedo: Inventing the Military-Industrial Complex in the United States and Great Britain* (London, 2014), p. 2.

19 M. Epkenhans, 'Military-industrial Relations in Imperial Germany, 1870–1914', *War in History*, 10 (2003): 17.

20 N. Arielli and B. Collins (eds), *Transnational Soldiers: Foreign Military Enlistment in the Modern Era* (Basingstoke, 2013).

21 J. Osterhammel, *The Transformation of the World. A Global History of the Nineteenth Century* (Princeton, NJ, 2014), p. 484.

22 R. Tombs, *The War against Paris 1871* (Cambridge, 1981).

23 S. Förster, 'Facing "People's War": Moltke the Elder and Germany's Military Options After 1871', *Journal of Strategic Studies*, 10 (1987): 219.

24 C. Trebilcock, *The Vickers Brothers: Armaments and Enterprise 1854–1914* (London, 1977).

25 H. S. Maxim, 'Experiments with High Explosives in Large Guns', *North American Review*, 168 (February 1899), pp. 142–50; R. Humble, *Before the Dreadnought* (London, 1976), p. 119. I am grateful for the advice of Andrew English.

26 R. Friedel, *A Culture of Improvement: Technology and the Western Millennium* (Cambridge, MA, 2007), p. 372.

27 *Hansard*, 26 July 1861, vol. 164, cc. 1629–40.

28 J. W. M. Hichberger, *Images of the Army: The Military in British Art, 1815–1914* (Manchester, 1988).

29 L. Brown, *Victorian News and Newspapers* (Oxford, 1985), p. 98.

30 L. Cole, *Military Culture and Popular Patriotism in Late Imperial Austria* (Oxford, 2014).

31 T. Buk-Swienty, *1864. The Forgotten War that Shaped Modern Europe* (London, 2015).

32 R. Bassett, *For God and Kaiser. The Imperial Austrian Army* (New Haven, CT, 2015).

The Challenges of Total War and Ideology, 1900–50

1 *Poilu. The World War I Notebooks of Corporal Louis Barthas*, translated by Edward Strauss (New Haven, CT, 2014). Barthas, in the French army, refers to a bombardment preparatory to an offensive the following day.

2 D. Geppert, W. Mulligan and A. Rose (eds), *The Wars before the Great War. Conflict and International Politics before the Outbreak of the First World War* (Cambridge, 2015).

3 J. Encke, 'War Noises on the Battlefield: On Fighting Underground and Learning to Listen in the Great War', *German Historical Institute London Bulletin*, 37 (May 2015): 7–21.

4 L. Sondhaus, *The Great War at Sea: A Naval History of the First World War* (Cambridge, 2014).

5 J. Krause, 'The French Battle for Vimy Ridge, Spring 1915', *Journal of Military History*, 77 (2013): 112–13.

6 M. B. Barrett, *Prelude to Blitzkrieg: The 1916 Austro–German Campaign in Romania* (Bloomington, IN, 2013).

7 J. Boff, *Winning and Losing on the Western Front: The British Third Army and the Defeat of Germany in 1918* (Cambridge, 2012).

8 A. Watson, *Ring of Steel: Germany and Austria-Hungary in World War I* (London, 2014).

9 War Cabinet, 2 Jan., 9 Feb. 1917, NA. CAB. 23/8; D. Welch and J. Fox (eds), *Justifying War: Propaganda, Politics, and the Modern Age* (Basingstoke, 2012).

10 W. Klinkert, *Defending Neutrality: The Netherlands Prepares for War, 1900–1925* (Leiden, 2013).

11 M. Alpert, *The Republican Army in the Spanish Civil War, 1936–1939* (Cambridge, 2013).

12 L. Ward, *The London County Council Bomb Damage Maps* (London, 2015).

13 C. W. H. Luther, *Barbarossa Unleashed: The German Blitzkrieg through Central Russia to the Gates of Moscow, June-December 1941* (Atglen, Pennsylvania, 2013); D. Stahel, *Operation Barbarossa and Germany's Defeat in the East* (Cambridge, 2009).

14 D. Stahel, *Operation Typhoon: Hitler's March on Moscow, October 1941* (Cambridge, 2013); W. Z. Goldman and D. Filtzer (eds), *Hunger and War. Food Provisioning in the Soviet Union during World War II* (Bloomington, IN, 2015).

15 R. M. Citino, *The Wehrmacht Retreats: Fighting a Lost War, 1943* (Lawrence, KS, 2012).

16 C. L. Symonds, *Neptune: The Allied Invasion of Europe and the D-Day Landings* (New York, 2014).

17   J. Ludewig, *Rückzug: The German Retreat from France, 1944* (Lexington, KT, 2012).

18   A. Beevor, *Ardennes 1944: Hitler's Last Gamble* (London, 2015).

19   N. D. Risser, *France under Fire: German Invasion, Civilian Flight, and Family Survival during World War II* (Cambridge, 2012).

20   C. J. M. Goulter, 'The Greek Civil War: A National Army's Counter-insurgency Triumph', *Journal of Military History*, 78 (2014), p. 1055.

The Erosion of the Nation-Army, 1950–2000

1   J. Hoffenaar and D. Krüger (eds), *Blueprints for Battle: Planning for War in Central Europe, 1948–1968* (Lexington, KT, 2012).

2   D. Sanders, 'The Bulgarian Navy after the Cold War. Challenges of Building and Modernising an Effective Navy', *Naval War College Review*, 68, 2 (Spring 2015): 71.

3   P. Germuska, *Unified Military Industries of the Soviet Bloc. Hungary and the Division of Labor in Military Production* (Lanham, MD, 2015).

4   D. Dimitrov, *Civil–Military Relations and Defence Budgeting in Bulgaria* (Groningen, 1999).

5   Y. Kiss, *Arms Industry Transformation and Integration: The Choices of East Central Europe* (Oxford, 2014).

Modern Society, 2000 to the Present: The Abandonment of War?

1   Henry Kissinger interview, 'The World at One', BBC Radio Four, 8 March 2015.

2   *Times*, 2 Ap. 2015, p. 1.

3   *Times*, 25 June 2015, p. 37.

4   C. Howard and R. Pukhov (eds), *Brothers Armed: Military Aspects of the Crisis in Ukraine* (Minneapolis, 2014).

5   R. Sakwa, *Frontline Ukraine: Crisis in the Borderlands* (London, 2015).

6   I have benefited from a conversation with the Belgian ambassador in London.

Conclusions

1   F. Braudel, *The Mediterranean and the Mediterranean World in the Age of Philip II* (2 vols, London, 1972), I, 16, 21. The French original appeared in 1949.

2   For differing views, P. Daix, *Braudel* (Paris, 1995); J. Marino (ed.), *Early Modern History and the Social Sciences: Testing the Limits of Braudel's Mediterranean* (Kirksville, MO, 2002); C. A. Aguirre Rojas, *Fernand Braudel et les sciences humaines* (Paris, 2004); G. Piterberg, T. Ruiz and G. Smycox (eds), *Braudel Revisited: The Mediterranean World 1600–1800* (Toronto, 2010).

3   J. Howorth, *Security and Defence Policy in the European Union* (Basingstoke, 2007); M. H. A. Larivé, *Debating European Security and Defence Policy: Understanding the Complexity* (Farnham, 2014).

4   For example, B. F. Braumoeller, *The Great Powers and the International System: Systemic Theory in Empirical Perspective* (Cambridge, 2012).

5   'Kremlin Trying to Start New Revolt in Ukraine, Police Warn', *Times*, 2 May 2015, p. 42.

6   K. Chase, *Firearms: A Global History to 1700* (Cambridge, 2003); A. Stanziani, *After Oriental Despotism. Eurasian Growth in a Global Perspective* (London, 2014).

7   B. L. Davies (ed.), *Warfare in Eastern Europe, 1500–1800* (Leiden, 2012).

SELECTED FURTHER READING

Readers will profit most from staying in touch with current research, literature and controversies. The *Journal of Military History*, including its regular feature on 'Recent Journal Articles', is the best introduction. *War in History* is also helpful, while the journal of the Royal United Services Institute is particularly useful for recent developments. The bibliography offered here focuses on books recently published. Earlier material and articles can be approached through the footnotes and bibliographies of these books.

1. General

Beckett, I. *Modern Insurgencies and Counter-Insurgencies* (London, 2001).
Mortimer, G. *Early Modern Military History, 1450–1815* (Basingstoke, 2004).

2. 1450–1600

Black, J. *European Warfare 1494–1660* (London, 2002).
Parker, G. *The Military Revolution: Military Innovation and the Rise of the West, 1500–1800* (Cambridge, 1988).

3. 1600–1700

Frost, R. *The Northern Wars, 1558–1721* (Harlow, 2000).
Parrott, D. *Richelieu's Army: War, Government and Society in France, 1624–1642* (Cambridge, 2002).
Parrott, D. *The Business of War. Military Enterprise and Military Revolution in Early Modern Europe* (Cambridge, 2012).

4. 1700–1800

Duffy, C. *The Military Experience in the Age of Reason* (2nd edn, Ware, 1998).
Hill, J. M. *Celtic Warfare 1595–1763* (Edinburgh, 1986).
Starkey, A. *War in the Age of Enlightenment, 1700–1789* (Westport, 2003).

5. 1800–1900

Rothenberg, G. *The Napoleonic Wars* (London, 1999).
Showalter, D. *The Wars of German Unification* (New York, 2004).
Wawro, G. *The Franco-Prussian War: The German Conquest of France in 1870–1871* (Cambridge, 2003).

6. 1900–50

Buckley, J. *Air Power in the Age of Total War* (London, 1999).
Kennedy, P. *Engineers of Victory: The Problem Solvers Who Turned the Tide in the Second World War* (London, 2013).
Stargardt, N. *The German War: A Nation Under Arms, 1939–45* (Oxford, 2015).
Weinberg, G. L. *A World at Arms: A Global History of World War II* (Cambridge, 1995).

7. 1950–2000

Glantz, D. M. *Soviet Military Operational Art* (Totowa, 1991).
Haslam, J. *Russia's Cold War: From the October Revolution to the Fall of the Wall* (Cambridge, 2011).
Leffler, M. P. and Westad, O. A. (eds), *The Cambridge History of the Cold War* (3 vols, Cambridge 2010).

8. 2000–15

Black, J. *War in the Modern World, 1990–2014* (Abingdon, 2015).

INDEX